THE L___
ST. MARY'S COLL___
ST ___ ___LAND
0686

In the ancient world 'philosophy' included all branches of higher learning except mathematics and medicine. It was the keystone of a university education; and it helped to change the Christian Church from an obscure Jewish sect into a worldwide civilizing force. This book gives a brief, lucid and systematic account of its origin among the Greeks and its transforming influence on Christian thought. Based on up-to-date scholarship, but requiring no specialist knowledge, it aims at theological penetration supported by accurate logic.

PHILOSOPHY IN CHRISTIAN ANTIQUITY

PHILOSOPHY IN
CHRISTIAN ANTIQUITY

CHRISTOPHER STEAD

Ely Professor of Divinity Emeritus, University of Cambridge

CAMBRIDGE
UNIVERSITY PRESS

Published by the Press Syndicate of the University of Cambridge
The Pitt Building, Trumpington Street, Cambridge CB2 1RP
40 West 20th Street, New York, NY 10011–4211, USA
10 Stamford Road, Oakleigh, Melbourne 3166, Australia

© Cambridge University Press 1994

First published 1994

Printed in Great Britain at the University Press, Cambridge

A catalogue record for this book is available from the British Library

Library of Congress cataloguing in publication data
Stead, Christopher.
Philosophy in Christian antiquity/Christopher Stead.
p. cm.
Includes bibliographical references and index.
ISBN 0 521 46553 2 (hardback). – ISBN 0 521 46955 4 (paperback)
1. Christianity–Philosophy–History. 2. Philosophy, Ancient. 3. Theology, Doctrinal–
History–Early Church, *c.* 30–600.
I. Title.
BR100.S754 1995
189–dc20 94–5960 CIP

ISBN 0 521 46553 2 hardback
ISBN 0 521 46955 4 paperback

Contents

Preface

Christian theology begins with the New Testament. The earliest Christians, it shows us, were ready to expound the Scriptures and to defend their faith in Jesus against Jewish and pagan opponents. But before long they faced the new task of expressing their beliefs in a way that well-educated pagans could understand and appreciate. And as the Christian movement expanded, new expressions of the faith were devised, and had to be examined and approved so that as far as possible disagreements and misconceptions could be avoided. The great development of early Christian theology took place in the three hundred years extending from the mid-second century to the Council of Chalcedon in 451: the age of Irenaeus, Origen, Athanasius and Augustine.

At this time the various schools of philosophy gave their adherents many of the benefits we now expect from religion. The conventional state religion was often little more than a formality; the so-called 'mystery cults' offered comfort and reassurance, but provided no explanations and made few demands; the worshipper could enter one, two or several such fellowships as he wished. The Jews had largely detached themselves from the main stream of ancient culture. It was the philosophers who both called for commitment and presented a way of life based on a rational view of the world and man's place within it.

Christians therefore began to present their faith as a 'new philosophy', and thus were drawn into debate with the established schools. In this process Christians often learnt from their pagan critics, sometimes corrected them, and often borrowed their ideas. And this dialogue has left its mark on the classical structure of Christian theology, which passed from Augustine to the Schoolmen, and so to Luther and Calvin, to Schleiermacher and to Karl Barth, and is the common inheritance of Orthodox, Roman Catholic and Anglican churchmen.

The work before you sets out to explain the influence of philosophy on early Christian thought, and the way in which Christian writers contributed to philosophy. For convenience I have included in Part I a brief account of the birth of philosophy among the Greeks; this of course can be checked and confirmed by the numerous books, both concise and extensive, which deal with this ever-fascinating topic; while those who are already well informed should feel free to omit this part, or possibly begin reading at Chapter 6. Part II, on the other hand, breaks new ground by bringing together some results of modern study which are not conveniently accessible, and in places extending them by new research. Here I have thought it best to arrange my material by topics rather than by authors. The reason, as I shall explain, is that early Christian writers differ so greatly in their knowledge, competence and sympathy with regard to philosophy that there is no continuous development of Christian philosophy to set beside the well-known development of Christian doctrine and theology. In this part I have concentrated on the basic articles of Christian belief, the existence and nature of God himself, and the philosophical terms employed in expressing the doctrines of the Trinity and the Incarnation.

In Part III I have written a brief sketch of the philosophy of Augustine. Historians of philosophy can, at a pinch, pass over all earlier Christian writers; but Augustine is the one figure which no student of late antiquity can ignore, and no philosopher should disparage. I hope my treatment of him will not be thought dismissive. Philosophers delight in learning from each others' mistakes, and are well prepared to acknowledge their own; whereas theologians, who have responsibilities towards their whole worshipping community, are expected to set forth saving truths, and may understandably feel wounded if they, or their revered authorities, are taken to task. As a philosopher, Augustine will stand up to the toughest criticism. But it has long been difficult to find a comprehensive work on him which takes account of the new philosophical methods and insights developed over the past hundred years. Fairly recently, a good study by Christopher Kirwan has partly met this need. But it is not altogether easy reading, except for those well acquainted with the language of modern professional philosophers. There is room, I would think, for a much briefer and simpler critical study.

The work I now present is a revised, and I hope improved, edition of my *Philosophie und Theologie I*, published at Stuttgart in 1990. Warm thanks are due to Professor Geoffrey Lloyd and to Professor Rowan Williams, as they then were, who read parts of my original manuscript and offered invaluable suggestions; also to Dr Christian Wildberg and Professor Martin Ritter, who gave much careful thought to the translation. Subsequently Professor Peter Geach made kind but annihilating comments on one chapter, which I hastily rewrote; but probably not to his satisfaction. The English version was further revised with generous help from Dr William Horbury, on Old Testament scholarship, and from Professor Michael Frede, who gave thoughtful and expert advice both on ancient philosophy and on St Augustine. And I must thank Professor Goulven Madec for the loan of an unpublished work on Augustine. I hope he will not mind if I borrow his prefatory words: 'I had to leave the philosophers for love of thee', *philosophos transgredi debui prae amore tuo, Confessions* 3.6.10. But our love is founded on God's love for us; and we should try to believe that that love extends even to philosophers.

Abbreviations

DG	H. Diels, *Doxographi Graeci*, Berlin 1879, 4th edn 1965
DTC	E. Amann *et al.* (eds.), *Dictionnaire de Théologie Catholique*, Paris 1903-72
ECD	J. N. D. Kelly, *Early Christian Doctrines*, London 1958, 5th edn 1977
GNO	W. Jaeger *et al.* (eds.), *Gregorii Nysseni Opera*, Leiden 1920–
GPT	G. L. Prestige, *God in Patristic Thought*, London 1936, 2nd edn 1952
JThS	*Journal of Theological Studies*
LCC	J. Baillie *et al.* (eds.), *Library of Christian Classics*, London, 1953–
LGP	A. H. Armstrong (ed.), *Later Greek Philosophy* (see Bibliography 6)
MSR	*Mélanges de Science Réligieuse*
PCF	H. A. Wolfson, *The Philosophy of the Church Fathers*, Cambridge, Mass., 1956
PG	J. P. Migne, *Patrologiae Cursus Completus, Series Graeca*
PGL	G. W. H. Lampe (ed.), *Patristic Greek Lexicon*, Oxford 1961
PL	J. P. Migne, *Patrologiae Cursus Completus, Series Latina*
RAC	*Reallexikon für Antike und Christentum*, Stuttgart 1950–
SC	*Sources Chrétiennes*, Paris 1941–
SVF	H. von Arnim, *Stoicorum Veterum Fragmenta*, Stuttgart 1903–24, repr. 1964–8
TRE	*Theologische Realenzyklopädie*, Berlin 1977–
ZKG	*Zeitschrift für Kirchengeschichte*

PART I

The philosophical background

CHAPTER I

From the beginnings to Socrates

Philosophy was invented and given to the world by the Greeks. Although in some departments they drew on the experience of other nations (for instance, on Babylonian astronomy), it was the Greeks who developed philosophy into a wide complex of studies, which included the beginnings of what we now call natural science, and which was later to be summed up in the three headings of logic, ethics and physics. Physics was the name given to the study of the natural world and its explanatory principles; it therefore took in the question whether there are gods, or a single God, and whether the world was made, and is governed, by such beings. For those who believed in divine existence, theology was a branch of physics.

The Greek philosophers broke new ground through their ability to ask abstract and wide-ranging questions. Before their time, much common-sense observation was embodied in the working knowledge of sailors, farmers and builders, or expressed in proverbial sayings about human conduct. But for the large general questions about the world men had to resort to a primitive mythology which associated each of the main components of the world with a particular divine being; the heavens with Zeus, the sea with Poseidon, and so on. A philosophy recognizably distinct from mythology began when the sages of Miletus, in Asia Minor, attempted to explain the world in terms of inanimate things which could be expected to behave in a regular way in accordance with a few simple laws. It thus became possible to account for unusual events by looking for some combination of previously known factors, instead of attributing them to the caprice of all-too-human gods.

Of course the method of identifying natural causes was not established at once; the early sages continued to name the elements or processes which interested them as if they were divine beings. Moreover there was a long-established and persistent belief that objects capable of moving themselves, such as fire or fountains, must be in some sense alive and so presumably animated. It was perhaps for this reason that Thales, traditionally regarded as the founder of Greek philosophy, pronounced that 'All things are full of gods'; and it is still legitimate to speak, with W. Jaeger, of 'the theology of the early Greek philosophers'.

Our accounts of them derive in the main from Aristotle (384–322 BC), though a few details were given about a century earlier by Herodotus; these are certainly incomplete and sometimes untrustworthy. But it appears that the Milesian philosophers were not only interested in speculative questions, but were capable and practical men. Thales studied astronomy and is said to have predicted an eclipse of the sun which occurred in 585 BC; but he also showed King Croesus of Lydia how to get his troops across the river Halys by diverting part of its water. Anaximander is said to have been the first to draw a map of the inhabited world. But their main significance as philosophers lies in their attempts to account for all natural phenomena in terms of a few simple substances or principles.

Thales took over the ancient belief that the earth floats on water, but is said to have developed the much more important idea that water – or perhaps rather, moisture – is the principle from which all things are derived. He may have reflected that moisture is essential to life, and so might be the cause of all growth and development. Moreover water itself can exist in three distinct forms, as a solid, a liquid or a vapour; it could therefore be the hidden principle which gives rise to the varieties of things.

Anaximander, who is said to have been fourteen years younger than Thales, attempted to account for phenomena by a principle which he called *apeiron*. This word is sometimes translated 'infinite', and Anaximander may well have thought that an enormous amount of something was needed to produce the earth and the heavens. But more probably it means 'formless' or 'indeterminate', and it is just possible that he had some idea of the important axiom that any explanatory principle must be distinct from all the phenomena which it purports to explain; it is illogical to assert, say, that all things are derived from fire, when fire itself is one of the 'all things' which need to be explained. Starting with his basic principle, Anaximander evolved a striking theory of the origin of the universe, in which fire does indeed play a prominent part; amongst other innovations he held that the earth, shaped like a cylinder, rests freely in space without needing any support.

Anaximenes, the third of the Milesian philosophers recognized by tradition, identified his basic principle as air or vapour. This might seem to be a less sophisticated conception than the *apeiron* of Anaximander; on the other hand Anaximenes had an explanation to show how the basic material could be modified so as to produce the various phenomena we see; it could be compressed into a solid state, or rarified again, and these dynamic changes were associated with heat and cold; it is possible also that he compared the air which permeates the world with the breath within living bodies, and so saw the world as a kind of living organism.

Miletus was now declining in importance, as the Persians conquered Ionia in 546 BC, and the city itself was destroyed in 494. Meanwhile the spirit of enquiry was arising at the opposite end of the Greek world, in the Greek-speaking cities of southern Italy, and was taking a very different form. The great originator was Pythagoras, who emigrated from the island of Samos, some 40 km from Miletus, about 530 BC, and founded his school at Crotona in south Italy. Pythagoras appears to have been influenced by Orphic religion, which saw human nature as a blend of earthly and divine elements. Body and soul were sharply divided; the body was seen as a mere receptacle or instrument; it was the soul, the divine element, that gave us the power of thinking and acting. Orphics taught a doctrine of reincarnation, a return to this world in another body. But they also promised their followers a blessed life in another world, provided that they observed a strict regime of purification and asceticism.

Thus while the Milesian sages were talented individuals and

men of affairs, the Pythagoreans pursued their studies in the context of a religious community; though naturally some came to attach more importance to their ascetic discipline, while others valued intellectual enquiry. About Pythagoras himself it is difficult to get reliable information; it is said that he left no writings, and that his followers were sworn to secrecy. Nevertheless his sayings were passed on, and also embellished; legendary tales were told in his honour, and he was given credit for theories which in fact were discovered after his time. His leading thought, no doubt, was that the soul can be purified and regulated by 'music', understood rather generally as an education or culture in which a man acquires knowledge of pure and unchanging truths; and this element of rational order in the world is revealed above all by the study of numbers. The Pythagoreans considered music itself, in the modern sense, to be a means of purification, and tried to draw an analogy between the intervals of the musical scale and the movements of the heavenly bodies. The most striking discovery attributed to Pythagoras was that musical intervals can be explained by mathematical ratios, using the first four integers. Thus the octave corresponds to the ratio 2:1; for if a string is halved without altering its tension it sounds an octave higher.

In reaching this discovery, the Pythagoreans were perhaps using an idea derived from Anaximander, namely the contrast between 'limit' or 'measure', including that which is limited or measurable, and the unlimited; for instance, the contrast between music and mere sound. Later Pythagoreans developed a table of opposites representing such order and disorder, with odd numbers assigned to the first column and even to the second; and so also with the male and female sex. Unity is of course ranged on the side of order; but the number one came to occupy a special position: we are told that it was regarded as both odd and even, and as the source and origin of all numbers, and thus of the rational order in the universe. But the system failed to distinguish clearly between physical and non-physical realities; it thought of numbers as having spatial extent, while units seem to be treated sometimes like points, sometimes like atoms.

Ionia, despite its political decline, was to produce one more figure of first-rate philosophical importance, namely Heraclitus (*c.* 544–480 BC). But something should first be said about another Ionian, namely Xenophanes. Xenophanes is difficult to place chronologically because of his unusually long life (*c.* 570–475 BC); moreover he is more of a theological poet than a philosopher; but he put forward religious ideas of great and permanent significance. In the modern phrase, his starting-point was comparative religion; he observed that the different nations pictured their gods as resembling themselves; the Thracians' gods had red hair and blue eyes, and so on. The Homeric gods indeed imitated men's vices. But why suppose that a god had a human form at all? Xenophanes therefore pictures God as a simple, unchangeable being, who needs no bodily organs for particular purposes but who perceives and wills and acts as a whole and in the same instant. Xenophanes may possibly have pictured this God as spherical, by association with the cosmos; but he does not seem to have made it clear whether God is coextensive with the cosmos or somewhere outside it.

Heraclitus was born and spent his life at Ephesus, some 60 km north of Miletus. He propounded a new and striking view of the world, though he professed to have acquired it simply by the intelligent use of observation, which most men fail to achieve. He expressed this view in boldly paradoxical epigrams, which puzzled both his contemporaries and later critics, and caused him to be known as 'the obscure'.

Heraclitus taught that the world is a unity, but a unity of a peculiar kind, in which opposing components or forces are held in tension. He seems to have interpreted this tension both in static terms, as a coexistence of opposites, and dynamically, as a rhythm in which sometimes one force prevails, sometimes the other. Thus he says that the sea is both poisonous (to men) and health-giving (to fish). Again 'day and night are the same', meaning probably that they have an underlying unity, since they cannot both be present together; they are not two *independent* phenomena. The theme of perpetual change is vividly expressed in the saying 'you cannot step twice into the same river'; we might say, there is indeed a river in the same place when you revisit it, but you will not encounter the same mass of water. More generally, the things which appear as parts of the world, namely fire, water and earth, are perpetually changing one into another, both downwards, from fire through to earth, and vice versa; but always in fixed proportions. And it is fire that controls the changes. Fire, because of its lightness and rapid movement, is associated with thought – hence, *per contra*, 'it is death for souls to become moist' and 'dry souls are wisest' – and so with the rational pattern of the world-process, its *logos*. Heraclitus appears to have been the first thinker to make philosophical use of the term *logos*, though its meaning is not precisely fixed. It can mean simply his own teaching; but also, the rational order which he detects. This same rational order can be described, in appropriate contexts, either as fire, or as *logos*, or as God; for although Heraclitus was critical of contemporary religion, his philosophy was theistic.

He sees divine order in all things; though of course he insists that, among men, only a few are good and wise. Wise and disciplined souls, he believes, can survive death and unite themselves with the cosmic intelligent fire.

Heraclitus was unfairly treated in the later tradition. He saw, correctly, that processes of change can take place in a regular course and can be measured. This is taken for granted today, when we measure not only the velocity of moving bodies but their acceleration, the change in their velocity. But Heraclitus was directly contradicted by Parmenides, who denied the reality of change, and was misjudged by Plato, who encountered his teaching in a debased form presented by his follower Cratylus, and associated it with the subjectivist views of Protagoras (see below). Plato's own theory of knowledge gave a central place to timeless truths such as those of mathematics, and he assumed in consequence that Heraclitus' doctrine of universal change made genuine knowledge impossible. Nevertheless some authentic details of his teaching are recorded by scholarly Christians such as Clement, Hippolytus and Eusebius.

Parmenides of Elea in southern Italy (*c*. 515–450 BC) is said to have been introduced to philosophy by a Pythagorean named Ameinias. Parmenides wrote in the somewhat old-fashioned medium of hexameter verse, and a good part of his work survives. Its opening allegory introduces a goddess, who promises to reveal 'the steadfast heart of well-rounded truth'. This 'way of truth' is contrasted with 'the way of seeming', which most men tend to follow, and which is later described. The way of truth is defined by a contrast expressed in the phrases 'is' and 'is not'. The subject of the verb is left undefined, and the argument turns on the implications of the Greek word *esti*, '(it) is'. This conveys both the existential sense '. . . exists' and the predicative '. . . is such-and-such'; moreover the present tense suggests unchanging persistence or timeless fact (as in, for instance, 'gold is a metal'); and the notion of existence shades into that of reality and truth. 'Is not' therefore conveys the notion of something unreal and delusive which can neither exist nor be known; and Parmenides goes on to argue that real being must be unchangeable and all-pervasive ('what is not' cannot be anywhere, so there is no empty space) and indivisible; moreover, since it must have a limit and be totally uniform, it is finite in extent and spherical in form. The 'way of seeming' then presents a view of the universe which is false, but seems obvious to ordinary men. This is of less interest; it seems to have included a corporealist view of perception and thought.

Parmenides' 'real being' resembles that of Xenophanes, as ancient critics observed, but is deduced by a totally different method. Although his conclusions are quite unacceptable to most modern thinkers, he set new standards of logical rigour by exploring every possible alternative and eliminating the impossible. He stated a fundamental principle of rationalist philosophy in arguing for a correspondence between thought and reality, expressed in an enigmatic phrase which perhaps means 'thinking and being are the same' (though Kirk, Raven and Schofield, *The Presocratic Philosophers*, prefer 'For the same thing is there both to be thought of and to be', despite the active infinitive *noein*). 'Thinking' of course refers to his own 'way of truth'; and there is some force in his claim that human thought at its best must correspond with the structure of reality; after all, no sensible thinker would argue for a *total* lack of correspondence.

But modern logic has increasingly shown that the correspondence is imperfect; it has revealed logical distinctions which our traditional thinking obscures.

Parmenides' teaching was enormously influential; the next generation of philosophers had to make a crucial decision for or against. Again, he was deeply respected by Plato; and his concept of unchanging being left its mark on the traditional Christian doctrine of God.

The most talented of Parmenides' disciples was Zeno of Elea, born about 490 B C. Zeno defended his master's teaching by a dialectical method, attacking the common-sense assumptions that the world consists of a plurality of things, and that these are capable of motion. These assumptions, he argued, lead to contradictions and so must be false. Some of Zeno's paradoxes are still familiar, the best known being 'Achilles and the tortoise': the faster runner can never overtake the slower, since by the time he reaches the other's starting-point, he will have moved on; and by the time he reaches *that* point . . ., so that an infinite number of steps are required. This argument of course assumes that space and time are continuous; other arguments are intended to show that we fare no better on the assumption that space and time are discrete, i.e. are composed of 'points' having a minimum but finite extension, a view which compares with the Pythagorean view of numbers. Another argument may perhaps be presented as follows: if an arrow is in flight, it must be moving now. But any 'now' is an instant, which gives the arrow no time in which to move. It appears, however, that Zeno was not the only one to use such arguments; Plato tells us that he was replying to (unnamed) opponents who used similar *reductiones ad absurdum* against Parmenides.

Other philosophers of the fifth century B C tried to respond to Parmenides' radical conclusions in such a way as to account for the apparent variety and change in the world. This required, at the least, the assumption of a plurality of things and the possibility of locomotion. Only three such thinkers can be mentioned here.

(1) Empedocles of Acragas (Agrigento) in Sicily, *c.* 495–435, was highly regarded as a religious and moral teacher with a

strong sense of the contrast between this world and the higher world to which he believed his soul would return. To explain this world he assumed four elements, fire, air, water and earth; but also two entities called Love and Hate (or attraction and repulsion) which operate by turns, so that the elements are now drawn together so as to interpenetrate and form a unity, now completely separated. At present we are in an intermediate stage, in which individual beings are born and die. Empedocles also formulated a theory of development in which plants and animals arise by stages from the element of earth.

(2) Anaxagoras of Clazomenae (*c.* 500–428) was an Ionian who migrated to Athens. Like Empedocles, he denied the possibility of things having an absolute beginning or ending, and explained qualitative changes in things as combinations and separations of minutely small particles; these, however, have the same properties as the larger masses, and so were later called *homoiomeries*, i.e. 'similar parts'. This theory, it might be said, enabled him to explain such processes as depend on the simple interpenetration and mixture of molecules (e.g. water blending with wine, or penetrating into porous clay), but could not account for chemical change, which produces new substances with quite different properties; cf. p. 48 below. Anaxagoras thought that the rational order in the universe could only be explained by postulating a single directing intelligence, *nous*, which exists in a pure state, unmixed with matter, and caused the world to evolve from an undifferentiated mass into an ordered structure.

(3) Democritus (*c.* 460–370) was born at Abdera, on the northern coast of the Aegean, and after extensive travels settled in Athens. Reacting against both Parmenides and Anaxagoras, whom he met, he explained phenomena in terms of 'being' and 'not-being', identified with matter and empty space. Matter consists of small dense bodies or atoms which persist eternally, and differ only in their shape and size; it is their position and arrangement which give rise to the perceptible qualities of things; 'sweet, bitter, hot, cold, and colour are subjective [*nomōi*, literally "conventional"]; atoms and empty [space] are real'. Thus unlike Parmenides he makes 'reality' include 'what is not';

it is a fact that there is nothing in between the atoms. Democritus developed this theory in great detail in the fields of cosmology, zoology and the study of mankind; even the soul, the divinest part of man, was explained in physical terms; it consists of smooth, round atoms of fire dispersed throughout the whole body. This applies also to the gods, who are conceived as powerful beings having human form and inhabiting the air. Much of Democritus' teaching was revived by Epicurus about a hundred years later, including his emphasis on contentment as the supreme value in life.

Each of these three thinkers left his mark on the later tradition. Empedocles' theory of four elements was widely accepted, either in its original form or with Aristotle's addition of a fifth element reserved for the heavenly bodies. It is taken for granted by Plato (*Timaeus* 32bc etc.), and by many Stoics (*SVF* 1.495–6, 2.413, 2.473), by Philo and by numerous Christian writers, for example Eusebius, Basil, Ambrose and Nemesius,[1] as well as Neoplatonists. In fact it held the field until the seventeenth century, when it was disproved by the work of Robert Boyle and others; Boyle's 'Sceptical Chymist' appeared in 1661.

Anaxagoras' theory of 'similar parts', which accepted the maxim that the part must resemble the whole, was less influential; as a physical theory it compares badly with Democritus' much more radical atomism. More important was his evolutionary view of the universe, assuming an original chaos, indeed a singularity, on which order was imposed by a cosmic mind, *nous*; the Church historian Eusebius gives a tolerably accurate summary of the opening phrases of his book, later quoted in full by Simplicius. Anaxagoras is commended for his theistic world view by the generally scornful Hermias (*Irrisio* 6, *DG* p. 652); but Eusebius also retails the criticism attributed to Socrates (Plato, *Phaedo* 97b ff.) that he failed to explain the workings of the cosmic mind in terms of the good, i.e. by showing in detail that the arrangement of the universe is the best that could be conceived.

---

[1] Eusebius, *Laus Const.* 6.5, 11.8; Basil, *Hex.* 1.7, 2.3, 4.5; Ambrose, *Hex.* 1.6.20, 3.3.18; Nemesius, *Nat. Hom.* 1.1.6 and 5.54.

Democritus' influence on the later tradition was largely indirect; his name was remembered, but his views were perpetuated in a modified form in the philosophy of Epicurus.[2] When this faded from the scene, in or about the third Christian century, the atomic theory of matter was upheld chiefly in the geometrical form proposed in Plato's *Timaeus* (56a ff.) which appealed mainly to professional scholars. Lucretius' exposition of Epicurus of course survived, but was no longer authoritative; more credence was given to Aristotle's explanation of the four elements in terms of the four primary qualities, hot and cold, wet and dry. A revival of atomism began with Galileo, and was continued by Gassendi and Boyle; after some setbacks it formed the basis of the major advances in chemistry in the nineteenth century; indeed the concept of atoms as minutely small solid bodies was still being taught by conservative schoolmasters in my own early years.

[2] Epicurus certainly made his atoms too small to be visible, but Democritus may not have done so; Dionysius of Alexandria, cited by Eusebius, *Praep. Ev.* 14.23.3 (ed. Feltoe p. 133), credits him with large atoms. Could he have taken diamonds to be atoms?

CHAPTER 2

Socrates and the Platonic Forms

Plato is probably the greatest of the Greek philosophers; without question he made the greatest contribution to Christian theology. Not that he himself set out to expound a system or doctrine; his genius lay rather in raising profound and far-reaching questions in an informal style with the minimum of technical terms. To some of these questions he gave definite answers; in many cases he was content to demonstrate the complexity of a problem and the considerations to be borne in mind, partly as an exercise in rational discussion, but mainly from a deeply serious conviction of the difficulty of attaining the whole truth, and a dislike of premature solutions. The later Platonist philosophers seldom imitated this open, undogmatic approach, but made selections from his writings which seemed relatively consistent and could be defended against opposing schools. Among Christians an open, uninhibited approach to philosophy was revived for a time, especially under the influence of the Alexandrians Clement and Origen, in the third and fourth centuries, when bold speculations could be excused as 'exercises', *gymnasiai*; and in this period the influence of Platonist writers made itself felt on Christian theology. But this in turn developed a fixed dogmatic outline, reinforced by the authoritative decisions of Church councils. From that time on most Christians quoted Plato solely where he appeared to confirm established doctrines of the Church; the reality of God, his creation and providence, the heavenly powers, the human soul, its training, survival and future judgement, could all be upheld by appropriate choice of Platonic texts.

Plato has left us a large corpus of writings, which include works of great beauty and power; but he himself regarded the written word as secondary, and preferred the exchange of ideas viva voce, in conversation or 'dialectic'. In this he was following the example of his master Socrates, who wrote nothing. We must begin by saying something about this remarkable man.

Socrates is known to us from Plato's dialogues, which give an idealized impression of his aims and methods; from Xenophon's favourable, but more conventional, portrayal; from a light-hearted caricature sketched by Aristophanes; and from other scattered reports, including those of Aristotle. Aristophanes makes it clear that Socrates was popularly regarded as a 'sophist'; Plato presents him as a radical critic of the sophistic movement; but in any case this movement forms the background to his life and work.

The word 'sophist' originally meant an 'instructor'; it was only later that it came to imply captious or dishonest reasoning. The Sophists were a class of professional teachers who offered both public lectures, at which a fee was demanded, and private instruction to the sons of well-to-do citizens. Hitherto Greek education had been limited in its range, comprising grammar, elementary arithmetic, some acquaintance with the poets, music and athletics; the Sophists, partly by adapting and developing the work of the philosophers, were able to offer a much more varied and ambitious programme.

Though the Sophists were colourful and highly individual figures, and possibly cultivated distinctive styles of life to advertise their talents, they shared two main characteristics. First, as compared with earlier philosophers, they paid less attention to large questions about the cosmos, and focused their vision on human behaviour. Protagoras, one of the most famous, began a notable book with the resounding sentence 'Man is the measure of all things, of those that are, that they are, of those that are not, that they are not'. Secondly, they were less interested in pure theory; they claimed to impart an all-round competence which would ensure success in civic and political life; and since political questions need to be debated, they taught their pupils the arts of public speaking, of literary style, and of persuasive argument. Thus they have sometimes been seen as continuing and popularizing the work of earlier thinkers, sometimes as reacting sharply against them. The truth is, perhaps, that they have something in common with the school of Miletus, but little or nothing with that of Pythagoras.

The wider horizons opened up by philosophers and Sophists alike tended to undermine the traditional morality based on local customs and religious cults; moreover the doctrine that morality was a matter of human convention, rather than natural necessity or divine command, could easily suggest that it was artificial and could be ignored at will. This view was not taken by the distinguished Sophists of the first generation; but already by the time of Socrates some of their pupils had drawn the immoralist conclusion.

Socrates shared the Sophists' interest in human affairs; he abandoned his early studies in cosmology in order to concentrate on moral issues. He did not aspire to social or political eminence, nor encourage his pupils to do so. He held that a man's soul, and its goodness, should be his chief concern; and one of his principal questions was whether such goodness, like other virtues and skills, could be taught. But he also challenged and perplexed the traditional moralists. On the one hand his reputation for moral integrity was confirmed by his manner of life; he was content to live simply, inured to physical hardship, and cheerfully faced unpopularity while upholding the law; and though he valued his affectionate friendships with handsome young aristocrats, he demanded intelligence and willingness to learn. On the other hand his enquiring temper and his exposure of commonly accepted wisdom laid him open to the charge of moral scepticism; he was condemned and executed on a charge of impiety and improper influence on young men.

Xenophon represents Socrates as 'constantly discussing human affairs; considering what is pious and impious; what is noble and ignoble; what is prudence, and madness; what is courage, and cowardice', etc. Socrates himself regarded these as practical questions; indeed he was constantly sounding craftsmen and experts about their special skills; he assumed that 'knowing what (e.g.) medicine is' was the same as 'knowing how to practise medicine'. He thus demanded that a man should give an account of his craft; and this amounted to giving a definition. He is often represented as testing a whole series of definitions of some commonly accepted notion, making some progress at each attempt, but rejecting each in turn, so that no conclusion is reached. More generally, indeed, he came to the conclusion that he knew nothing; his one advantage was that he recognized his own ignorance.

In enquiring what virtue (or some particular virtue) is, Socrates aimed at completeness and consistency. He rejected answers which failed to cover all possible cases. And he sought for some standard which was independent both of changing conventions and of changing circumstances, thus opposing the views both of Protagoras and of Heraclitus. But it is difficult to discover how far he exploited this line of thought, since Plato depicts him as putting forward an elaborate development of it, the so-called theory of Forms, which Aristotle assures us was originated by Plato himself. This theory plays a prominent part in the *Phaedo*, a dialogue which purports to reconstruct Socrates' last conversation of the day of his execution, in which he defends his belief in the survival and immortality of the soul, and which later was naturally of much interest to Christians. But Socrates is represented as depreciating the body, with its perceptions and feelings, in a manner which seems more consonant with Pythagorean theory than with his own lively practical curiosity. He may indeed have believed, as the Orphics and Pythagoreans did, in the survival of a fully conscious and active personality; but Plato makes him defend it with arguments of his own coinage, for which, however, he claimed no credit, regarding them as only the natural outcome of his master's teaching.

Plato can be approached with greater confidence than the thinkers we have so far considered, since his writings have come down to us *in extenso*. Many of them are literary classics, and the thoughts expressed have so influenced the intellectual tradition of Europe that the reader will find himself on familiar ground. Moreover it is now possible not merely to summarize Plato's thought but to give some account of its progress and development, for scholars have detected changes both in thought and style by which his works may be arranged in a rough chronological order. They comprise some twenty-five dialogues, together with the *Apology*, which purports to be the speech made by

Socrates at his trial, and thirteen letters. To these have been added other dialogues which are imitations by unknown authors; some dialogues besides, and some at least of the letters, are of doubtful authenticity. It is customary to divide the genuine works approximately as follows:

Early works: *Apology, Crito, Laches, Lysis, Charmides, Euthyphro, Hippias Minor* (? and *Major*), *Protagoras, Gorgias, Ion.*

Dialogues of the middle period: *Meno, Phaedo, Republic, Symposium, Phaedrus, Euthydemus, Menexenus, Cratylus.*

Later dialogues: *Parmenides, Theaetetus, Sophist, Statesman* (= *Politicus*), *Timaeus* (perhaps earlier), *Critias, Philebus, Laws.*

The first five dialogues of the middle period are works of outstanding distinction and importance; the *Gorgias* also is unforgettable.

The early dialogues appear to aim at giving a portrait of Socrates' activity and method of discussion. In the great dialogues of the middle period Socrates still plays the leading part, but the thoughts expressed are Plato's own, and go far beyond his master's basic ideas. Some of the later dialogues no longer have Socrates as the central figure; the characterization is often less vivid and the thought becomes more technical and more sophisticated as Plato develops his theories in the face of criticism.

Plato's most distinctive doctrine was his theory of Forms or 'Ideas', by which he meant, not 'thoughts', as we now understand the word, but eternal objective realities which make up an intelligible system or world. We must explain how he formed this conception on the basis of Socrates' teaching.

In the early dialogues we find Socrates asking questions of the form 'What is *x*?', referring most commonly to moral qualities; how can piety, courage, beauty or justice be identified and defined? This clearly reflects Socrates' concern to base his conduct on real knowledge as opposed to mere opinion; there must be some agreed and constant measure by which puzzling cases may be judged. Plato suggests that Socrates was demanding, not just examples of courage etc., but the unique reality named by the expression 'courage itself', which would be present in each genuine instance. This is correct, though in some cases it seems that Socrates was concerned to recognize concealed distinctions rather than a common factor; thus he was inclined to answer the question 'Is *x* good?' by replying 'Good for what?'; indeed it sometimes appears that the best way to know what *x* is is to find out what *x* does, or is fitted to do – that is, its function.

This idea is explored in the *Cratylus*. But Plato's quick imagination led him to see further possibilities; and a more important development soon follows. It appears that a question such as 'What is justice?' can only be answered if we can point to some unchanging reality, independent both of human conventions and of changing circumstances: that which truly is, and always is, justice. Plato may well have been thinking of the timeless and objective quality of mathematical definitions; equality, which he discusses, is after all closely related to justice. But the theory came to embody at least two separate lines of thought which Plato himself never effectively distinguished.

First there is the problem of the one and the many. Why do we apply a single word, for example 'just', to a multitude of actions? Plato replied, because all these actions 'resemble' or 'participate in' the single Form or standard which is what the word 'justice' properly means. This theory can be made to cover a wide range of cases; Plato naturally thinks first of moral notions, following Socrates, and of mathematical concepts, following Pythagoras; but already in the *Phaedo* the list is extended, and we find references not only to justice and equality but to health and disease, to heat and cold; and in the Seventh Letter Plato recognizes Forms 'of shapes and surfaces, of the good, the beautiful and the just, of all bodies natural and artificial, of fire and water and the like, of every animal, of every quality of character, of all actions and passivities'. Plato was here foreshadowing what was later to be called a theory of universals; and such a scheme can be applied without restriction to any class of similar entities.

On the other hand there are questions of value and disvalue. Plato thinks of the Form of justice as being always just and perfectly just. But no human action can attain to this perfection, just as no two pairs of clothes or utensils can be mathematically and perfectly equal. In this connection the Forms are seen as ideal standards, to which material objects or human actions have some resemblance but never perfectly conform. Plato marks this distinction by saying that the Forms must exist 'apart from' their instances, on a different level of being; indeed they are imaginatively pictured as occupying a heavenly region, the 'plain of truth'. But are there such Forms for every class? As we have seen, Plato mentioned disease, as well as health, as instances where a Form is required to explain why a single name applies to a multitude of cases. (It will not do to explain disease simply as the absence of health, for we need to distinguish and classify specific diseases.) But how could there be a perfect disease? In one of the later dialogues, the *Parmenides*, Plato himself admits this difficulty; he presents Socrates as faced with the question whether we can imagine ideal Forms of hair or mud or other nasty and worthless things. Socrates himself demurs; but the answer given by Parmenides implies that the theory should be applied consistently in every case. Plato does not pursue the problem further in this dialogue; the Seventh Letter, mentioned above, implies that the difficulties can be resolved; but the later dialogues suggest reservations; the *Politicus* (263b) claims that we must not imagine a Form corresponding to every 'part', or class-concept; these might be definable at will, whereas the system of Forms is objective; it determines the unchanging structure of the universe.

Does the concept of function assist this claim? A thing's function normally implies some greater good which it subserves, as shoes are for walking, and walking for health. But in practice the shoemaker's craft is governed by a complexity of factors; the terrain to be traversed, the formation, or possibly malformation, of the wearer's feet. It seems difficult to claim that things which fulfil their function are beautiful, and therefore relate to a single ideal, that of beauty. And even if such a Form of beauty is one and unique in relation to its instances, we need to consider its relation to many other Forms.

In particular, if the Forms are seen to be good, it should follow that they themselves participate in the Form of goodness. This concept receives its most impressive development in the *Republic*, where Plato describes it as a mystery for which no words can suffice (506c–e), though a remote parallel can be suggested; just as the sun enables living beings both to exist and to be seen, so the Form of goodness confers both existence and intelligibility on all other Forms; they are what it is best that they should be. Another impressive allegory depicts the contrast which obtains between the perceptible world and the world of Forms; the experience of ordinary men is compared to that of prisoners in a cave who can watch only a play of shadows; and even the objects which cast those shadows are not realities, but lay figures within the cave, unseen by the prisoners. If in some case a man can escape into the world above, his eyes will be dazzled by the unaccustomed light; and if he attempts to return to the cave and explain his vision, his words will be confused and his account of the higher realities will not be believed. In this way the wisest of men will be discounted as fools.

This doctrine, however, is not presented merely as an apologia for philosophy; the *Republic* begins with an enquiry into the nature of justice, but Socrates is made to respond by sketching the outlines of an ideal state which will be ruled by a carefully selected caste of guardians who are to be trained in those sciences which encourage temperate and enlightened behaviour. The programme of education comprises arithmetic, geometry, solid geometry, astronomy and music; by studying proportion and regularity the soul is to be led onwards to the apprehension of a transcendent harmony which can only be described in mystical terms, in the hope that this vision will inspire the practical decisions of the governing class.

This development of political theory is accompanied by a new conception of human personality. In the *Phaedo*, which considers human destiny from the viewpoint of an idealized philosopher, Plato works with a rather simple contrast between body and soul, and argues that the soul is a simple unitary being and as such is indestructible. In the *Republic* he has to provide for a community in which only a select minority will possess philosophic abilities. The others will be guided in their actions by their natural desires, or at best by honourable but unconsidered impulses; so for practical purposes Plato distinguishes three sources of action in the soul – desire, impulse and reason – and correspondingly divides his ideal state between three classes of men, according to the type of motive which principally governs their actions. Whatever its original purpose, this division was soon taken as an authoritative psychology; indeed Plato himself underlined it in a roughly contemporary dialogue, the *Phaedrus*, which represents the human soul as a chariot driven by a charioteer (its reason) and drawn by two horses, one of which (representing 'desire') is ill-tempered and hard to control. In later tradition, this led to some distortion of moral judgement; the human desires for food and drink and sexual satisfaction came to be regarded as the enemies of reason and virtue *par excellence*, whereas anger and aggression, symbolized by the relatively tractable horse, were not so readily condemned. Moreover this Platonic division of the soul led by a somewhat indirect route to the later Christian division of the human personality into flesh, with its 'carnal' desires, soul (i.e. unreformed soul) and the (God-given) mind or spirit; this again prompted many Christians to regard the flesh not as a God-given instrument for the soul but as intrinsically vicious and a source of temptation.

Plato's genius largely consists in an extraordinarily vivid appreciation of the dimensions of beauty and goodness, and his imaginative skill in conveying this vision. It could perhaps be said that beauty is his basic value; but physical beauty in people is insignificant unless it consorts with beauty of character. In the *Symposium* and the *Phaedrus* he shows how one can make the transition – or pilgrimage! – from love based on admiration of physical beauty to a universal vision of transcendent beauty; and in the *Gorgias*, one of his most powerful pieces, he makes Socrates argue that it is better – not just morally better, but preferable – to suffer wrong than to do wrong; since the man who does wrong injures his most precious possession, his own soul. Not unnaturally the later Platonists, both pagan and Christian, tended to value Plato as a moral and religious teacher; his political ideas were coolly received, and his pioneering work in logic and metaphysics was often overshadowed by the developments carried forward by his pupils and successors.

CHAPTER 3

The philosophy of Plato's maturity

As literature, the dialogues of Plato's middle period are among the world's greatest creative achievements; the later dialogues fall short of them in imaginative power and dramatic skill. Nevertheless they advance considerations of great importance for the future of logic and metaphysics. Plato was now much concerned with the theory of knowledge. A fairly early dialogue, the *Meno*, had pointed the way; Meno, an intelligent but uneducated slave, is questioned by Socrates and shown to discover a simple mathematical truth without being told. Some truths, then, can be known independently of experience; and Plato concludes that the soul became acquainted with the Forms in a previous existence which we have forgotten; the discovery of such truths is in fact a recollection (*anamnēsis*). This clearly marks a distinction between knowledge of the Forms and knowledge of everyday facts; but the proof of our pre-existence gives little support to the theory of transmigration, which Plato presents in several dialogues with a wealth of imaginative detail; for we are said to recollect a previous *ideal* existence, whereas the transmigration theory would make it probable that other imperfect incarnations have preceded our present life.

In the *Theaetetus*, where the problem of knowledge is more fully discussed, there is surprisingly little reference to the Forms; but the dialogue is important, *inter alia*, for its demonstration that perceptual knowledge involves more than mere perception, and again for the suggestion that knowledge is a disposition; knowing is not something like seeing or sleeping which we do from time to time; to know something is to be able to act or answer correctly when required.

23

The problem of knowledge is aired in a much more surprising fashion in the *Parmenides*, which we have already mentioned as expressing Plato's misgivings over the theory of Forms. The theoretical objections raised here have been of great interest to philosophical critics, but will be briefly treated here, since they had little direct influence on Christian tradition. It is argued first that if everyday realities 'participate in' the Forms, they must participate either in each Form as a whole, or in a part of it; but whichever is true, it seems that the Form loses its unity. (Socrates should have chosen the first alternative and insisted that *nothing* need be divided merely because it has many relationships; the sun is one though it is seen by many.) A second objection is that named by Aristotle as 'the third man'. Socrates thinks that like things are like because they participate in the Form of likeness; but they also resemble this Form; so the likeness of this Form and its participants has to be explained by assuming a further Form, and so on *ad infinitum*. (This cannot be briefly answered, as different Forms raise different problems; but one might, for example, suggest that the Form of goodness is good, and simply makes an exception to the general rule of goodness by participation.) A third objection seems to depend on the principle that like is known by like; the Forms are transcendent, and so could be known only through a transcendental knowledge, which we do not possess.

In the latter part of this dialogue Plato presents a series of hypotheses, of which the first is expressed in an untranslatable phrase which may mean either 'If there is a unity' or 'If it [the cosmos?] is one'. Plato reasons that if this is so, then nothing whatever can be said about it; but he continues by assuming the same hypothesis and arguing, conversely, that if it is so, it possesses all possible predicates. In all, four hypotheses are put forward and contradictory conclusions are drawn from each, ending with what looks like a grandiose *reductio ad absurdum*. Scholars have puzzled over Plato's intentions, some even suggesting in desperation that the whole thing is an elaborate joke. I think myself that the two halves of the dialogue are connected by the thought that a philosopher must not be afraid of criticism; having aired the drawbacks of his own theory, he demolishes the logic employed by Parmenides, using much the same weapons as Zeno had used in its defence. Parmenides' metaphysics can only stand if it survives this attack. The positive conclusion suggested is, no doubt, that we need a more sensitive account of both unity and being, a task which Plato was soon to attempt. But the Platonists of late antiquity developed a totally different interpretation, as we shall see.

The relationships between the Forms are further explored in the *Sophist*, though here again only the briefest account can be given. Ostensibly the question at issue is, how to define a sophist? Seven proposals are made, all of them of course uncomplimentary. But Plato's more serious concern is with the logic of classification, which involves the Forms in their guise as class-concepts, arranged by genera and species. He shows that they must be interrelated, rather than each one exhibiting a single property to the exclusion of others; in Plato's own rather imprecise terms, some Forms 'mingle with' others.

A crucial problem is raised quite early in the dialogue (237a): can we explain false statements without making the 'risky assumption', condemned by Parmenides, that 'not-being is'? In Plato's time it seemed natural to treat 'being' as a single notion; his tangled discussion is an attempt to elicit different senses which we can now readily distinguish. In some senses, clearly, a false statement 'is'; as an event, it occurs; as a sentence, it has a meaning. But in Greek to say '*X* is' can be understood as '*X* is so', or 'is true', the very suggestion that we have to rule out. Plato concludes that a false statement 'states things that are other than realities' (or 'truths', *tōn ontōn*); it 'speaks of things that are not as though they were' (263b). The second of these formulations seems more helpful than the first; for to say that a falsehood is other than some particular true statement may be true, but does not prove it false; to say that it is other than all true statements must be true, but is not illuminating; it amounts to saying that it is not true.

Plato conducts his arguments by separating what he calls 'five greatest kinds' (genera, *genē*) – namely being, motion, rest, sameness and otherness – and asking which of them combine with or exclude each other. He pronounces that 'sameness' is other than 'being'. This amounts to a fairly clear recognition that the 'is' expressing identity is a special case; 'Ilium is Troy' is not like 'Socrates is wise'. Should it also be said that he distinguishes the latter, where 'is' is used predicatively, from the existential statement 'Socrates *is*', or 'exists'? Certainly some hints are given; Socrates 'participates in' wisdom; but it seems to me that the distinction is not clearly grasped; and, very certainly, misleading phrases are not eliminated. Moreover his treatment of false statements does not formally distinguish the sense of 'being as truth', as Aristotle does.

An equally important and controversial point is raised at 248e 6. A discussion of idealist philosophy leads to the suggestion that what is known cannot in all respects be changeless; to be known is to be acted upon, and so to suffer some sort of change. Socrates then breaks out in protest: 'But tell me, in heaven's name: are we really to be so easily convinced that change, life, soul, understanding, have no place in that which is perfectly real – that it has neither life nor thought, but stands immutable in solemn aloofness, devoid of intelligence?' This has suggested to some critics that Plato is proposing a radical revision of his doctrine of Forms. He had regularly argued that they must be unchanging, though they can be causes of change; the *Republic* had affirmed that goodness, like the sun, causes things to exist and to be known. It would be a bold step to argue now that the Forms are subject to change and possess life, soul and understanding; and a number of critics have held that Plato retained his belief in the immobility of the Forms, which he asserts in some later dialogues, and meant only that change, life, etc., are realities which call for explanation. But the case for the 'bold step' has been ably argued; and whether or not it was Plato's intention, this interpretation left its mark on some later Platonists, as we shall see, who closely assimilate the Forms with souls.

But it is not easy to trace in the works that immediately follow. In the *Timaeus*, one of his most influential dialogues, Plato gives an imaginative picture of the origin of the universe. It was made, he says, by a divine Craftsman or Artificer (*dēmiourgos*), following the pattern of perfection laid down in the world of Forms. Christians came to value this work as affording confirmation of the Book of Genesis. Nevertheless on Plato's showing the Crafts-man does not seem himself to be the highest perfection; he only imitates, he does not initiate, the perfection he sees. On the other hand he represents an active principle, which the Forms them-selves apparently lack; the notion that they themselves could be causes of movement and change is but faintly suggested (as at 50d, where they are said to play the role of 'father'). Some modern scholars indeed have claimed that the whole notion of a divine Craftsman is a product of Plato's myth-making art; for dramatic purposes he personifies the active principle, which in more reflective moments he takes to reside in the Forms them-selves. At all events an active principle is required; we cannot both interpret the Craftsman as merely figurative and the Forms as merely static. But in any case there is evidence in two late dialogues, the *Philebus* and the *Laws*, that Plato was moving towards a more definitely theistic conception of a world-con-trolling mind or soul; indeed the *Laws* could be said to offer the first draft of a rational proof of such a being, a first essay in natural theology. Even so, the 'best soul' is not an unlimited supreme cause, for there is disorder in the world, which must be produced, we are told, by one or more bad souls.

Plato's latest reflections on the Forms, if we may trust the reports given by Aristotle, seem to have been dominated by logical and mathematical interests. He had always regarded mathematical concepts and figures as prime examples of real being, though he also suggested that the soul is 'akin to the Forms'. As regards numbers, we now begin to hear of a distinction. Two can be added to two; thus the number two, or any other number, can be repeated; it must therefore be distinguished from the pure Form of duality itself; on the other hand it is not identical with any actual pair of objects. Duality itself is an 'ideal' or 'non-addible' number; and Plato was clearly interested in the theory that such non-addible numbers might be the basic reality from which the whole system of Forms is derived. But the details of any such system are difficult to plot; can one maintain that there is just one such Form to match each of our general notions, when these notions themselves form a hierarchy, with several species collected under each genus? Plato himself assumed this was possible; but if there is an ideal man, an ideal horse, etc., it seems that there must be several ideal animals besides the ideal 'animal itself' which the theory requires; an ideal city, again, presupposes a number of ideal citizens. Moreover the suggestion that the Forms might be endowed with life and operative power would make them seem much more like souls; Plato may have already encountered Xenocrates' definition of the soul as a 'self-moving number', where the strange idea that a number can move and take action perhaps derives from the older definition of the soul as a harmony; for harmony can be defined in terms of number, and harmonic vibration can constitute speech, or demolish a bridge.

Such reflections could lead one to suppose that there might be a Form corresponding to each individual, at least among human beings; an ideal self, or 'daemon', or in Christian terms a guardian angel; such a Form would be hard to distinguish from the individual soul. We must consider these developments in the context of later Platonism; they can hardly match the poetic and imaginative appeal of Plato's earlier conception, still assumed in the *Timaeus*, that the Forms compose not simply a theoretical system but a structured whole, an 'intelligible world', whose beauty and perfection are faintly reflected in the things we see; a beauty which our souls enjoyed in the forgotten ages before we were born, and to which the best of us may hope to return.

Plato's work was discussed and developed by a long series of thinkers who carried on the traditions of his school, the Academy. Many Christians also read at least some of the best-known dialogues, or extracts from them, for themselves. We can give some indication of their estimate of his achievement.

In general, among all the philosophers, Plato was by far the most warmly and widely accepted. There were of course opinions which provoked dissent and indignation: the rejection of marriage in the *Republic*, with its proposal that children should be communally brought up; the tolerance of homosexual love; the rigid division of society based on intellectual ability. Nevertheless outright condemnation was comparatively rare, and some Christians regarded him as the only wise man among the Greeks. No difficulty was found in accepting his dualistic picture of the universe, with its contrast between the perfect world of unchanging realities and the imperfect world perceived by the senses; this could readily be assimilated to a biblical world view which contrasted earth and heaven. The Bible of course speaks also of invisible powers of evil; but Plato himself accepted the possibility of good and evil *daimones*, and in the *Laws* had canvassed the possibility of an evil world soul. On the other hand he had left many problems unsolved in regard to his intelligible realities. Few Christians were interested in discussing their interrelations, or in the theory of ideal numbers; they commonly seem to have interpreted the intelligibles very generally, as symbols of heavenly perfection, but to have followed Plato in assuming that this could be brought within view by intellectual contemplation. Considered in detail, the Forms assumed three main guises: (1) thoughts in the mind of God, collectively entertained by his Word or Intelligence, his Logos; (2) moral and spiritual ideals, to some extent personified and thus identified with, or similar to, the angels of Hebrew tradition; and (3) God's constructive designs, the prototypes of the created world. All these equations are found at the very beginning of the Christian era in Philo of Alexandria.

In regard to human nature, Plato's teaching afforded both incentives and problems. In general, Christians accepted his rather sharp opposition of body and soul, and his insistence that the soul is principally responsible for our intellectual and moral life. He had also suggested that the soul retains its powers of consciousness and thought after the death of the body; this was naturally welcomed as confirming Christian belief in survival of death, but was not easily harmonized with the alternative, and biblical, doctrine of the resurrection of the body. The Jews had assumed that there could be no life or consciousness without a body, and so postulated a long interval of unconsciousness followed by a general resurrection and reconstitution of the body in a more glorious form (so 1 Cor. 15, etc.); though in the individual's experience this interval could be 'telescoped' and pass unnoticed (cf. Luke 23:43). Plato, however, had seemed to suggest that any commerce with perceptible things was a corrupting influence; and believing the soul to pre-exist, implied that its entry into the body must be due to a 'fall', a culpable attachment to sensuous and physical pleasures (though more creditable motives were also suggested). Thus no Platonist could welcome a revival of the body. But the language of Plato's myths gave some grounds for accommodation, since the souls were often pictured as if in bodily form; for instance, the charioteers of the *Phaedrus* myth who traverse the heavenly regions. In some other myths, we have noted, Plato suggested that vicious souls might be penalized by being assigned to animal bodies in a subsequent life, and that there could be a long cycle of rebirths and deaths for individual souls. Origen accepted at least the second of these views, but in general Christians rejected both; on the other hand they welcomed Plato's adumbrations of a divine judgement assigning rewards and punishments after death.

CHAPTER 4

Aristotle

Plato's most important pupils were his nephew Speusippus, who succeeded him as head of the Academy on his death in 347; Xenocrates, who followed Speusippus, 339–314; and Aristotle, who broke away from Plato's influence and after spending a period away from Athens returned in 335 to found a school of his own, the Lyceum. Meanwhile he had acted as tutor to the young Alexander the Great. On Alexander's death in 323 an anti-Macedonian movement in Athens induced him to leave the city, and he died the next year.

Aristotle's influence on Western thought can hardly be exaggerated; but he was not a major influence on Christianity during its first four centuries, and for that reason will be rather briefly treated here. Indeed the scope and originality of his thought were not generally appreciated for several centuries after his death. The reasons for this change of fortune can be found in the history of his writings.

The works which were accessible to early Christians and other non-specialist enquirers were in the main those which he called his 'exoteric' or popular writings, which though lacking Plato's literary genius were carefully written to appeal to the general reader. These works have not survived, though to some extent they can be reconstructed from surviving fragments. It appears that they were written early in life, while Plato's influence was still powerful, and that they take an idealistic view of the aims of philosophy, besides showing signs of personal religious feeling.

The works which we now possess, and on which Aristotle's enduring reputation is founded, bear a very different character. Many of them read like memoranda set down for the use of students; some appear to be notes on which to base a course of lectures, or even transcripts of lectures taken down by pupils; the language is concise and allusive, intelligible only to those familiar with the master's ideas. At this stage Aristotle still refers to Plato with respect and affection, but repeatedly criticizes his theory of Forms; moreover he has enormously widened his programme of studies, making fundamental new discoveries in logic and the natural sciences, and including influential writings on ethics, politics, rhetoric and poetry. During the first few Christian centuries most of these impressive but difficult works were studied only by professional scholars; serious study by Christians begins with Marius Victorinus in the late fourth century, and was continued, for example, by Boethius and John Philoponus. A few earlier Christians such as Clement of Alexandria knew the elementary logical treatises and the work on ethics. In this last case, two versions exist of what is basically the same course of lectures, presented with some attempt at a popular style. The shorter version, the so-called *Eudemian Ethics*, continued to be read and was indeed attractive to Christians, as showing rather more sympathy with religious ideals, though the longer *Nicomachean Ethics* in the end established itself as Aristotle's definitive statement. Indeed it was long considered to be the later and more mature work; but a powerful challenge to this view has been presented by Dr A. Kenny.

In general, however, some progress has been made in sorting out Aristotle's earlier and later works, thanks to the studies of Werner Jaeger and others. Jaeger assumed that the young Aristotle adopted the ideas of Plato's middle period, but moved steadily away from them with advancing years, thus progressing from idealist philosophy to empirical science. This now seems too simple a picture, even if we need hardly agree with I. Düring that he was never a Platonist at all. Jaeger rightly observed that in some books of the *Metaphysics* Aristotle associates himself with the Platonists, while in other, presumably later, books he writes as an independent critic. But nowhere in this work does he defend the theory of Forms. Indeed signs of independence appear in what is probably his earliest surviving work, the *Categories*; conversely, traces of Platonic thought pervade the scientific works of his maturity, as will shortly be shown. But he certainly changed his position, and this change enables us to explain inconsistencies for which he was criticized by scholars in antiquity. Some of these, again, may be due to his teaching methods; with a group of lively minded pupils, Aristotle was likely to discuss in passing far more suggestions than he could ever hope to synthesize.

Aristotle's divergence from Plato can be traced very clearly in his handling of the theory of Forms. He returned to this topic repeatedly in his lectures, and several drafts of these discussions are preserved in the *Metaphysics*, which is not a unitary treatise but a loosely organized collection of papers on 'first philosophy', probably put together by pupils after Aristotle's death and inserted 'after the *Physics*' in the corpus of his writings. He discusses several distinct versions of the theory, but consistently rejects the concept of Forms as independently existing, or 'separable' (*chōrista*), namely as eternal, unchangeable and ideal realities which are 'participated in' or 'imitated' by perceptible things. The criticisms themselves are remarkably acute, but cannot be detailed here; Aristotle notes, for instance, that the Platonic arguments fail because they prove too much; they entail consequences which are known to be false, or again they lead to an infinite regress (cf. p. 24 above). Hence for polemical purposes he can say 'The Forms do not exist'. But he continues to teach that the existence and development of things, especially living beings, is governed by their form in the sense of an *immanent* principle which is characteristic of the species; indeed the same word *eidos* is used both for the species, the group of individuals, and for the 'specific form' which defines and controls it. This specific form, he thinks, is expressed in the formula by which the species is defined; but it also governs each individual's development towards its mature or perfect state. This close association of a controlling principle with a formula or verbal definition comes to light in the puzzling phrase *to ti ēn einai*, the 'what it is to be' so-and-so, or what is involved in a thing's being the sort of thing it is. Even in the scientific works of his maturity Aristotle attaches an importance to definition which surprises many modern readers, who assume that a skilled scientific observer should be an empiricist. It is part of his Platonic inheritance, which thinks of mathematics as the ideally perfect science; thus he conceives the universe at large as having a fixed unchanging structure, whatever accidents may occur in detail, so that all its constituents fall into definable classes; a picture unacceptable to modern scientists, not to mention existentialists, though quite compatible with the doctrine of Creation.

Plato had tended to associate truth with permanence, and to regard change, including changing standards of judgement, as an obstacle to knowledge. Aristotle also thought that knowledge relates to what is invariably and eternally true; but he also gave careful attention to the subject of change. First, he discusses the causes of change, and points out that the word 'cause' (*aitia*) can be understood in four senses: (1) as the material from which a thing is made; (2) as the pattern to which it conforms; (3) as the agent, father or maker; and (4) as the end or purpose or perfect state for which it is made. In living things the 'essence' or 'what-it-is-to-be' discussed above seems to combine senses (2) and (4); such things tend to conform to type (sense (2)) but also develop as if seeking their perfect form (sense (4)). Aristotle thinks that the growth of living beings is goal-directed though not necessarily controlled by conscious intelligence (cf. Kant's 'Zweckmässigkeit ohne Zweck'). But clearly this explanation applies best to constructive change; Aristotle gives a separate account of natural decay and does not, I think, take much account of accidental or deliberate destruction, which is one of the ways in which things cease to be.

He also seeks to remove some confusions through which the verb 'to be' was often thought to imply unchanging being and to exclude change. When a thing comes to be so-and-so, he explains, it was always so potentially (*dunamei*); the change is not strictly one from not-being to being, but from potential being to actual being. Aristotle applies this theory in a number of contexts, and possibly stretches it beyond its useful limits. Again, there is a range of cases, not very clearly explained, between 'What must become *x*', 'What will normally become *x*' and 'What may become *x*', like the bricks which could be used to build a house, but could find other uses. For our purposes, it is worth noting that his usage introduces an ambivalence into the important word *dunamis*, commonly translated 'power'. In ordinary cases this implies, or does not exclude, the actual exercise of power; in Aristotle *dunamis* often indicates what is merely possible, as contrasted with what is actual. The very common concrete sense, in which *dunamis* means 'a powerful being', for example an army or a spirit, falls somewhere in between; such beings have power, which they can exercise when required.

Although he discarded Plato's transcendent Forms, Aristotle attached much importance to the notion of unchanging being, which he finds represented in the order and regularity of the heavenly bodies. In his view they are composed of a fifth element, or 'quintessence', purer and better than the four elements found in the lower world. They move in regular paths, though of course a complicated explanation has to be found for the movements of the planets; and their regular motion stems from an appropriate number of 'movers', cosmic intelligences headed by a supreme God who 'moves them by being loved', inspiring them to seek and imitate his own perfection. But Aristotle's God does not exercise providence; still less, providential care for individual beings. As Ross puts it: 'God, as conceived by Aristotle, has a knowledge which is not knowledge of the universe, and an influence on the universe which does not flow from his knowledge; an influence which can hardly be called an activity, since it is the sort of influence that one person may unconsciously have on another, or that even a statue or a picture may have on its admirer' (*Aristotle*, p. 183).

In the lower world, despite many appearances of purposive order, things are liable to unpredictable disturbances; hence Aristotle was popularly supposed to have taught that providence does not operate 'below the moon'. But some later writers, especially Platonists, endorsed this impression of disorder by a very common confusion over the word *hulē*, matter, which could be used to denote the material world as a whole, but also stood for the highly theoretical notion of 'prime matter', or 'formless matter', a pure substrate, something to which qualities attach but which has of itself no qualities at all. Such writers are perpetually confusing the change and instability which they detect in the material world with the total lack of *all* determination – even instability! – which is implied by the theory of prime matter.

Aristotle ranked for many centuries as the final authority on the discipline of logic. We cannot deal here with his theories of syllogistic inference, or of scientific method; they make difficult reading, and many students contented themselves with the little work which was put first by the editors, namely the *Categories*. Aristotle here attempts to clarify the various types of thing that can be said about a subject; though it is clear that he did not regard this as a mere classification of terms, but as indicating the major distinctions in the things to which they applied. He sets out a system of ten categories, though only four are discussed in detail, namely what a thing is (*ousia*, its 'essence' or 'substance') and its quantities, qualities and relations. As an elementary guide to our classificatory concepts this book was an outstanding success; attempts to produce an alternative system of categories made far less impact, and Aristotle's work remained influential right down to the Middle Ages and beyond. But at first it was strongly criticized, and it was not until the third century AD that an authoritative defence was provided by Porphyry.

In a somewhat later work, the *Topics*, Aristotle develops a distinction between a thing's substance, namely what belongs to it in virtue of its definition, and 'accidents', or predicates which do not necessarily and always attach to it. Unfortunately his treatment of accidents is not always consistent; sometimes they are taken to include even invariable attributes, provided these do not follow from the definition; more commonly, only those that are non-necessary or occasional; contrast, for example, 'cold snow' with 'soft snow' or 'falling snow'. And a further confusion was introduced when the term 'accident' was used as a label for the categories other than substance; for in some cases these are required for the definition of a substance, and are not freely variable in the way the term 'accident' suggests. One cannot define a triangle without using the number three, which falls within the category of quantity. In this case, therefore, a quantity is part of the definition, and it is quite misleading to call it an accident. The term became popular, however, as a means of expressing the contrast between timeless or necessary truths and contingent facts.

In the *Categories* itself Aristotle's programme is not perfectly consistent. We can illustrate his difficulty by considering the phrase *ti esti*, which sometimes stands as an alternative to *ousia*. It can mean either 'What *is*' or '*What* it is', and the meanings are not clearly distinguished. Aristotle thus seems to be arguing two distinct theses:

(1) What is (or exists) most truly, is that which is naturally expressed by the subject of a sentence, and never by a predicate; namely the individual man or thing, S; for example 'S is a man', or 'S is white'. But by extension we can say, for example, 'Man is an animal'; and by a further extension, 'White is a colour'. The 'first existents' or 'primary substances' are things like 'this man', 'this horse'; though 'man', 'horse', 'animal' and so on, qualify as 'secondary substances'. Other predicables (qualities, quantities, relations, etc.) are contrasted with substance.

(2) The question 'What is it?' is best answered by indicating an individual substance. Next best (*according to the* Categories) is to state the character which it must have in order to be itself (e.g. 'man' in the case of the man S). This can be expressed in a definition, which states 'what *x* is'. A sentence like '*x* is white' does not state *what x* is, but how *x* is; it is *coloured* white, and possibly will not always be so.

In the second thesis Aristotle has to modify his initial claim about subjects of sentences, for he gives the name 'substance' to items like 'man', which can figure as predicates. Hence the paradox that 'substance' appears in the list of categories, though 'category' means 'type of predicate'. Indeed, very occasionally, the word *ousia* itself appears where we might expect to find the purely general term 'category'.

Aristotle was strongly criticized by the Platonists for giving the imposing title 'primary substance' to perceptible individuals; they understood it rather as 'highest reality', a title which they reserved for the Forms. But in late antiquity, and still more during the Middle Ages, the distinction between two types of substance was accepted as the normal way of distinguishing between the individual and the species; though confusion could result from the failure to distinguish between the species as a collection of individuals and the species in the sense of 'specific form' which they possess in common; just as 'humanity' can indicate either the characteristics thought to be common to the human race, or the human race itself; see pp. 33 and 49. But most earlier Christian writers, it needs to be emphasized, attach no special importance to this part of the *Categories*, and when discussing substance are primarily interested in the question whether or not immaterial, ideal substance takes precedence over matter.

Aristotle bases his ethics on the concept of well-being or happiness (*eudaimonia*), defined as 'activity in accordance with virtue' (*N.E.* 1.7); other subjects explained include the definition of virtue, the virtues in particular (including virtues of the intellect), moral freedom and responsibility, the causes of moral infirmity, the nature of friendship and the ultimate good for man. Although Aristotle treats virtue as an indispensable condition of happiness, he regards other advantages (health, prosperity, good looks, etc.) as contributory to it; he thus opposes the rigorist views espoused by Speusippus and later by Stoics and Christian ascetics; he follows Plato (in the *Philebus*) in holding that not all pleasures are bad, and that some activities are both pleasant and morally valuable. He develops the view that virtue consists in well-regulated action, explaining in detail how each virtue can be seen as a mean between two undesirable extremes. This theory was influential; but it tended to emphasize the value of self-knowledge and moral discrimination while understating the emotional appeal of true goodness – so dear to Plato! – and the difficulty of attaining it. It was also misunderstood, or maligned; although Aristotle expressly declares that in point of value, virtue is not a medium but a maximum, he was often represented as arguing for a half-hearted commitment to virtue. As to moral freedom, he gives an admirably clear statement of common-sense principles, explaining what kinds of ignorance or compulsion excuse a man from blame when he acts wrongly; but he hardly touches the difficult problem whether any of our acts are free in the radical sense of 'not determined by natural causes'.

Aristotle's theory of the mean, and his teaching on pleasure and non-moral goods, led many Christians, following the trend towards asceticism, to discredit him as the exponent of an unheroic and worldly morality. His achievements in logic and the natural sciences were often dismissed as pedantry (*minutilo-quium*) or as idle curiosity. He was criticized also for restricting the scope of divine providence (see above p. 35), and, perhaps with more justice, for remaining rather cool and formal in his attachment to a theistic world view. The last book of the *Ethics*, however, commended itself by exalting the value of 'contemplation' (*theōria*) as opposed to the pursuit of physical pleasure or fame. Contemplation is good because of the goodness that is contemplated; but it is not at once clear what this should be in a system which rejects the ideal Forms upheld by Plato. Aristotle's supreme example of contemplation, however, is God, whose activity is the contemplation of the best possible object, namely himself, and who moves the intelligent heavenly bodies in their perfect circular paths by arousing in them a desire to resemble himself. Here at least the attractive power of true goodness is clearly in view; though it is a very Greek form of goodness, in which splendour is valued, rather than self-giving or sacrifice.

CHAPTER 5

Epicurus and the Stoics

The philosophy of Epicurus and that of the Stoics developed at Athens from about twenty years after Aristotle's death. Epicurus, born c. 341 BC, came to Athens in 307–6; Zeno of Citium, some seven years younger, began to teach there c. 301. They soon acquired, and for some centuries maintained, an influence that eclipsed that of all rival schools. Xenocrates' attempt to create a coherent system of Platonism had not won widespread acceptance; both Speusippus and Aristotle had been notable innovators. Aristotle was succeeded by his pupil Theophrastus, best known for his pioneering work in botany, and later by Strato, another scientist; while many later members of his school – the 'Peripatetics' – turned towards critical scholarship. Platonists such as Polemo gave much attention to the intricate problems raised by logicians such as Stilpo at Megara, and Diodorus Cronus; and a sceptical movement was emerging under Arcesilaus, head of the Academy from c. 273. Both Epicureans and Stoics offered a practical policy for ordering one's life which could appeal to the ordinary man. It has been argued that this was especially needed in the disorientation caused by the decline of the Greek city-states in the face of Alexander's empire.

Epicureanism was to an unusual extent the unaided work of its founder. It remained an intellectual influence for some five hundred years, during which time its teaching altered remarkably little. Christians accepted a few points of Epicurean doctrine, but rejected its basic assumptions for various reasons, both good and bad, which we shall soon understand.

Epicurus taught that pleasure is the primary good, and that a happy life is one in which pleasure predominates. But he also

40

believed that we should choose only those pleasures which we can enjoy without tormenting ourselves or harming our neighbours. Pleasures, again, cannot be increased beyond a certain limit; and our natural desires for food and clothing, sex and friendship can be agreeably fulfilled without elaborate contrivance. Epicurus thus in practice advocates a simple life-style in which tranquillity of mind plays an important part, and the society of like-minded friends is especially valued. He did not withdraw completely from civic life, but he had no use for political ambition.

Epicurus' teaching about the universe involves two elements which seem strongly contrasted. In the first place, he maintains that all human knowledge begins with sensation. Our senses work, he believes, by detecting certain 'effluences' or images thrown off from the surface of the bodies we encounter, a process roughly analogous to the sense of smell as we now understand it. If our sense-impressions are clear and are not contradicted by other impressions, we can put them together to form concepts and judgements. One striking by-product of Epicurus' sensationalist theory was his view that the sun really is of the same size as it appears to us, namely about a foot in diameter. He argued that distant objects on the earth look both smaller and less distinct; but the heavenly bodies can be seen quite distinctly, thus there is no reason to think that they appear smaller than they really are.

On the other hand Epicurus accepted a physical theory which certainly could not be established by direct observation, namely the atomic theory of Leucippus and his more influential successor Democritus. The atomists pictured material bodies as collections of minute unchanging solid bodies colliding and rebounding in empty space. In this way they could account for a variety of physical processes, such as the movements of liquids and vapours and the passage of solid bodies through them, the mixing of one substance with another, as with solutions and alloys, and the digestion of food; the consistency of solid bodies was also explained, rather crudely, by a theory of hook-shaped projections upon the atoms which linked them securely together. Epicurus failed, however, to provide a convincing account of the emergence and persistence of orderly structures, such as the planetary system, or animal bodies. He held that the universe originated in a swarm of atoms falling freely through space. At some moment, for no assignable reason, some of them began to swerve from their downward path and began a series of collisions and interactions which eventually produced the more or less orderly world in which we live.

Most ancient thinkers condemned the notion of an uncaused swerve as illogical, and rejected Epicurus' explanation of the order in the universe as a result of purely random events. The objection is convincing; given infinite time, an orderly pattern might conceivably emerge by chance; but that would not explain its persistence.[1] Nevertheless the doctrine coheres with his philosophical intentions. He held that religious beliefs were a cause of needless anxiety and a threat to the tranquillity of mind which he prized. He was not in fact an atheist, for here as elsewhere he endorsed the commonly accepted beliefs, holding that there were gods in human form, such as they were commonly represented, who lived in peace and contentment in the spaces between the worlds. But such gods, he thought, could not concern themselves with human affairs; he therefore rejected any view of the world as created or governed by divine providence. The blessedness of the gods and likewise their immortality, had a physical basis in the fineness and regularity of the atoms that made up their bodies. In the same way, human thought and character was simply an effect produced by the harmonious movements of the atoms within our bodies. But human bodies die and disintegrate; so there could be no persistence of consciousness or survival of death. Yet death was not to be feared. It meant a simple extinction of life; no heavenly reward or satisfaction could be awaited; conversely, there was no judgement or punishment impending.

It is clear that such a philosophy could have little attraction for Christians. Its physicalism, its polytheism, its denial of divine providence, of a judgement and of a future life, were directly opposed to basic Christian affirmations. But in one respect their

---

[1] Cf. Ambrose, *Hex.* 1.2.7.

attacks were unjust; whether misled by propaganda from Epicurus' opponents, or willing to blacken their adversaries by any means, Christian writers tended to tax Epicurus with the indiscriminate pursuit of pleasure that was actually advocated by Aristippus and his school, the Cyrenaics. For all their divergences, Epicurus' ideal of tranquillity had more in common with the aims of Christian asceticism than his detractors cared to admit. Indeed Christian writers often echoed Epicurus' view that scientific research is valuable only in so far as it brings reassurance; further pursuit of it was denounced as *curiositas*.

Both Epicureans and Stoics have been represented as reacting, in their different ways, to the conquests of Alexander and the decline of the Greek city-states, trying to present a way of life that could be followed by all men everywhere, whatever their political setting or social class. But there the resemblance ends. Epicureans, we noted, continued to teach the ideas of their master without substantial change. Stoicism, by contrast,[2] was developed and modified by a succession of able exponents; there were exchanges of ideas with the later Platonic and Aristotelian schools; and a modified Stoicism made important contributions to the thought of Philo of Alexandria, and, both by his influence and independently, to that of the Church Fathers. But the details of its early history are hard to unravel, since the great mass of early Stoic writings has been lost, and only fragments can be recovered from quotations and reports by later writers, augmented by a few tattered papyrus documents. The sheer lack of evidence has tempted many critics to regard Stoicism as a complex but static system whose details have to be discovered and fitted together. The true situation is far more baffling; within a broad general framework, there are many dissensions and changes of view; the later Stoics continue to quote the simple and trenchant ideas of their founding fathers, especially Zeno, along with subtler and more reflective theories elaborated in later controversy. An evolution of ideas has clearly taken place; but many aspects of it cannot now be discerned.

Stoicism was founded by Zeno of Citium in Cyprus (*c.* 332–

---

[2] The contrast is noted by Numenius, fr. 24 des P., cited by Eusebius, *Praep. Ev.* 14.4

262), who came to Athens perhaps about 311 and began to teach there some ten years later in the *stoa*, or colonnade which gave the school its name. As a young man he was influenced by the Cynic philosopher Crates, and this influence appears in his rejection of social conventions unsupported by reason, religion among them. Zeno's successor Cleanthes was a man of a different stamp; though wide-ranging in his interests, he gave the school a more theological impetus; his 'Hymn to Zeus' came to be widely acclaimed as an expression of monotheism. Chrysippus, who succeeded in 232, was a versatile and hugely industrious dialectician, who both strengthened the theoretical basis of Stoicism and impressively developed its logic, ethics and physics alike. 'Without Chrysippus', it was said, 'there would have been no Stoa'.

In Chrysippus' day the Stoics were in controversy, not only with Epicureans, but with a sceptical movement within the Platonic school, headed by Arcesilaus, and later continued by the formidable Carneades (203–129). This led to a modification in the Stoics' moral teaching. Originally they had taken an 'all-or-none' view which tolerated only the wise man and his virtue, and regarded every deviation from perfect wisdom as inexcusable 'folly'. They now came to recognize the importance of non-moral values, or of natural goods, and of a gradual moral progress towards wisdom. Such teaching was continued by Stoics at work away from Athens. Panaetius of Rhodes (*c.* 185–109), an exponent of this common-sense ethic, spent many years in Rome before succeeding as head of the school in 129; his ideas were later publicized by Cicero in his *De Officiis*. The most important and original figure of the first century BC was Posidonius (*c.* 135–50), a native of Apamea in Syria, who succeeded Panaetius at Rhodes. His philosophical stance is not wholly clear, and at one time he was credited with transcendental and mystical interests foreshadowing those of Neoplatonism. This is not wholly false, but is certainly one-sided; it neglects the enormous variety of Posidonius' work, which included logic, mathematics, ethics, astronomy, geography and history. He wrote five books 'about the gods', and condemned Epicurus' anthropomorphic view of them as a sop to convention, or atheism in disguise; he seems to have thought of divinity as a single controlling power or intelligence pervading the heavens and extending to every part of the universe. He wrote on Plato's *Timaeus*, and unlike earlier Stoics appears to have adopted the Platonic theory of a tripartite soul.

Later Stoicism is represented by three writers who have for us the advantage that their work has survived *in extenso*, but the limitation that they became increasingly dominated by moral interests to the neglect of logic and natural philosophy. These are the well-known Roman littérateur and statesman Seneca (*c.* 2 BC to AD 65), who did, however, publish a book of *Naturales Quaestiones*; the freed slave Epictetus (*c.* 55–135 AD), who taught at Rome till AD 89 and later at Nicopolis, and whose lectures were recorded by Arrian; and the Emperor Marcus Aurelius (*b.* 121, Emperor 161, *d.* 180). These thinkers were all viewed with sympathy by Christians, and Seneca was even supposed to have corresponded with St Paul (the spurious letters in fact date from the third or fourth century). All three believed in an overruling providence, and the first two adopted a definitely theistic view, teaching the kinship of the human mind with God and its survival of death. Marcus Aurelius' *Meditations*, which expound a less optimistic doctrine of resignation, were also acceptable to Christians, though he himself tried to suppress Christianity as a corrupting influence.

The Stoics divided their teaching under the headings of logic, ethics and 'physics', the last-named being understood to cover the whole study of what exists in the world, including its supreme principle, or God. For our limited purposes little space need be given to their logic, though it has recently attracted much interest among specialists; their ethics will concern us later; but, perhaps surprisingly, it is their physical doctrines which are most important for their bearing on Christian thought.

They regarded the world as a process of perpetual change. On this point they were consciously following Heraclitus, in contrast to most subsequent thinkers; for Plato and Aristotle, though they believed in cycles of cosmic history, gave prominence to a static pattern of Forms or species; and Epicurus explained only the origin of the world, seeing no consistent trend in its later history.

For the Stoics, the whole universe had a life and development, and also a rational governing principle, analogous to that of a living creature, especially man himself; hence man could be called a 'microcosm', a 'little world', in contrast to the 'macrocosm', the universe at large. Since the Stoics had only one world, a better parallel might be the mythical phoenix, a unique creature, which reproduces itself by dying and being reborn in fire.

The Stoics have sometimes been called materialists; but this term can be misleading. For the atomists, inanimate matter is the ultimate, irreducible reality; life and thought arise out of peculiar configurations of atoms. The Stoics, however, taught that all matter is permeated and controlled by a rational principle, but also conversely, that rationality is always and necessarily embodied in matter. They thus distinguished between two principles, the passive recipient matter and its active directing power. But this is conventional and relatively unimportant; the two, we have seen, are separable only in thought. What is more significant is the continuity of all natural processes, a smooth gradation from inert matter to a fiery and luminous matter which actually exercises directive reason, such as the Stoics attributed to the sun and the stars.

This universe, therefore, had its origin in fire; but this was not a mere amorphous blaze; it embodied a controlling principle; it was *pur technikon*, 'constructive fire'. The connection of fire with rationality will seem bizarre to ourselves, who have rightly observed that great heat is inimical to life. But like most users of the four-element theory, the Stoics could speak of the elements in either a precise or a broad sense. 'Water' could mean either the pure liquid, or any liquid; 'fire' could simply indicate warmth, including the moderate warmth on which our life and thought depend. But pure fire had a special importance in their system; the primeval constructive fire gave rise to the universe by differentiating itself, and so producing the other elements – air, water and earth – and from them the various compound substances and forms of life. The lowest of these have no self-directing power, but only a consistency (*hexis*); plants, however, are controlled by their organizing principle, their nature or 'growth' (*phusis*) – an important word which will concern us later; and men by their intrinsic rational principle or soul (*psuchē*; or *hēgemonikon*, the 'directive part'). Thus the whole universe is organized with a rational end in view, namely to promote the good of rational beings, including men; and its overall rationality is reproduced in varying degrees in the organizing principles which control the development of its parts, the so-called 'seminal principles', *spermatikoi logoi*. Ultimately, however, this rational order will be reabsorbed by fire in a cosmic conflagration, in which, however, it persists in a latent form as 'constructive fire', by which a new cosmos will be produced.

We appear to have described two cosmic principles, fire and reason (*logos*); but more properly, there is a single principle which in its physical aspect is described as fire, and in its functional aspect as *logos*. Other aspects are indicated by the designations spirit (*pneuma*), nature (*phusis*, in a broader sense), cosmos and God. The Stoic doctrine of *pneuma*, though important, is not quite clear or consistent. It was conceived as a kind of vapour which could exert pressure and could carry a pattern of vibrations (*tonos*, 'tone') which varied in frequency and intensity. A problem here was that this *tonos* was supposed to explain the varying consistency of material substances; but the Stoics also attempted to explain *pneuma* itself in terms of these substances, regarding it as a blend of air and fire, and so producing a *circulus in definiendo*: *pneuma*→its *tonos*→air and fire→*pneuma*. The connection of *pneuma* with rationality is not at once apparent; but the human voice, which can convey rational directions, depends precisely on rhythmic variations in air-pressure; and the Stoics, having no adequate knowledge of nerves or brain, postulated a similar mechanism to transmit information received from all the senses to the central directive organism, the *hēgemonikon*, from which similar impulses proceed to control the whole body. An archaic feature of their theory is that the *hēgemonikon* is located in the chest. Moreover, certain basic differences of temperament in men were explained by differences of the *pneuma* in their localities; as we would say, by differences of climate.

The atomists' theory of the universe had been based on the

principle that material bodies could not interpenetrate one another. Water and wine, for instance, may appear to blend, but only because the minute atoms of which they are made are mixed together like peas and beans in a sack. The Stoics held that there is no empty space, and that matter is continuous; but also, as this view requires, that material substances can interpenetrate at any level; red-hot iron, for instance, is a mixture of fire and iron, in which both substances are present throughout. Again, the rational principle of the universe, its divinity or God, is itself a special sort of matter which can diffuse itself through the universe 'like honey through honey-combs'. The Stoics thus had available a very simple physical explanation of divine immanence, which is echoed in a less definite form by many religious writers. But on a more commonplace level the Stoics distinguished several types of mixture; the mere 'juxtaposition', say of peas and beans; the 'blending', say of water and wine, where each ingredient, even if enormously diluted, retains its properties in a weaker form (whereas Aristotle had held that these would eventually disappear); and 'complete fusion', where a new substance is produced with its own distinct properties. This seems to point to chemical combination as we now conceive it. Blending produces a compromise, as milk blended with ink produces a greyish liquid. But sodium and chlorine, two violently reactive poisons, *combine* to produce the stable and harmless common salt.

We have had to ignore Stoic logic, though it embodied some insights into the meanings of words and the interdependence of statements which are now regarded as important. But we may note some points that lie on the boundary between logic and physics. The Stoics taught that only 'substances' were fully real, by which they meant individual beings, like the sun or Socrates; general terms, like 'man' or 'animal', denoted only *ennoēmata*, mental constructs or notions. This 'conceptualist' theory was one that Plato had expressly disowned, though it attracted some of his followers; its obvious drawback is that it gives no account of the facts that justify such conceptions and distinguish them from fictions. For Plato, a term such as 'man' indicates a permanent and objective reality, the Form or Idea of manhood; it was the

Stoics who used the term 'idea' to mean simply a mental conception or notion, a meaning which it commonly bears today.

Aristotle, we noted, recognized three orders of generality – individual, species and genus – though both he and Plato attached particular importance to the species. The Stoics adopted the simpler plan of distinguishing between the (real) individual and the unreal, or merely mental, general conception. But one could form a conception of individuals too; and such individuals are frequently indicated by the word *eidos* and its derivatives – the very word that had previously indicated the species! This too has affected our modern usage; when we speak of a 'special case' (*specialis* = *eidikos*) we normally mean an individual case; it is much less common to use such a phrase to single out one *species* from another. To say 'man is a special case' is certainly legitimate, but less usual.

The Stoics are credited with a system of four categories; they distinguished subjects, things qualified, things disposed and things relatively disposed (*hupokeimena, poia, pōs echonta, pros ti pōs echonta*). The second item represents the species (which indeed Aristotle occasionally calls *poiotēs*, 'quality', though he normally means thereby a condition or state of something, corresponding roughly to the Stoic *pōs echonta*). In any real situation, for the Stoics, all four items are present together; the first category – perhaps also sometimes called *ousia*, substance – implies 'is material', and therefore 'is real'. In fact the Stoics often avoid speaking of 'qualities' in the abstract, and prefer to speak of 'qualified subjects'; in much the same way 'knowledge' was defined, not as a state of the *hēgemonikon*, but as the *hēgemonikon* so disposed, i.e. well instructed; just as a fist is not any *state* of a hand, but simply a closed hand. Such reference to concrete things was not always possible; but the Stoics insist that apart from subjects or substance, qualities and the rest are not fully real. But of course they are not purely fictitious; hence the Stoics describe the meanings of words (*lekta*), and indeed space and time, as not *onta*, but *tina*; not real, but nevertheless distinguishable facts.

Turning to theology, we may observe a certain tension and

some inconsistency in the Stoic school. They held that the cosmos as a whole exhibits a rational structure and governing principle; but obviously some parts of it – human beings, for instance – are distinguished by having a rationality of their own, and are called 'microcosms' on this account. On the whole a pantheist tendency is dominant; indeed the Stoics were accused of teaching that 'the world is God'. But Cleanthes apparently held that the rationality and divinity of the universe is concentrated in its purest and most intelligent part, the sun; or by other accounts, in the all-encircling element of ether; thus it was not too difficult for some later Stoics to adopt the notion of a transcendent deity. The Stoics, again, were often tolerant of contemporary myths and cults; they could identify their cosmic reason with Zeus, and regard the lesser gods as mythical representations of particular 'powers' of the cosmic reason, or parts of its domain; thus Hera was held to stand for *Aēr*, the air. Such 'powers' of the supreme God find an important place in Philo and the Christian tradition.

The Stoic doctrine of an all-embracing providence crystal-lized into the theory that all events are determined; in its extreme form this view could even suggest that there is a fixed pattern of events which applies not only to this world, but to all other worlds which have preceded and will follow it, so that every event and every action is repeated *ad infinitum*. Determinism poses well-known difficulties for the moralist; if all our actions are bound to happen as they do, why do we advise or deprecate them, and praise some actions but condemn others? The Stoics put forward two alternative answers. One, the so-called 'Cylinder' argument, suggests in effect that our own character is part-cause of our actions; but this is little comfort if our character is represented as a datum which we cannot alter. The other answer was to say that we have the freedom to accept or reject the providential order of things, though it will run its course whatever choice we make. This is clearly true in some part; we ought to accept, for we cannot avoid, the approach of old age and death. But as a complete answer, it also fails; for if the providential order embraces literally all events, it must embrace my choices of attitude; while if these were undetermined, they would necessarily lead to other undetermined events. It is thus foreordained whether I shall accept or oppose.

Whether determinism is in fact compatible with the freedom which the moralist rightly requires is a point on which philosophers are not yet agreed (though I myself think it is not). In antiquity the Stoic teaching was challenged by Carneades, who himself rejected not only strict determinism but every notion of providential order. On the other hand he produced telling arguments to prove that rational beings can exercise a genuinely undetermined choice. But the debate was confused by the disputants being too ready to argue for a global view, neglecting the obvious fact that some events are much more predictable than others. Carneades, however, held that there could be no absolutely certain knowledge of anything, let alone the future, but only a reasonable working belief; whereas the Stoics taught that sense-perception, in favourable circumstances, could give us a 'cognitive impression' (*katalēptikē phantasia*) which was proof against error.

The Stoics thus came to be charged with denying the freedom of the will and teaching a fatalist doctrine akin to that of the astrologers. But this was not their intention. The notion of freedom had always been important for them. The Cynics had urged men to attain it by disregarding social conventions and dispensing with comforts which made one dependent on society. Contempt for convention was very evident in Zeno; as Christians later observed with distaste, he taught that in certain circumstances both homosexuality and cannibalism could be approved on rational grounds. And an ascetic life-style was commended by the Stoics throughout their history; though as time went on their social morality became more conformist.

As originally presented, the Stoic wise man was completely devoid of *pathē*, or irrational impulses; his actions were governed solely by reason. This teaching was modified as *pathē* came to be distinguished from *hormai*, simple natural impulses, by their immoderate strength or unsuitable objects; it then became possible to approve moderate and well-directed emotions. But some confusion was caused by the Stoics representing *pathē* and the acts they inspired as faulty 'opinions' or 'judgements' and their results. This involves a good deal of over-simplification. As a general rule, it may be that good men act reflectively, coolly and consistently, and again, that bad men act irrationally. But they do so in very different senses. Some are coolly and consistently selfish; others habitually yield to their immediate impulses; yet others, Aristotle's *akrateis*, have some aspirations after goodness but are swayed by disorderly impulses, which conflict not only with the former, but with each other. Such facts, and others like them, can be better explained if we distinguish between a man's conflicting impulses and the judgements and opinions which he may in a sense retain even when actually yielding to impulse.

Nevertheless the Stoics portrayed the wise man as different in kind, not only in degree, from all others, the 'fools'; a man who fails to float, even by two inches, will drown. And in principle the Stoics maintained that moral virtue is the only good. But in practice this exclusive stance came to be modified. Since the cosmos as a whole is rational, the ideal of rational action could be presented as 'acting in accordance with nature'. But it could not be denied that certain emotions and instincts (e.g. self-preservation) were natural to men, and that health or reasonable prosperity were natural advantages. Thus while still maintaining the unique value of moral goodness, the Stoics came to recognize a set of secondary values – *proēgmena*, 'things approved' – which one might reasonably wish to secure for one's friends and dependents, if not for oneself; and of secondary moral obligations towards one's associates and society as a whole.

Christian moralists, it is often said, drew largely on popular Stoic ethics. It was this modified code which influenced the New Testament writers; though the ideal of the 'passionless life' became increasingly important from the second century onwards. But Christian thinkers, in common with the main Greek tradition, tended to refer to all strong emotions as *pathē*, instead of reserving the term for 'emotions contrary to reason'. This led to confusion; the ideal of 'metriopathy', properly 'moderating one's passions', could suggest 'discreet indulgence in them'; and *apatheia* could suggest the absence of any emotion whatsoever. Christians claimed that God was *apathēs*, 'impass-ible'. On a strict interpretation of *pathos* this was appropriate. Even so, its negative emphasis could sound as a strange contrast to the biblical ideal of God's outgoing love.

CHAPTER 6

The Middle Platonists and Philo of Alexandria

The first century BC witnessed the emergence of a new movement in philosophy which, though it involved no really distinguished creative thinkers, was to prove an important
influence on Christian thought. The philosophy of this period is
sometimes called 'syncretistic', which implies a merging of
previously distinct systems; but this suggestion is true only in
part. Certainly there was no general merging of the older
schools. Most of them retained a clearly marked individuality.
Epicurean doctrines were expounded, for example, by the Latin
poet Lucretius; scepticism was taught by Aenesidemus, and the
sceptical, 'academic' brand of Platonism was expounded by
Cicero; work on Aristotle continued, and a collected edition of
his writings was produced by Andronicus of Rhodes, perhaps
c. 65–40 BC.[1] But as we have seen, there had already been
contacts between Stoics, Platonists and Aristotelians. The new
movement begun by Antiochus of Ascalon about 80 BC claimed
to be a revival of genuine Platonism which rejected the sceptical
tradition, and moreover claimed that there was substantial
agreement in doctrine between Plato, Aristotle and Zeno (!), the
founder of Stoicism. Clearly the conflict with scepticism was of
prime importance. At the same time the Pythagorean number-
theories which had attracted Plato and his immediate successors
enjoyed a revival of interest.

The new Platonism of the so-called 'Fifth Academy', as most

---

[1] For the date see N. Gottschalk, 'The earliest Aristotelian commentators', in R. Sorabji
(ed.), *Aristotle Transformed* (see Bibliography 4), p. 63: 'Andronicus began his work in
the sixties and published his edition . . . during the following decades' as against I.
Düring's view (at Rome, and some twenty years later).

commonly taught, soon showed itself to be markedly theistic in character. This is clearly seen in its treatment of the Ideas or Forms (*eidē*); in Plato himself, transcendent, unchanging prototypes; in Aristotle, immanent principles of development; for the Stoics, mere conceptions in our minds (though they admitted that some conceptions were common to all men, and had a rough equivalent for Aristotle's *eidē* in their *seminae rationales*, see p. 47 above). Plato himself, in the *Republic* and the *Timaeus* especially, had left many questions unanswered. Was the Craftsman in the *Timaeus* intended to represent the supreme perfection in the universe? Or was this position occupied by the Form of the Good, so that the Craftsman merely observes and imitates this perfection? Or could one identify them, either by personalizing the Form of the Good, or by treating the Craftsman as merely a mythical presentation of the life, thought and action which in fact resides in the Forms and the supreme Form? The new Platonism, possibly reviving a view which goes back to Xenocrates, held that the supreme reality was a mind or intelligence, and that the Forms were 'ideas' or conceptions which originated in that mind and were used as 'examples' (*paradeigmata*) for creating the various kinds of things which the world contains. This usage may have been suggested by a phrase in Aristotle's *Physics* 2.3, 'the form and the example'; some thinkers drew a distinction which he did not intend,[2] and so could interpret the 'example' as the transcendent prototype, and the 'form' as its imprint on the familiar object, thus roughly reproducing both Plato's and Aristotle's conceptions. Sometimes, indeed, the 'example' is treated as a fifth kind of cause, alongside Aristotle's original four.

Suppose, then, that the world originates from a creative intelligence applying the Forms to unformed matter. This doctrine has been entitled a 'Dreiprinzipienlehre', a doctrine of three originative principles; and it is well to remember that this expression does not refer to any form of trinitarian theology; of the three principles it indicates, only one is divine. Moreover the term 'Dreiprinzipienlehre' should properly imply three *indepen-*

---

[2] For contrary view see P. Merlan, *LGP* p. 54.

dent principles; but for those who conceived the Forms as
products of the divine mind, there are properly speaking only
two ultimate principles, God and matter. Such a doctrine was
taught, for instance, by the Hermogenes attacked by Tertullian.
Another competitor was the view that there could be only one
ultimate principle; so, for example, Philo, *Leg. All.* 3.7, was
perhaps influenced by Eudorus (see below, p. 107). To Christians this could suggest that God himself created matter, and so
made the world *ex nihilo*. But this argument assumes the biblical
doctrine of an act of creation, whereas most Platonists held that
the world was *timelessly* dependent on its creative principle(s);
only a minority took the *Timaeus* at its face value as implying a
creative act.

Many Platonists, however, agreed with the Stoics in treating
the forms as conceptions in a mind, but made them real and
objective as belonging to a supreme mind from which all
perfection is derived. The marriage of the Stoic 'common
notions' with the Platonic transcendent Forms was not so absurd
as it might appear, since the Stoic doctrine of men as a
'microcosm' could suggest that human minds correspond in
principle with the divine creative reason. To this scheme was
added the Pythagorean view that the ultimate source must be a
perfectly simple unity, the One, or Monad. Paradoxically this
theory, which stressed the total simplicity and uniqueness of the
supreme being, soon led to developments and complexities in
theology. For the word 'one' is itself ambiguous, as we shall
explain; it can stand for something unique, or something
undivided, or for the first number (which on Pythagorean
reasoning would be the origin of all things), or again for a mere
unit which can be repeated, as when we say, 'two ones are two'.
There was some reason, therefore, for distinguishing between
the supreme One, the ultimate origin, and a lesser principle of
unity which, as source of the Ideas, conceives and expresses itself
in multiplicity.

It will not be possible to consider the exponents of this
philosophy in any detail; for our purposes it will suffice to
explain its contribution to the thought of a single writer, who,
however, exerted his influence on many Christian theologians,

namely Philo of Alexandria. Philo was a Greek-speaking Jew, a member of a noble family who played a prominent part in civic affairs; he had received a comprehensive education and was widely read in Greek philosophy; he lived approximately from 25 BC to AD 45. His religious life centred on the Jewish scriptures, the Pentateuch in particular, which he read in Greek, in the Septuagint version; he regarded the Torah as accurate and authoritative in every detail, though he does not seem to show much acquaintance with the Temple ritual as actually performed in his day at Jerusalem. The larger part of his extensive writings consists of allegorical commentaries on Genesis and Exodus, with some other treatises on particular topics like creation and providence, and biographies of some biblical heroes. He sought to demonstrate that the Jewish scriptures in themselves were able to present not only divine truth but a liberal education; and by the use of allegory he claims that the precise wording of the biblical text, and even the names which it introduces, yield moral and spiritual guidance which coheres with the philosophy of the contemporary Greek schools. Among these, he gives whole-hearted allegiance to Platonism, using even sceptical Platonism where it serves his turn, though in general opposed to scepticism; he makes considerable use of Aristotelian and Stoic concepts, while utterly rejecting Epicurus and all other exponents of materialism. But his philosophic learning, though abundant, is very often adduced incidentally to explain some point arising from the sacred text; he has no opportunity, even if he had the ability, to produce a consistent philosophical scheme.

Philo is of course aware of the practical bearing of philosophy as offering a way of life; he exhibits the patriarchs, not simply as devout and virtuous men, but as wise and reflective moralists. More striking, perhaps, is his determination to present Moses in particular (to Philo the author of the entire Pentateuch) not only as an authoritative teacher but as a Platonist philosopher. We may attempt to illustrate these traits from the work in which he discusses Genesis 9:20, 'Noah ... planted a vineyard', commonly called *De Plantatione*: 'It is related in Leviticus "He called Moses" [Lev. 1:1]; but Bezaleel also, who is given the second rank, will have been called; for God calls him to prepare and supervise the sacred utensils [Exod. 31:2 ff.]. But he will have a secondary calling, while the all-wise Moses takes first place; for he works on shadows, like the painters who may not create anything living; for "Bezaleel" means "shadow-maker"; but Moses is charged with reproducing, not shadows, but the originative natures of things themselves.' Bezaleel is in fact a craftsman who fashions material objects used in worship; to call these 'shadows' is a reminiscence of Plato's *Republic*, especially 7.514–17 (the allegory of the cave, see p. 21 above) and 10.595–8 (the painter, who makes likenesses rather than real objects). Moses, however, has access to the originals, namely the system of Platonic Forms, which Philo tells us are themselves the conceptions of the supreme God conjoined in his reason, the Logos, and acting as 'seals' or patterns for his work in creation.

Of God himself Philo tells us, negatively, that he is not in human form, despite the biblical references to his 'face', 'hands', etc., and to his emotions, like love or anger; positively, that his nature is mysterious; we can know *that* he is, or exists, but not *what* he is. Philo refers to him as 'He who is' (Exod. 3:14 LXX), where the present tense suggests unchanging being; God is eternal and unchanging, outside space and time, though capable of acting within them; he is occasionally called the 'mind' or 'soul' of the world; but his transcendence is emphasized by calling him 'the Monad' or even 'above the Monad'. His moral attributes are described with rather more assurance; God is the source of all goodness, the creator and ruler of the world; though said to be free from passion (*pathos*) he rejoices in goodness and shows kindness (*eleos*) to all, but rejects, judges and punishes what is evil. Like Plato's Craftsman, he is generous in his creative work; the world itself is his gift; so also the human mind, and human virtues.

Philo's sense of God's holiness and transcendence is coupled with a certain reluctance to speak of God as acting directly on the world; he speaks of God acting through his 'powers', *dunameis* (like other Jewish teachers of his time; cf. also [Aristotle] *De Mundo*). It is often unclear whether these 'powers' represent God's own action expressed in terms of condescension, or whether they are subsidiary beings created to serve him and deputize for him. Pre-eminent among them is God's reason or Logos; in other passages Philo speaks of God acting through, or conferring with, his Wisdom (Sophia), who is envisaged as a female being, and even described as God's 'consort'. Again he describes God as employing two principal powers, his Goodness and his Sovereignty, which are entitled respectively 'God' and 'Lord', but are subordinate to Him who Is. This clearly derives from earlier attempts to explain the use of two names, 'God' and 'Lord', for a single divinity. But when Philo expounds Genesis 18, he affirms that God can be viewed either as one or as three. This theology has naturally interested Christian scholars investigating the doctrine of the Trinity; but it must be said that Philo shows no consistent inclination to a trinitarian theology; thus although he speaks both of God's Word and his Wisdom, comparing them respectively to his Son and his Consort, he treats them as alternative conceptions; they are seldom combined to form a *Familientrias*.

When examined in detail, Philo's doctrine of the 'powers' also proves elusive. He uses a whole group of terms, some of which represent attributes or functions of God himself, some clearly stand for assistants or mediating principles, some recall the Platonic Forms; but their meanings overlap and no clear distinctions are drawn; God's 'powers' thus overlap with 'principles' and 'virtues', with 'angels', 'demons' and 'souls', and with 'Ideas', 'images', 'seals' and 'examples' (in Greek, *dunameis*, with *logoi*, *aretai*; *angeloi*, *daimones*, *psuchai*; *ideai*, *eikones*, *sphragides*, *paradeigmata*). In part this reflects Philo's attempt to amalgamate Platonic philosophy with Hebrew traditon (thus *daimones* = angels); but it also points to complex developments in the Platonic tradition itself.

We have noted, on p. 27, the problem whether the Forms are to be regarded simply as 'examples' or 'seals', requiring some further power to reproduce them in matter, or whether they are to be seen as themselves productive. The creation of the world could be explained by an active Creator using mere inert 'patterns'; but one still needs to know what part, if any, is played by the Forms in the continual recurrence of natural phenomena and the reproduction of living creatures. Some Platonists used the term 'secondary intelligibles' to describe the imprint of the Forms on perceptible things, or took over the Stoic concept of immanent seminal principles; but this did not explain how the simple, eternal, unchanging Forms could produce their multiple reflections in a changing world. Philonic and Gnostic texts influenced by Platonism sometimes picture God or his Logos as presiding over a cosmic ladder or some similar device by which life-giving principles are transferred from heaven to earth and vice versa (see, e.g., Philo *De Somniis* 1.133–59, Hippolytus *Ref.* 5.17); but we have little knowledge of the way this problem was tackled by professional philosophers. In some cases, at least where human beings are involved, the imprint of the Form must have been assimilated to the incarnation of a soul. One way or another the Forms must be shown to be active; though we may note that even those who conceived them as numbers did not necessarily make them purely static; Xenocrates had already defined the soul as a 'self-moving number', see p. 28 above.

In Philo, therefore, the Logos is regarded both as the 'place' or the totality of the Forms, and as an active ruling and organizing power, sometimes described in Stoic terms as 'fiery', and of course subordinate to the supreme God. Sometimes, indeed, one seems to detect a compromise already established in middle Platonism, putting the Platonic–Pythagorean divinity, the pure Monad, in the first place, with the Stoic cosmic deity as his subordinate. Philo, we have seen, explains Jacob's vision of the ladder as representing the ascent and descent of *souls*, the purest of which are God's attendant angels, with the Logos 'set up' (Gen. 28:12) to preside over the whole. Later Christian theology came to draw a sharp distinction between uncreated beings, God himself with his divine attributes together with his Word and Spirit, and created beings, including angels and men. In Philo this distinction is by no means clear; the sharp contrasts are those between the mind and the senses (seen respectively as male and female); between the intelligible and the perceptible worlds; and then lastly between the pure uncharacterized Godhead and all nameable attributes, virtues, assistants and creatures.

Philo was not, of course, the only channel through which this type of Platonism came to affect the early Church; but his influence was long-lasting, and he can serve as an example. Philo himself was intrigued by the properties of simple integers, and gives learned arithmetical explanations aimed at showing the special importance of the number seven, to justify the Sabbath, or ten, for the Commandments; but his Platonism was one in which serious logical and mathematical interests had been displaced by moral and spiritual concerns. But virtue, for Philo, was an intellectual affair; and the intelligible order, the *cosmos noētos*, had in practice supplanted the biblical picture of God's heavenly dwelling-place located above the firmament, the solid vault of heaven, in which even the infant angels could behold God's face. It was, moreover, essentially conformist, since the pattern of everything that should exist was laid down in the world of Forms, themselves the production of an unchanging God. Although in practice the Platonists could recognize men of exceptional wisdom or holiness, their theory tended to discount individuality, since goodness was seen simply in terms of conformity to a predetermined ideal. Philo himself does indeed enlarge on the distinctive virtues of Abraham, Isaac and Jacob; but he still sees them as ideal representatives of distinctive *types* of human goodness; no genuine moral creativity can be looked for. Our approach to the 'intelligible world' called for intellectual activity inspired by the beauty of true goodness and buttressed by self-discipline; but simple unreflective piety must take second place. The perceptible world could, of course, be appreciated as evidence of its Creator's generosity, or as affording instructive symbols of spiritual realities; but interest in, or love for, perceptible things was sternly discouraged. And the dualism of body and soul suggested, not merely that men should use and govern their bodies wisely for the benefit of the soul, but that hostility to the body – unless indeed prompted by unworthy motives of ostentation or the like – was a reliable means to spiritual benefit. In the end, with the rise of Christian monasticism, the intellectualist strain just mentioned was largely suppressed by the growing tendency to asceticism, so that many devout Christians discounted, or professed to discount, not only pagan learning but any form of liberal education.

Certain other faults of the early Christian mentality, traceable
to the same tradition, should be set against the immense benefits
which Platonism brought to the imagination and thought of the
Church; notably the almost universal failure to look upon sex as
an acceptable product of the Creator's wisdom; since any violent
emotion which even temporarily displaced the reflective reason
was regarded as 'passion' and so condemned. Few New Testament texts were so consistently disregarded as Hebrews 13:14, *hē
koitē amiantos*, 'intercourse' either is, or should be, 'free from
defilement'. Christians commonly viewed it with alarm.[3] The
Stoics had considered it allowable only with a view to procrea-
tion; Christians could add that it was only enjoined as a result of
the Fall (Gen. 3:16), and some even held, like Philo, that the
ideal man was asexual ('male–female', Gen. 1:27). An attempt
by the Valentinians to regard sex as a form of sacrament failed to
win much support. One might also point to an accentuation of
the male dominance already present in the Israelite tradition as
well as in pagan society, partly through failure to recognize the
unconscious rationality present in the typically feminine intuition; and an over-confident acceptance of orthodox Christian
tradition, leading to a bitter intolerance of heretics where
persuasion had failed to produce agreement. This was the
reverse side of that love and mutual self-sacrifice within the
orthodox Christian fold which won the reluctant admiration
even of pagan satirists like Lucian of Samosata.

---

[3] A notable exception is Augustine, *Gen. ad Litt.* 9.2.5: Adam and Eve could have enjoyed
innocent sexual intercourse in Paradise if they had not sinned.

CHAPTER 7

The philosophy of late antiquity

During the first two Christian centuries Platonism gradually became the dominant philosophy. The Epicureans had lost their appeal by the end of this period, which witnessed a revival of religious interests, both good and bad. Second-century Stoicism is represented for us by the freed slave Epictetus and the Emperor Marcus Aurelius, who were widely respected as moral teachers; but its theoretical side is unknown to us, though Cornutus, an associate of Seneca, commented on Aristotle's logic in works now lost. A general acquaintance with both Epicurean and Stoic doctrine of course persisted much longer, as part of a general philosophical education. Meanwhile, many Pythagoreans were closely allied to the Platonists, and only a minority considered themselves a distinct school. The Aristotelian Aspasius (*c.* 100–150) wrote a range of commentaries on Aristotle, of which that on the *Nicomachean Ethics* survives in part. More important are the extensive surviving works of Alexander of Aphrodisias, early third century, the last really distinguished member of the school. His *De Fato* especially, which deals with the problems of determinism and free will, retains an interest for the non-specialist today.

Opposition to the Platonists came chiefly from a revived scepticism, which claimed to be pursuing the tradition of Pyrrho of Elis, *c.* 365–275 BC, who himself may have been indirectly indebted to Socrates and more closely to Democritus. We have noted that the Academy went through a sceptical phase under Arcesilaus and Carneades (p. 44), which was perpetuated by Cicero. But after the Academics' revival of 'dogmatism' (see p. 54) an independent sceptical movement claiming Pyrrho's authority was promoted by Aenesidemus, who seems to have argued both for the unreliability of sense-perception and for the relativity of our moral notions, commending suspense of judgement (*epochē*) as the only rational course. Our information comes largely from Sextus Empiricus, *c.* 180 AD, who has left extensive surviving works. Sextus himself is a tedious writer, whatever his merits as a critic, and is mainly valued for the information he provides on more significant thinkers. But it seems that scepticism continued to present a challenge; Augustine encountered it in its Academic form, and considered it important enough to oppose in an early work, the *Contra Academicos*.

The dominant tradition, however, in late antiquity was a Platonism of a positive and spiritualizing trend incorporating some Pythagorean and Stoic elements; Aristotle's importance was a matter for debate, as we shall see. We can distinguish three periods, dominated by (1) the Middle Platonists from Eudorus to Atticus, roughly 40 BC to AD 200, of whom the best known, and certainly the ablest writer, is the essayist and biographer Plutarch (AD 45–125); (2) the Neoplatonists, especially Plotinus (AD 205–69), his immediate successors Porphyry and Iamblichus, and much later Proclus (*c.* 411–85); Plotinus was an important influence on Augustine; but the term 'Neoplatonism' is a modern coinage; they saw themselves as continuing an unbroken Platonic tradition; (3) the Aristotelian scholasticism of late antiquity, whose representatives still treated Plato as their main authority, but accepted and developed Porphyry's defence of Aristotle's logic; for our purposes the most significant figures are Marius Victorinus and Boethius in the West, and John Philoponus in the East. These three were Christians; but the leading pagan Neoplatonists continued at work until, or somewhat after, Justinian closed the philosophical schools at Athens in 529; among them the learned Aristotelian scholar Simplicius.

Of all these, there is little doubt that the Neoplatonists are the most original and powerful thinkers; indeed many historians of philosophy have passed immediately from the later Stoic moralists to Plotinus. But for our present purposes they are less important, since they had less influence on Christian thought. The four we have mentioned were all strongly anti-Christian;

Porphyry, the most readable of the group, wrote a treatise against the Christians and had his writings condemned to be burnt by Constantine the Great. Accordingly Christian theologians of the fourth century, even as late as St Basil (*c*. 330–79) drew mainly on earlier Platonist writers. Intelligent study of Plotinus begins about a hundred years after his death with Marius Victorinus and Augustine; and by this time Christian theology had developed firm dogmatic outlines as a result of the fourth-century controversies, and was well able to criticize its Neoplatonist opponents. 'The crucial doctrines of a graduated divinity, of the world as existing without beginning, of the once-for-all primordial revelation of the Logos, of the transmigration of souls and the homecoming of (only) the enlightened soul . . . were all without exception rejected by the Church', states H. Dörrie, correctly.[1] But they were not all rejected at once; for instance, a 'graduated divinity', as taught by Numenius, was acceptable to many Christians before the Council of Nicaea; it appears as 'subordinationism' in histories of doctrine. Moreover, the Church never discarded certain philosophical tenets which it had taken over from the Middle Platonists at an earlier and more suggestible stage of its development; notably the view of God's nature as a simple unchangeable unity, and the cult of intelligence which, even when qualified by tenderness for the simple believer, still bred a distrust of emotion and an assumption that every human shortcoming could be traced to sensuality. Even Augustine, on any showing the most independent and creative thinker of late antiquity, never completely freed himself from the Platonising tendency of his early years.

The Middle Platonists after Antiochus can be roughly classified, following the recent survey by John Dillon. We thus distinguish (1) Plutarch, a voluminous, imaginative and religiously minded writer, who largely recaptured the spirit and literary flavour of Plato's own dialogues, and made effective use of the Platonic myth; (2) a more prosaic and scholastic group, supposed to derive from a certain Gaius, who incorporated much of Aristotle's teaching into their system; they are repre-

---

[1] 'Was ist spätantike Platonismus?' (see Bibliography 20), p. 300 (= *Platonica Minora* p. 522).

sented for us by the text-book writer Albinus, who was studied by Clement of Alexandria, and by the more colourful Latinist Apuleius; (3) an opposing group, based on Athens, who sought for a pure Platonism free of Aristotle's influence, their most remarkable representative being Atticus; and (4) Platonists owning a special respect for Pythagoras, among them Eudorus, Moderatus, Nicomachus and the extremely influential Numenius, between about 50 BC and AD 200.

In the longer perspective we should not exaggerate the importance of these writers. In particular the potentially fruitful idea that the world could be explained in terms of numbers – a Pythagorean speciality – brought no useful results except in the field of musical theory, harmonics. Authentic discoveries were achieved rather by thinkers on the fringe of the main philosophical schools, in mathematics, optics and astronomy. On the other hand it is clear that Porphyry and Iamblichus, and indeed the later Neoplatonists, deserve more respect than they have often received. Acute thinking is sometimes concealed in what look like mere laborious commentaries.

The Middle Platonists thus call for attention primarily because of their influence on Christian writers of the second to fourth centuries, especially Justin, Clement, Origen and Eusebius. Among the problems discussed we may mention the following, some of which will be reviewed more fully in Part II:

Our knowledge of God's existence.

The question whether and how God can be described.

Unity and plurality in the divine nature.

The world as eternal or as created.

Human nature, spiritual and bodily.

It is convenient to begin with a problem arising from Plato's creation narrative in the *Timaeus*. Plato does not suggest that the divine Craftsman made the world out of nothing, but rather that he made an orderly world out of a previous confusion; so 30a, 'Desiring that all things should be good . . . he took in hand all that was visible, which was not at rest but in discordant and disorderly motion, and brought it from its disorder into order'. This seems to agree with the biblical account, since Genesis 1:1 as originally written probably implies that God made an orderly world out of chaos, the *tohu-wa-bohu* (see the commentary on this passage by G. von Rad, Bibliography 20); but it also raises a problem. Plato seems to be describing a definite act, the first in a series; the difficulty is that he then describes the making of time in a later chapter (38c): 'Time in fact came into being together with the heavens'. But how could any action take place *before* the beginning of time?

Plato's immediate successors, Aristotle, Speusippus and Xenocrates, all taught that the universe has existed from all eternity. Aristotle held that Plato was simply mistaken; the other two excused him by saying that he was using figurative language designed to show that the visible world is eternally dependent on its divine origin. This view continued to be held by the majority of Platonists; but a minority, including Plutarch and Atticus, taught that the world had a real beginning, though not precisely a beginning in time as we know it. Some others took a less clearly defined position. Thus Philo condemns the view that the cosmos has always existed (*Opif.* 7) and argues that there was no time before it began (*ibid.* 26); but he also paraphrases the *Timaeus* passage on the goodness of the Craftsman (29e) and uses it to explain God's ordering of the cosmos in accordance with his pre-existing designs (*Opif.* 21–2). His reading of the *Timaeus* therefore allows of a definite creative act which in fact was instantaneous (*ibid.* 13). This seems to rule out an allegorical explanation of the past tense, though Philo uses one to explain away the 'six days' of creation. Other points are simply left unclear, for instance, how time began 'either at or after' the creation of the world (*ibid.* 26).

Some time earlier Cicero had apparently taken the *Timaeus* in a literal sense (*Nat. Deor.* 1.18–19); and the Wisdom writer (11:17) says merely that God's all-powerful hand created the world out of formless matter, an opinion which the Christian apologist Justin was content to reproduce.

Nowhere in these writers do we find the view later defined by orthodox Christians, that God created the world *ex nihilo*; but the position is unclear because this phrase was current before its meaning became fixed. In Greek thought it is often hard to distinguish the notion of being as mere existence from that of 'being so-and-so'; accordingly 'that which is not' need not indicate sheer non-existence; it may mean simply 'that which has no definite character'. Even much later thinkers found it difficult to conceive absolute non-existence; Athanasius describes God as addressing 'things that are not' (!) and calling them into being (*C. Ar.* 2.22). So the writer of 2 Maccabees who refers to God 'making the world out of that which is not' (*ex ouk ontōn*) may not have envisaged the later doctrine. Some suggestions may have come from pagan thinkers of the first century BC; Eudorus seems to have taught that God created not only the Ideas but also matter;[2] and Cicero knows, but rejects, the view that matter was created by divine providence; see the fragment preserved by Lactantius, *D.I.* 2.8.10. But Eudorus at least probably meant that matter, like the Ideas, was eternally dependent on its divine origin; it was, after all, a fairly natural development of the Pythagorean theory that all things proceed from the One. Nevertheless the notion of a momentary creation was also current, as just explained. Creation *ex nihilo* was expounded with great clarity by Basilides early in the second century; see Hippolytus *Ref.* 7.22.2, who treats him as a Gnostic heretic; it was adopted into orthodox Christianity by Theophilus of Antioch, *c.* AD 180, and is taken for granted by Irenaeus. An argument commonly used was that it is impossible to imagine matter existing eternally without interference or improvement alongside an almighty God.

The *Timaeus* raises a further problem. Plato begins his creation narrative with the much-quoted phrase 'The Maker and Father of this universe is hard to discover' (28c). It was natural to ask how far this dictum could be pressed; does it mean that we have *no* knowledge of our ultimate source? But setting this aside, the two titles themselves called for comment. Are they equivalent, or do they refer to the same being in two different capacities, or to two different beings? To view God as Maker sets all his workmanship on a lower level. But the title Father could suggest that God, in creating man, communicated to him something of his own spiritual nature; as indeed might be

---

[2] H. Dörrie, *Platonica Minora*, p. 306.

suggested by Genesis 2:7, with its mention of 'the breath of life', or even simply by reflecting on the Greek word *poiētēs*, which can mean 'poet' as well as 'maker', for a poet expresses himself in his works. Man was admittedly an embodied creature; but in regard to his soul at least he might be regarded as God's son in the sense of sharing in his nature. Certain New Testament texts, written before the issue had been clearly thought out, could point in this direction, for example 1 John 2:29–3:2 and 4:7.

The doctrine that man on his spiritual side is actually akin to deity has good support from the philosophers. Pythagoreans, for instance, spoke of a 'divine spark', an offshoot of the divine nature, imprisoned and submerged in our gross and recalcitrant bodies. The notion of divine self-giving seems appropriate, and had been eloquently expressed by Plato: 'God, being generous, desired that all things should become as like as might be to himself... that all things should be good' (*Timaeus* 29c–30a); the Bible adds, 'God saw that all he had made ... was good'. But why need there be any limit to the goodness which God could confer upon his creatures, once we have discarded the notion – assumed by Plato – that his action is limited by the shortcomings of uncreated matter? True, God could not deny his own nature by making other beings equal to himself; but what other restraint need there be?

These problems open up a wide range of possibilities, ranging from what we may call graduated monism to extreme dualism. One can believe that God's goodness is reflected in various degrees throughout the heavenly realm and the natural order, of which the human soul is simply the noblest part. Or one can postulate an abrupt discontinuity, so that the human soul is seen either as itself corrupted, or as a divine spark imprisoned in an alien and hostile world of dead matter and malignant spirits. Even Numenius had thought of the 'Maker' of this world as a second God, distinct and subordinate to its supreme 'Father'. But there were many others who were ready to paint the Creator–God in far more depressing colours.

These questions come to the fore in the three-sided debate between the Gnostics, Plotinus, and the Christian opponents of them both. We shall not deal with the Gnostics at any length;

few of them could be described as philosophers; there was a bewildering variety of conflicting schools; and the evidence is difficult to summarize in view of the new data provided by the Nag Hammadi discoveries. But it is clear that most of them took a dualistic position; the material world was seen as the product of a misguided or a malignant creator; the divine spark was present only in certain chosen souls, who could escape the creator's influence by means of *gnosis*, 'knowledge' or 'enlightenment', revealed as a message by the Gnostic teacher, and well summarized as 'who we were and what we have become; where we were or where we have been made to fall; whither we are hastening, from what we are being redeemed; what birth is, and what is rebirth'.[3] And since the body, and the material world in general, is devalued, Gnostic practice tended to opposite extremes; one might either oppress the body, as necessarily hostile to the spirit, or else insult and degrade it, as an irrelevance to spiritual progress that had to be outfaced.

However, some Gnostics introduced a contrary tendency, which is commonly described as 'emanationism'. This seems to me a somewhat confusing term conveying three suggestions which, so far as I can see, have no logical connection, though they are often found together. They are:

(1) God imparts his own life to other beings, who are thus in some sense 'consubstantial' with him.
(2) This action is a necessary consequence of God's nature.
(3) Nevertheless it is not complete; at each stage something of the original divinity is lost, and imperfection creeps in.

Thus Valentinus, one of the most talented among the Gnostics, and also among the nearest to orthodox Christianity, conceived of God's being as developing out of a primal mysterious unity into a series of powers or 'aeons', collectively called 'the *plērōma*' or 'fullness' (of the Godhead); the starting-point being the process by which the mysterious Godhead arrived at a conception of himself, which has to be in some degree incomplete. The process is then repeated and produces a series of powers, which are not mere aspects of functions of the Godhead,

---

[3] Clement, *Excerpta ex Theodoto* 78.2

but are, or become, endowed with personalities and wills of their own. But as these moved away from the original unity and acquired a distinct individual form, the divine perfection was progressively limited or diluted to the point at which actual error or sin could arise; all this in some eternal or pre-temporal state before this lower world was mistakenly created. A thoughtful and suggestive version of this theory is now available in the *Tractatus Tripartitus* from Nag Hammadi. God has all the attributes that make for perfection. God's attributes, however, can only mirror the divine life if they themselves acquire life and consciousness. But they then fall into error by forgetting their own limitations and their need of each other to represent the whole divine fullness.

Some elements in this myth are clearly drawn from philosophy. Platonists would naturally assume that a copy must be inferior to its original, in the light of the theory of Forms. Philo thus uses the simile of diminishing power in a chain of magnets (*Opif.* 141) to show the inferiority of God's works to Himself. (This 'dilution' theory must not be confused with the view that the *original* itself is weakened by producing its replica, which crops up later as an objection to the doctrine that God produced his own Logos 'from his substance'; here both Christians and Neoplatonists could reply that the divine original suffers no loss, just as a lighted torch is not cooled when it kindles another.)

Irenaeus, who became bishop of the Greek-speaking Christian community centred on Lyons in the Rhone valley *c.* 180, replied to the Gnostics in his five-volume treatise *Against the Heresies*. He opposed both the tendencies we have traced in the Valentinian school. On the one hand he attacked their emanation theory, on the grounds that there can be no continuity between the perfect God and fallible sinful creatures. If the Aeons are in any sense divine and part of God's own being, it is blasphemous to represent any one of them as involved in error and sin. On the other hand he argued that the created world is not evil in itself; the origins of evil lie rather in the gift of free will to men, and their misuse of it. Nevertheless free will is a condition of moral life and moral progress; in the long process of history the mistakes arising from man's immaturity and weakness of will can be corrected, so that humanity is fit to share in the wonders of the age to come. Some other objections which he makes to the Gnostics rest on Christian tradition rather than philosophy; thus he argues that there is no warrant in the Bible for postulating another God beyond the Creator (*A.H.* 2.2.6, 3.6.1, etc.). More generally he attacks what he regards as their fanciful interpretation of Scripture and their use of number-symbolism, a Pythagorean trait which of course had been prominent in Philo. Irenaeus also condemned the Gnostics' eccentric morals, as well as their reliance on individual teachers who lacked institutional authority within the Christian body, which he somewhat optimistically regarded as united in a common faith and Church discipline.

Plotinus also wrote in Greek, though he spent most of his working life in Rome, having migrated there from Egypt after an unsuccessful attempt to visit Persia and consult with Persian and Indian sages. His philosophy is a consistent working out of the principle underlying Plato's doctrine of the ideal Good, namely that the universal is more real than the particular – more inclusive, more simple, and better. He thus accepted the emanation theory in all its implications. The supreme principle in the universe is pure Unity, which is also pure Goodness, on which every other reality depends. The world order is fixed and eternal; there is no temporal or momentary act by which the highest reality gives rise to the rest; still less a cosmic catastrophe, like the presumptuous act of Sophia with Valentinus, or the Fall, whether of Lucifer or of Adam, in Christian doctrine. Rather, everything proceeds in an orderly and eternal outward flow, the first step being that by which the One causes itself to be known by generating Mind or Consciousness (*Nous*).

Some of Plotinus' contemporaries treated Mind as an alternative name for the supreme Goodness. Plotinus made a distinction, for two reasons: (1) No description, whether as Mind or anything else, can properly apply to the One; to describe it would mean adding some predicate to it, and so destroy its unity; and (2) Mind and its thinking imply a duality, the subject that thinks and the thought it conceives. The One therefore does not think; it gives rise to thought; but this is the work of a second principle or hypostasis, which contemplates and considers the One.

In stating these reasons, I do not of course defend them. In modern theory 'S is P' is not explained as a would-be identification, which half suggests 'S is not-S'. It does of course imply that S has distinguishable aspects or *epinoiai*, P, Q, R, etc.; but Plotinus himself implies this by naming his supreme principle, now as the One, now as the Good, and very occasionally, as God. The second point, that self-knowledge implies a duality of subject and object, should perhaps be broadened. It is hard to see how any thought can take place without a process of discrimination. If then the One is regarded as a perfect unity, it proves to be an indefinable source of all goodness, raised above the level of conscious thought, which gives rise to a reasoning Mind, but remains exempt from its limitations. It is this divine Mind which can express the original Unity in a plurality of Ideas; but not perfectly (as if the One could be exactly duplicated), since each Idea represents only a partial truth, and the whole complex falls short of perfect unity.

To resume: the outward progression duly continues, as Mind gives rise to Soul, an originative principle of movement and life, which issues in distinct souls, both the soul of the world and the souls of individuals. These however remain united with Soul itself by a bond of attachment which Plotinus views as a kind of identity. It is the world-soul which by reflecting on the higher realities produces the immanent Forms of material bodies. Here again we see the working out of Plato's doctrine: such and such things exist in the world because it is good that just these things should exist; cf. *Rep.* 6, 508e. All these levels of reality are good in their degree, since they all in some measure reflect the ultimate Unity and Goodness; and all have an innate tendency to return towards their source. Even matter itself is not evil; it is simply the lowest level of reality, the level at which ultimate Goodness and Unity are most dimly reflected; it is the limit of the outward movement, the edge of not-being.

It is not quite easy to understand the relation of our individual souls to the universal Soul. Rather unusually, Plotinus holds that each human individual exists on the ideal or transcendental level; more technically expressed, that there are Ideas of individuals. But on the empirical level our souls are self-directed; they may or may not remain true to their ideal Form. Evil arises in the world when our souls attach themselves to material things, crediting them with a reality which they do not possess, and thereby turning away from the One and the Good.

Plotinus came into contact with Gnostic Christians, possibly Valentinians, and wrote against 'those who say that the maker of the universe is evil, and the universe is evil'. Like Irenaeus, he attacked their complicated systems of Aeons, their elitist theory of salvation and their immoralism. True, his system has some similarity with Valentinus' emanationist process of expanding divinity which begins with the first principle's Thought of itself; and it agrees with Christian orthodoxy in treating evil as the result of faulty choice. However, by treating both the outward and the returning movement as eternal facts, he disallows all 'historicist' views of sin and salvation, both Gnostic and Christian, as explained above (p. 72).

The nobility of Plotinus' thought was amply seconded by his character; shrewd, kindly and practical in the common affairs of life, as well as disciplined, ascetic and mystical. All this makes it natural for Christians to claim him as *anima naturaliter Christiana*. But in practice Christian thought was little influenced by the distinctive features of his system; what he communicated to Augustine was mainly a vivid impression of the traits common to all Platonists; the reality of a transcendent world, the source both of truth and of beauty, and the high valuation of the intellect as the gateway to it. On the whole Christians paid more attention to his successor and biographer Porphyry; and that not so much for his own philosophical views as for his polemical writing against the Christians.

We have not the space to comment on the later Neoplatonists in any detail; but two points can be briefly outlined. First, whereas Plotinus is original, suggestive and often careless about his terminology, his successors from Porphyry onwards began to adopt a more rigid and scholastic method, paying much greater attention to verbal consistency. Partly as a result of their anxiety to comprehend all of Plato's legacy in a comprehensive scheme, their divine hierarchies tend to become more complicated, and so to diverge more completely from Christian conceptions of the divine Trinity. The correspondence had never been very close, since although the Platonic triads often contained fair approximations to God the Father and the divine Logos, their third member – Soul, or the cosmic soul, or the ensouled cosmos – have never looked very like the Holy Spirit. But secondly, the Christians themselves began to move away from any appearance of an alliance as a result of the movement which led to the Councils of Nicaea and Constantinople. Origen, Eusebius and the Arian party, whatever their differences, had all believed in a serial or subordinationist Trinity with three Persons ranked in descending order of dignity. Nicaea pronounced the Father and Logos coequal and led to a distinct conception of a Trinity as one God distinguishable into three Persons, rather than one God made into a Trinity by the addition of other Persons. It is the more remarkable that the complex divine hierarchy taught by Proclus in the fifth century was adapted and Christianized in the very influential work of the writer we know as Dionysius 'the Areopagite' about AD 500.

PART II

The use of philosophy in Christian theology

CHAPTER 8

The debate about Christian philosophy

During some four centuries in late antiquity, from the second till early in the fifth, two systems of belief and moral direction existed side by side. At the start of this period well-educated men in civilized Europe looked to philosophy for guidance; as we have seen, the Platonic tradition was already strong and would soon be dominant. Philosophy was taken to comprise logic, ethics and physics, which included the beginnings of what we now call natural science. Ancient logic led up to the theory of knowledge; ethics enquired what sorts of good we should aim at securing, and how to achieve them in practice.

At the outset of this period Christianity did not look like a counterpart to philosophy; indeed it was not always recognized as a distinct movement independent of the Judaism from which it sprang. But it developed very rapidly, and by the end of our period it had captured the intellectual allegiance of cultivated citizens in both the Eastern and the Western Empire. Compared with other religions of its time and place it was far more successful in organizing its beliefs into a coherent system. In doing this it borrowed largely from philosophy, and especially from Platonism. But it kept a sharply defined identity; its commitment to the Bible as a sacred book was far more uncompromising than the philosophers' respect for Plato; and it valued communal experience and tradition in a way which offended students accustomed to accepting the guidance of expert scholars. Nevertheless philosophy helped to mould its beliefs about God and the world, and taught it to uphold them in argument. Christianity itself could be termed a philosophy; 'the barbarian philosophy', it was sometimes called. It is a nice question whether we should call it a philosophy today.

There is no doubt about the contribution which philosophy made to early Christian thought; the fact is certain, though its value is sometimes disputed; and we shall try to describe it in detail. But we cannot speak with the same assurance about the contribution which Christian writers made to philosophy. Books have been written, indeed, which set out to describe 'Christian philosophy', not only as existing in the Middle Ages, where it is commonly recognized, but in late antiquity.[1] Such writers, I would argue, construe 'philosophy' in too large and too loose a sense. No doubt Christianity itself can be called, and was called, a philosophy, in that it offered a programme for living and gave reasons for adopting it. But if we relax our definition of 'philosophy' to this extent, *any* religion, no matter how fanciful, will count as a philosophy. The proper question is whether the use which Christian teachers made of philosophical doctrines and methods, in the sense accepted today, entitles them to be called philosophers. I myself would prefer to reserve the term for those who treat such doctrines and methods as an autonomous discipline to which they are committed. In this sense, only a few of the early Christian Fathers can properly claim to rank as philosophers; for the majority, the commitment to philosophical method was too uncertain and their achievement, as philosophers, too slight.

We need not criticize them for making religion, and the Christian religion, the centre of their interests. A philosopher is entitled to concentrate on the philosophy of religion, no less than on logic or the theory of knowledge. And we do find early Christian writers dealing with issues of acknowledged philosophical importance: the basic problems of theism, the origin of the world, the nature of evil and the interplay of fate and free will. Our point is rather that their allegiance to biblical and Church tradition left too little room, in most cases, for the dispassionate critical study that philosophy requires. Very few were interested in basic questions of logic or methodology for their own sake; fewer still developed new methods or established new results.

[1] For example, Henry Chadwick, 'The beginning of Christian philosophy', *LGP* Chapter 9; Eric Osborn, *The Beginnings of Christian Philosophy*; cf. H. A. Wolfson, *The Philosophy of the Church Fathers*.

Many of them welcomed and adopted current philosophical doctrines where these agreed with their Christian convictions. And they were ready to reply when these convictions were challenged by philosophers. In other cases, generally speaking, they were not interested. Thus what has been called 'Christian philosophy' generally proves to be Christian theology, systematically stated with the aid of elements borrowed from philosophy.

Gregory of Nyssa, for instance, has greatly influenced European culture through his theological writings. A distinguished theologian, he plainly drew upon contemporary philosophy; and one might easily infer that he must have been a distinguished philosopher. But a moment's reflection will put this claim in doubt. To Gregory, the Bible and Christian tradition were the source of all truth; he would have considered it frivolous to give comparable attention to Platonic scholarship or Aristotelian logic. And it would take some courage to argue that without such effort and training he was able to beat the philosophers at their own game.

But before going further we must dispose of an objection. Are we setting up unrealistic standards of excellence, attempting perhaps to judge early Christian writers by the standards of Aristotle? It is sometimes implied that in late antiquity the level of philosophical work was so low that Christians could easily pass for philosophers by the standards of their time. This again is misleading. Certainly there was some lack of original genius, with Plotinus and Augustine as the only great exceptions, but one could still distinguish between the mere dilettante and the competent professional scholar. Readers who are not philosophers can still appreciate the great difference between mere interest, however genuine, and professional skill.

We might take Justin as a case in point since, rather unusually for a Christian, he was a teacher of philosophy at Rome in the second century. Justin was a sensible man who did good service in formulating the primitive Christian tradition. There is not the slightest reason to think him inferior to his professional rivals among the Roman pagans; indeed his attachment to Christianity was in many ways an advantage, as setting him new problems

outside the traditional agenda of the Platonic schools. Nevertheless in acumen, breadth of culture and philosophical discipline
he is not to be compared with the best minds of the second
century; with Plutarch, perhaps, or Galen. His importance is
that of a Christian teacher, one of our founding Fathers.

In the first four Christian centuries, then, we can find sound
professional work emerging from the pagan schools, like that of
Alexander of Aphrodisias in the Aristotelian tradition, and of
the Neoplatonists. Christian handling of their themes was
usually derivative, except where attacks on the Church and its
theology called for refutation. Apart from such controversial
pieces on both sides, there was admittedly some lack of genuinely
creative writing in a popular idiom, as achieved by Plato and
Augustine, and later by Anselm or David Hume. Many pagan
writers were content to treat philosophical questions as a theme
for oratory, where elegance rather than enquiry was the desired
end; here, we must admit, the seriousness of Christian writers
often gave them the advantage. A few, like Porphyry, did
combine philosophical competence with an easy style of exposition; Plotinus, and later Proclus, though more powerful
thinkers, were too esoteric and too difficult to have much
immediate influence.

After Augustine's time the situation changes perceptibly.
Christian theology becomes more rigid, more self-confident,
more inward-looking, and correspondingly less open to positive
suggestions from the philosophers. On the other hand the
Neoplatonists, now supreme in the philosophical schools, maintain the anti-Christian attitude adopted by Porphyry; their
speculative systems become more complex and esoteric, and
much of their work is expressed in the arid and technical form of
commentaries on Platonic and Aristotelian texts. Late in the
day, as Christianity strengthens its hold as the official religion of
the empire, we begin to find Christian Neoplatonist scholars;
among these John Philoponus has recently come to be recognized as a thinker of some distinction; conversely, we have noted
the mystical theologian Dionysius 'the Areopagite', surprisingly
indebted to the philosophy of Proclus. There are the beginnings
of a Christian scholasticism, in which philosophical methods are

used to work out the details of what are basically dogmatic decisions approved by Church councils. But as a rule the philosophers have little influence on their Christian contemporaries, and the influential churchmen cannot rank as philosophers; Cyril of Alexandria, say, or Gregory the Great, have studied philosophical texts but have absorbed little in the way of philosophical discipline. An interesting exception is Boethius, whose interests are fairly evenly balanced between philosophy and theology, and who shows ability in both, besides writing an immensely influential popular work, the *Consolation of Philosophy*.

Where then did Christian writers make original contributions? The question can be approached by recalling that the ancients commonly divided philosophy into the three departments of logic, ethics and physics. Serious Christian engagement with logic begins in the fourth century, with Marius Victorinus and Augustine, and was continued by Boethius. But some work was done earlier in the related field of the theory of knowledge, or epistemology. Clement of Alexandria compiled notes on this subject in the tradition of Albinus, using Aristotle's logical writings and also Chrysippus; these have come down to us as Book 8 of his *Stromateis*. A rather elementary treatment of rational knowledge is also presupposed in discussing the virtue of faith and in proofs of the existence of God, which we shall examine in due course. In both these cases Christian writers had an interest in refuting scepticism. On the other hand many of them actually use traditional sceptical arguments in order to show that philosophy as such cannot yield assured truth, which must then be found in Christian theology: a conclusion directly contrary to scepticism. Some writers allow themselves an indiscriminate attack on the philosophers; examples are found in Tertullian, Lactantius, Athanasius, Basil and Gregory Nazianzen; the philosophers' dissensions, it is claimed, prove that they have failed to discover the truth. Augustine takes a more positive line, at least in his early writings; he states the case against scepticism and writes elementary treatises on the theory of knowledge, the *Principia Dialecticae* and the *De Magistro*, as well as a far more important critique of the sceptics, the *Contra Academicos*. He also uses human knowledge as a datum from which to prove the existence of God (see pp. 118–19 below). But his most penetrating reflections are delivered in passing, in works written after his main interest had moved from philosophy to theology; the *Confessions* (e.g. Book X) and the *De Trinitate*.

The Christian contribution to ethics is less easy to summarize because of the difficulty of deciding what the term 'ethics' ought to include. Is ethics involved wherever moral issues are discussed? It goes without saying that Christian writers concerned themselves with morality, both by setting out the standards of character and conduct at which Christians should aim and by considering what practices are inadmissible for members of the Church; they distinguish, then, between virtues and vices, but also rather differently between acceptable conduct and recognized offences. Much of this writing is tolerably familiar, and general surveys are to be found; on the social side we have the classic work of E. Troeltsch;[2] an impressive book by K. E. Kirk[3] considers both personal ideals and Church disciplines; and recent studies have appeared from G. W. Forell and Eric Osborn.[4]

But clearly a mere assemblage of moral directives, however wise and lofty, cannot as such be called philosophy. No well-defined frontier can be drawn; but provisionally we suggest that moral teaching can count as philosophy if it discusses moral questions in relation to larger philosophical problems, such as the nature of man, of his soul and intellect, or that of fate and free will; or again, if it brings together its practical recommendations into a coherent and inclusive system; or again, naturally, if it does both. Some early Christian writers amply fulfil these conditions. Clement of Alexandria has a well-conceived educational programme which coheres with his metaphysics and theology, and aims at leading the mind away from material things to the study of transcendent realities. His near-contemporary Tertullian, in striking contrast, writes as a severe and

---

[2] *Die Soziallehren der christlichen Kirchen und Gruppen* (Tübingen 1912); Eng. trans. *The Social Teaching of the Christian Churches* (London 1931).

[3] *The Vision of God* (London 1931).

[4] G. W. Forell, *History of Christian Ethics*; Eric Osborn, *Ethical Patterns in Early Christian Thought* (Cambridge 1976).

mainly unphilosophical moralist. A more reflective idiom appears with St Basil, who defends recourse to non-Christian authors and collects together a rule of life for his monastic communities. But the details of his programme hardly square with his commendation of the 'philosophic life'; they reflect the experience of monastic life untouched by philosophy. Augustine offers a far more imaginative and integrated ethics based on a synthesis of Christianity and Platonism.

Thirdly we should enquire what the Christian writers contributed to philosophy under the heading of physics. For the ancients 'physics' was a wide and inclusive term; it denoted the study of the natural world, including its first principles or causes, its origin and its ultimate fate, with an important subsection on the nature of man, his body, mind and soul and his claim to free will; some thinkers also included the gods and their dealings with the world and mankind. Thus the second volume of von Arnim's *Stoicorum Veterum Fragmenta* treats physics under nine headings: (1) fundamental principles, including the definition of reality, categories, causes, elements, space and time; (2) the universe in general; (3) astronomy; (4) animals and plants; (5) the human soul; (6) fate; (7) the gods; (8) providence; and (9) divination. But this catalogue is adapted to the Stoic assumption that there is no reality, even of the most rational and intelligent kind, which has not some sort of material embodiment. This view was of course opposed by the Platonists (discounting those of the sceptical, 'academic' school), who taught that material things constitute only half, and far the less important half, of the totality of things. The first place belonged to the world of immaterial realities, the Forms or 'intelligibles' (*noēta*), often thought to be not only intelligible but also intelligent, and thus including uncorrupted human souls together with demons or angels and a supreme creative principle or god. By and large the Christian writers, like Philo before them, accepted this division of reality into *aisthēta* and *noēta*, the perceptible and the intelligible order. But this division was crossed by another, native to Christianity, which acquired special prominence as a result of the Arian controversy; namely the distinction between God the Creator and all created beings whatsoever, including immaterial spirits or angels. Viewing the material world as God's creation, it was natural for Christians to include at least an outline account of it under the heading of theology. Nevertheless Christian writers generally approved the Platonic theory of *noēta* for the support it gave to their own doctrines of an immaterial Godhead with attendant angels or spirits and the immortal human soul, while remaining somewhat sceptical towards the doctrine of Forms, which was the starting-point of the whole scheme.[5] Tertullian stands by himself in claiming that God, since he is real, must be a *corpus*.

Many Christian writers found it unnecessary to argue in a philosophical idiom that God exists, or that He is one; they had the assurance of Scripture and Christian tradition. Others adopted current arguments against atheism and polytheism, but were slow to devise new methods (see Chapter 10 below). Positive arguments for God's unity and transcendence, deriving ultimately from Plato and Aristotle and already presented by Philo, are found in Justin and Irenaeus and are rather more coherently stated by Clement (especially *Str.* 5.81–2). A more considered approach to Christian theism begins with Augustine.

Christian thought about the origin of the world is of course dominated by the general acceptance of Genesis 1 and 2 as a literal account of the 'Hexaemeron', the six days of creation. Writers such as Basil the Great and Gregory of Nyssa consult philosophers like Posidonius to confirm and develop various details of the biblical narrative, but do not allow them any independent authority (Basil, *Hom. Hex.* 1.2); Basil indeed regards the shape of the earth as a question of no importance (*ibid.* 9.1), whereas Lactantius had insisted that it is flat (*D.I.* 3.24). Here again Augustine is wiser; though uninterested in scientific research as such, he notes that well-established conclusions in apparent conflict with the Bible may pose a danger to Christian faith unless accommodations can be found (*Gen. ad Litt.* 1.19.39 etc.). Origen again, exploiting his allegorical methods, which give him great freedom in interpreting Scripture, presents a daring and wide-ranging conspectus which

[5] See, for example, Origen, *Princ.* 2.3.6; Gregory Nazianzen, *Orat.* 27.9 (= *Orat. Theol.* 1.9).

draws on both Platonic and Stoic teaching. If God is Creator, he must be so eternally; so this world is only one episode in an infinite succession of created worlds; he also discusses its approaching end, using Stoic theories of a final conflagration. Christian understanding of the nature of man is generally based on the widely accepted Greek distinction between the perishable body and the immortal soul, often modified to yield a trichotomy of body, soul and spirit. Plato provides some suggestions of this latter view, though his best-known scheme is that which contrasts the body with a soul which is itself tripartite (see pp. 21–2). For Plato it is *nous*, intelligence, which is the highest part of the soul (while God is 'either intelligence or something better', Aristotle fr. 46, p. 57 Ross). The Pythagoreans, however, spoke of an element in man, the 'divine spark', which is actually akin to God. Christians came to dislike the suggestion that sinful men could claim such a relationship with their Creator (cf. p. 71). Hence Christian thinkers mostly distinguish between man's soul, as the highest part of God's creative workmanship, and the spirit as a particular gift of inspiration accorded to men but not theirs to control.

Christian teaching about human nature is so largely dominated by Platonic thought that we find hardly any trace of the distinctive biblical anthropology as we now interpret it, regarding life and personality as a function of the human body when this is animated by the divine spirit. But one awkward legacy survives; the Hebrews could only conceive of survival as a resurrection of the body, and this belief was early integrated into the Creeds, with a powerful influence from St Paul. It proved something of an embarrassment; the notion was ridiculed by many Platonists, for whom the body was necessarily the source of sensuality and corruption, and ought to disappear for ever. On the other hand Christians found themselves accepting two distinctive concepts of survival, which it was difficult to bring together in a coherent scheme: the soul surviving without a body after death, but waiting to receive a glorious body at the last day. (How was it handicapped meanwhile? And how could a *body* enhance its spiritual life?)

The only comprehensive work on Christian anthropology

that survives is the *De Natura Hominis* by Nemesius of Emesa, a well-read though unoriginal writer of the late fourth century who has at least the merit of presenting a carefully worked out synthesis of Platonic and Christian ideas. There is a more considerable literature on the soul as such, including the striking and unconventional *De Anima* written by Tertullian, who borrows much of his material, including an account of the views already expressed by philosophers, from the medical writer Soranus.

The origin of the human soul was long debated. In the case of Adam an answer could be found in Genesis 1:27; but for his descendants various possibilities were open. Origen at one time accepted the Platonic view that our souls have previously lived in other bodies, and will do so again; though apparently our 'other lives' take place in past or future *worlds* (cf. Plato *Phaedrus* 249b). This view, however, was strongly criticized, and Christian opinion was divided between the alternatives of 'traducianism', the soul being transmitted from parent to child in the act of generation, and 'creationism', each soul being created individually by God, either at the moment of conception or shortly after.

A question of fundamental importance for ethics concerned the freedom of the human will. It was commonly conceded that our activities are circumscribed by nature and by chance; we cannot help growing old, or incurring various illnesses or accidents. But it remained a debatable question whether we enjoy a limited freedom or whether all our actions are determined and in principle predictable. The Stoics tended towards determinism, though they offered two rather inadequate replies, the freedom of self-determination and the freedom of accepting the inevitable, as discussed above (pp. 50–1). Determinism seemed also a natural conclusion from astrology, for those who accepted it, and from the doctrine that God foreknows all events. The contrary position, that human actions are at least partly undetermined, was argued by the sceptical Platonist Carneades; and he was followed by Christian writers who argued that if all our actions are determined one can give no rational justification for praise or blame, or for rewards and punishments after death.

Christian work in this field is apt to look amateurish compared with the rigorous argumentation (so far as we can reconstruct it) of Diodorus Cronus and Carneades and the surviving work of Alexander of Aphrodisias, partly because Christian writers did not address themselves to the fundamental problem posed by Aristotle (*Interpr.* 9) on the truth and falsity of propositions about future events. The best-known early Christian treatment is that by Origen in the third book of his *De Principiis*; Origen argues, *inter alia*, that God foresees human actions but does not determine them. Methodius takes up the subject in his *De Autexusio*, and Augustine in his *De Libero Arbitrio*.

We may conclude, then, that few Christian writers apart from Augustine would be accepted by dispassionate critics as having made original contributions to philosophy. But an objection must now be considered. It may be claimed that the main structure of Christian orthodoxy was argued out in a continuous tradition with the aid of philosophical techniques, and that this work can properly be included in the philosophy of religion. This claim might be made for the basic doctrine of God, for those of the Trinity and the Incarnation, perhaps for that of the Creation (in principle, as *creatio ex nihilo*, though not in its biblical detail), and for doctrines concerned with mankind and the moral life. No doubt it is such an inclusive notion of philosophy which was adopted by Professor Wolfson when he wrote of *The Philosophy of the Church Fathers*.

I myself would resist this extension for several reasons. The most obvious is that it conflicts with accepted usage. Any competent librarian knows where to place books on Christian doctrine. Moreover, if these are removed to the philosophy section, theology is deprived of its basic discipline; it is reduced to an assortment of peripheral studies, biblical criticism, ecclesiology, liturgiology, and so on, with no intelligible connection.

Much more important, the proposal just made ignores the dimension of faith in Christian thinking. It is faith that gives the Christian imagination the power of advancing new perspectives within a continuous tradition of common devotion. This does not mean that it is impossible to present Christian orthodoxy within a rationally ordered scheme. One can, for instance, argue for the existence of a God who is personal and loving, from which it is reasonable to conclude that he reveals himself to men; the next step is to claim that such a revelation can be found in the Scriptures and in their record of the life and death of Christ. Such a scheme, whether or not it is convincing in detail, would bring dogmatic theology within the ambit of the philosophy of religion. But in the early Church it is clear that the main items of Christian belief were seldom, if ever, argued out in this way; they are the product of Christian reflection upon the Scriptures, accepted by faith as the word of God, in the context of a common life of devotion to Christ, accepted by faith as Lord, Illuminator and Redeemer.

If we then reject the larger definition of philosophy just considered, we may define the philosopher in terms of his commitment to a rational discipline and method, and his skill in pursuing it. I do not think that this particular kind of commitment, and this particular skill, was strongly represented among the Christian Fathers. The case should, of course, be argued in terms of individuals; and I will briefly set out my views on a few leading figures. But on so controversial a subject it seems best to set out the opinions of others, both for and against, attached as an appendix to this chapter.

Of Justin I have already spoken. Irenaeus is more problematic. He has, I suspect, more philosophical talent than is easy to detect in his surviving work. His *Adversus Haereses* is a *piece d'occasion*, written to meet a pressing pastoral need, no doubt in moments snatched from episcopal duties, clumsily constructed and unevenly well informed; its theology sometimes naive and archaic, but often surprisingly mature. But when philosophical methods are used, they are ably handled, and one regrets the disappearance of other works known to Eusebius, especially the treatise arguing that God is not the author of evil.

Eusebius of Caesarea does at least make his mark as a careful student of philosophy, and his sympathy with the Platonic tradition has left its mark on his theology. He is not, on the whole, an original thinker; though I believe the tendency of theologians to disparage him, whether because of his sympathy with Arius or of his uncritical admiration of Constantine, has been carried too far. He deserves a modest rehabilitation.

Of the Cappadocian Fathers, Basil and Gregory Nazianzen are of course far more influential and effective thinkers, and some basic philosophy plays an important part in their distinction between 'substance' and 'person' in the Trinity (see Chapter 15). Basil again can argue perceptively against Eunomius, drawing upon established theories of the nature of language. But on the whole he looks upon philosophy as an auxiliary to Christian tradition, rather than as an independent source of truth, or even a valid corrective in detail; it would be unrealistic to account him a notable philosopher. The same applies *a fortiori* to Gregory Nazianzen, whose gifts lie mainly in the effective expression of Christian teaching; but his telling phrases often do make points of real theological substance.

Gregory of Nyssa has already been mentioned, and I have discussed his case elsewhere. He has even been described as 'the greatest Christian philosopher among the Church Fathers',[6] to the surprising neglect of Augustine; but such a claim can only rest on a loose definition of philosophy which I have given reason to discount. He is a theologian of some note, as well as a much-loved devotional and mystical writer; and he makes some striking advances in a philosophical vein, for instance in contending for the infinity of God. Against this we may set his advertised contempt for non-Christian philosophers and his lack of consistency both in his terminology and in his conclusions (the latter, indeed, extending to theology; for instance in his conflicting opinions about the future life).[7] I would criticize his disrespect for philosophical technique more than the very surprising errors to be found, for instance, in his treatise *On Not Three Gods* (see pp. 182–3 below); for the greatest philosophers have not been proof against surprising errors.

There remain one or two writers who are more difficult to classify. Of these Origen is perhaps the most intriguing. He himself makes it clear that he does not regard philosophy as a primary authority; that role belongs to Scripture and Christian tradition. Nevertheless he is a careful and well-informed student of philosophy. He lived in a time and place where standards of Christian orthodoxy were liberal; and his allegorical methods of

---

[6] Basil Studer, *Gott und unsere Erlösung* (Düsseldorf 1985), p. 177.
[7] See T. J. Dennis, 'Gregory on the resurrection of the body' (Bibliography 20).

exegesis allowed him to claim whole-hearted allegiance to the Scriptures as God's inspired word while retaining considerable freedom to speculate. He thus adopted a number of beliefs, some of them Platonic or Stoic in character, which proved unacceptable to later theologians: the pre-existence of souls, including the soul of Christ; the resurrection of our bodies in an ethereal, discarnate form; the ultimate salvation of every soul, not excluding even the Devil, who (being God's creature) cannot be essentially evil. Origen can take a broad view; his four-volume work *De Principiis* presents a comprehensive account of God, the world and mankind. And although so widely separated from the main philosophical tradition by his often fanciful use of the Bible, he often writes in a philosophic style. His approach is dispassionate, inventive and judicial; he does not think in terms of unquestioned truths or patent heresies, but is willing to consider suggestions on their merits. A reader of his *Contra Celsum* – in some ways his worst book – might easily dismiss him as a close-minded polemist; but in his Commentary on St John he deals far more temperately with the Gnostic Heracleon, admitting on occasion that Heracleon is right, or at least not far from the truth (e.g. 6.26.126, 13.10.59, 13.10.62).

Clement, though on the whole a less gifted thinker, is a strikingly original writer and can also be thought of as a philosopher. The presentation of his thought in the *Stromateis* or 'Patchwork' is deliberately and tantalizingly unsystematic; but he has a consistent view of a Christian culture in which philosophy plays an essential part in the education of the intelligent believer. As we have seen, he thought it worth while to enquire into epistemology as part of his programme; he has also left us a study of a specific problem in Christian ethics, the *Quis Dives Salvetur*. He draws on the Platonic tradition to establish a negative theology, stressing God's transcendence to a degree which makes him virtually unknowable to man.

Tertullian is more of an enigma. Well read in the philosophers, his stormy temperament and his rhetorical bias lead him to assert contradictory views with uninhibited force and eloquence. His theory of Christian authority shows him in his most obscurantist mood; his moral teaching is severe and puritanical, and is developed without philosophic refinements. But he can on occasion argue skilfully and logically with the aid of his philosophic learning, as in his *De Anima*, or (with more lasting effect) in expressing the Christian doctrine of the Trinity by presenting God as a single substance deployed in three Persons.

In view of this uneven record of achievement, I do not present this book as a history of Christian philosophy. It would certainly be misleading to suggest that in these early centuries the Christian use of philosophy involved a continuous process of development in any way comparable to that of Christian theology; there are relatively few points at which philosophical work was incorporated into the accepted structure of Christian teaching. Even this degree of patronage is in some ways remarkable; for philosophy came into the Church from outside and was always liable to be attacked as a pagan aberration. Only a few Christian writers had any genuine commitment to philosophical study; fewer still became philosophers of distinction; suspicion, over-confidence and rhetorical showmanship – matched of course in contemporary paganism – were seldom completely eliminated. For this reason I shall not attempt to describe the interaction between philosophy and theology in the early Church as a developing process. It seems more appropriate to adopt a systematic approach; having given this cursory sketch of the whole field, I will try to investigate the main concepts which Christian thinkers either learnt from the philosophers or developed along lines which show their influence. This method of treatment may lack the human warmth which could be introduced if we treated the Christian thinkers one by one. But I believe it can be made interesting and intelligible enough to any moderately competent reader who preserves the spirit of enquiry.

For positive estimates of Justin as a philosopher, see H. Chadwick, *Early Christian Thought and the Classical Tradition* (Oxford 1966) pp. 20–2, and *LGP* pp. 160–5; Eric Osborn, *Justin Martyr* (Tübingen 1973) pp. 77–82, 109.
For Irenaeus, W. R. Schoedel, in *JThS* n.s. 35 (1984) pp. 31–49.
For Lactantius, E. Amann, *DTC* 8 (1924) cols. 2434–43.
For Eusebius, J. Moreau, *RAC* 6 (1966) col. 1081.

For Basil, G. Bardy, _RAC_ I (1950) col. 1264.

For Gregory Nazianzen, I. P. Sheldon-Williams, _LGP_ pp. 440–7.

For Gregory of Nyssa, E. Mühlenberg, _Die Unendlichkeit Gottes_ (Göttingen 1966) especially pp. 90–2; A. Dihle, _The Theory of Will in Classical Antiquity_ (Berkeley, Los Angeles and London 1982) pp. 119–22.

For negative estimates of Justin as a philosopher, see R. A. Norris, _God and World in Early Christian Theology_ (London 1966) pp. 33–56, especially 53.

For Irenaeus, A. Benoit, _S. Irénée_ (Paris 1960) pp. 65–73.

For Lactantius, O. Gigon in A. M. Ritter (ed.), _Kerygma und Logos_ (Festschrift for C. Andresen) (Göttingen 1979) pp. 196–213.

For Eusebius, D. S. Wallace-Hadrill, _Eusebius of Caesarea_ (London 1960) pp. 139–54.

For Basil, J. M. Rist, in P. J. Fedwick (ed.), _Basil of Caesarea_ (Toronto 1981) pp. 137–220, especially 219–20; Y. Courtonne, _Saint Basile et l'Hellenisme_ (Paris 1934) pp. 143–62, especially 144–5, 159.

For Gregory Nazianzen, R. R. Ruether, _Gregory of Nazianzus_ (Oxford 1969) pp. 167–75.

For Gregory of Nyssa, G. C. Stead in H. Dörrie _et al._ (eds.), _Gregor von Nyssa und die Philosophie_ (Leiden 1976) pp. 107–27; and see below, p. 184 n. 5.

CHAPTER 9

Greek and Hebrew conceptions of God

The Christian Doctrine of God gives rise to a problem of more general application. How important was the influence of Greek thought upon the early Church, and how should we estimate its value?

Christians will agree that their primary inspiration is the life and teaching of Jesus Christ as presented in the New Testament. Much of this teaching was based on the sacred Scriptures as he knew them, which roughly correspond to our Old Testament. We cannot demonstrate that Jesus himself treated all these Scriptures as having equal authority and value; most Jews of his time drew a distinction between the Law, the Prophets and the Writings; and certainly few modern Christians will equate them. But a general allegiance to the Old Testament has been an indispensable part of Christian discipleship ever since the second-century Church rejected the Marcionites' attempt to discard it.

Most Christians, again, accept the judgement of the early Church in supplementing the Gospel records with other documents which reveal how the life and death of Jesus was interpreted and imitated by his followers of the next generation; the documents added to the Gospels in our New Testament. Many scholars, of course, go much further than this; for example, they regard St Paul's letters as our primary authority, since they provide contemporary evidence for the life of the Church, whereas the Gospels attempt to recall the events of a generation or two before they were written. On the other hand there are those who argue that the original teaching of Jesus was complicated and distorted by Paul and others of his kind. It is claimed that whereas Jesus taught his disciples to worship God, his heavenly Father, Paul and others taught the Church to worship Jesus, presented a different scheme of salvation, adopted a different set of values, and so on.

This is a question which lies beyond the scope of this book; but it is clear that similar problems will arise in an acute form when we consider the further development of Christian teaching in and after the first century. It soon proved that the most active and influential Christian teachers were those who could appeal to cultivated Greek-speaking enquirers, offering the Christian faith in terms that they could understand, as a new philosophy, or again as the authentic version of an age-old philosophy which had been known to virtuous pagans in antiquity but had since been corrupted.

There is an enormous literature devoted to the question whether this process of hellenization was a justifiable development to meet the needs of a new situation, and whether, even in this case, some vital elements in the early Christian proclamation of Jesus were lost or submerged. Certainly the New Testament itself does not encourage the reader to think favourably of philosophy; it is condemned by name at Colossians 2:8, and although Paul is represented in Acts 17:18 as debating with philosophers at Athens, he seems to have had little immediate success (Acts 17:32–4); and it is commonly supposed that this disappointment partly accounts for his words to the Corinthians (1 Cor. 2:3) 'I determined not to know anything among you save Jesus Christ, and him crucified'. Moreover it may be thought that there are particular objections to applying philosophy to the basic belief in God himself; it may seem that we are substituting rational demonstration for authentic faith; faith in a divine mystery, which prompts us to worship a being who is infinitely greater and holier than we can understand; whereas rational reflection presents only that small measure of divine being that is accessible to our minds.

In some Christians there is no doubt that this objection takes the form of an irrational repulsion, which after all contains elements of honest simplicity; the believer whose devotion is fixed on 'Jesus Christ and him crucified' will tend to regard the more sophisticated developments of Christian theology as irrelevant distractions, if not as fatal corruptions of primitive truth. But more reflective characters will wish for a clearer understanding of what happened before they pass judgement. In dealing with the doctrine of God this historical development can be presented in its simplest form if we leave the New Testament on one side and consider the contrast between the Jewish picture of God presented in the Old Testament and the modified picture which resulted from taking over the most appropriate concepts offered by Greek philosophy.

For an account of the Hebrew conception of God I shall refer to W. Eichrodt, *Theology of the Old Testament*, whose systematic exposition suits the style of this book. Some readers may think he over-simplifies, and may be referred, for example to W. H. Schmidt, *The Faith of the Old Testament*, for a more historical treatment. It is of course true that Israelite theology was never perfectly consistent, but developed over a long period of conflict and change. Nevertheless, owning a common religious tradition it can be seen as a unity as compared with the extremely divergent speculations of the Greeks. This need not exclude a recognition of variety; in particular, during the two centuries preceding the emergence of Christianity, some Jewish writers – and notably the author of 'Wisdom' – accepted elements of Greek philosophy; others, for instance those of the apocalyptic school, ignored or rejected it.

Eichrodt, then, presents the Old Testament conception of God as follows. The Israelites' approach to their deity was cultic and devotional, sometimes also nationalistic, and Eichrodt quite rightly stresses those beliefs about God which were most characteristic of the Jewish tradition. In this tradition, he explains, God is personal; God is spiritual; God is one; and he goes on to list God's attributes under the headings (1) power; (2) loving-kindness or loyalty (*hesed*); (3) righteousness or faithfulness (*emeth*); (4) affection; (5) anger; and (6) holiness.

To say that God is personal indicates that he is an intelligent being who can have knowledge of our world and a purpose for it (he is 'not a blind natural force', Eichrodt p. 104, Eng. trans. pp. 210–11); he has a well-marked character, being powerful, righteous, holy, etc.; and he is in fellowship with his creatures, especially mankind, so far as their limited powers allow them to understand him. By saying that God is spiritual, we do not mean that he has no body (as will soon become clear) but rather that he is the source of a mysterious life-giving power and energy that animates the human body, and himself possesses this energy in the fullest measure. The spirit is an unseen power, like the wind or the breath; and God, who is himself unseen, can communicate with men, not only by visible apparitions but by unseen agencies, spirits. By saying that God is one, we are summing up a long process of development, which begins with the demand that Israel should worship and serve only one God, Jahweh, ignoring all others, but develops into the conviction that there *is* only one being, Jahweh, who deserves the title of God and claims our allegiance as ruler of all the world. On this view the so-called gods of the other nations are either mere lifeless images or wicked spirits; though in some Old Testament passages we find the notion that God has allowed some of his subordinate spirits to be worshipped by other races; they are 'the angels of the nations'.

God's power is seen both in the once-for-all occurrences of history and in the recurrent cycles of the natural world. In the earliest books he appears as a warrior chief who leads his people to victory or abandons them to defeat; his power can 'break out' also in terrifying and destructive events such as earthquakes or plagues; but it is generally seen as controlled by a moral purpose, for instance, to punish the rebellious Korah (Num. 16:31–3) or to drown the oppressing Egyptians; and it is recognized also in the fertility of the people's cattle and their growing crops. God's loving-kindness to his people proceeds from his special covenant relation to them; *hesed* implies his faithful keeping of his promises rather than the abstract impartiality which can be implied by our word 'justice', or the irrational emotion which can be denoted by 'love' or 'affection'. God's righteousness appears primarily in his watchful care for his people which is appropriate to his position as their creator and protector. His affection for his people appears in his choice of them, upheld despite all their shortcomings. But God, though ready to pardon, can never compromise with oppression, deceit or impurity; his absolute rejection of such human failings is the negative side of his holiness. But he also rejoices in the splendour and dignity of his heavenly court and in the beauty and fruitfulness of his created world and the innocent joys of his human creatures.

These beliefs sum up for us the religious and devotional ideals of the Old Testament. But we have to imagine the situation of early Christian converts reading the Greek version of it, some of them educated in the tradition of Greek philosophy and prompted by the spirit of detached enquiry that it encouraged. In pre-Christian times the Jews had already taken steps to present their religion in a philosophical form calculated to appeal to cultured pagans. When Christian apologists moved beyond the simple proclamation of their message (*kērygma*) and were challenged to give a reasoned defence of their faith, they largely adopted the assumptions and methods of their Jewish precursors, adding of necessity a defence of their own movement and their distinctive beliefs against Jewish criticisms – which soon developed into a spirited counter-attack.

One could imagine the enquirer posing a series of questions based on Aristotle's *Categories*. What is God? – i.e. what is his form, if he has a form, and what is he made of? How is he related to space and time? – or more concretely, Where is He? How large? In what sense eternal? – Is there only one such God, and if so, in what sense one? What does he do, and what happens to him? In practice, not all such questions were considered important – though Philo supplies answers to them all; but the answers either given or assumed by Christian teachers provide the basis of much early Christian theology.

It should of course be remembered that even cultivated enquirers in antiquity had nothing corresponding to the modern critical approach to the Bible. Its opponents might attack it as provincial, immoral and inconsistent; its defenders assumed that it must be treated as an inspired book, and therefore consistent, complete and correct in every detail. We can now speak of 'archaisms' and 'primitive elements' in the context of a theory of progressive revelation; Jewish and early Christian interpreters commonly dealt with inconsistent or offensive passages by adopting the theory of allegory already worked out by Stoics and others to defend the educational value of Homer. (Some examples will soon be given.) This left them with the task of choosing which texts should be given primary authority, either as literally interpreted or in the light of some traditional understanding; and inevitably these texts tended to be explained along lines which harmonized with the best contemporary pagan thought.

In practice, beliefs about the form of God are bound up with beliefs about his location; and neither the Old Testament nor Greek philosophy present a united view. Three early beliefs have been attributed to the Israelites: God dwells in the deserts of the South (Judg 5:4), or in the land of Canaan (2 Kgs. 5:17), or more specifically in its sanctuaries, as later in the Jerusalem Temple. But the impression most easily formed by the reader is that God's dwelling-place is 'in heaven', above the solid vault of the sky. Heaven is God's home; though for the earliest writers this does not prevent him from coming down to visit the earth (Gen. 11:5, 18:20–33). In the later books God is not conceived as descending to earth, since (1) he can see and hear at a distance (Zech. 4:5 N.E.B., Ps. 34:15, Jer. 23:24a, and more generally Ps. 139) and (2) he can act at a distance by his mere word of command, by his messengers or 'angels', or by his spirit instructing men. Even late and sophisticated writers retain the picture of a royal palace situated above the clouds, for example Wisdom 18:14–16: 'All things were lying in peace and silence . . . when thy Almighty Word leapt from thy royal throne in heaven into the midst of [Egypt] that doomed land'. But this does not imply his absence from the world; God makes his presence known in the Temple at Jerusalem (as formerly on Sinai) by a manifestation of glory, his *Shekinah*: he extends his presence in dwelling with the righteous ('round about them' or 'among them', Ps. 34:7, 125:2, rather than 'within them') and in a few passages he is described as present everywhere, for example Psalm 139:7–10 and Jeremiah 23:24b, 'Do I not fill heaven and earth?', a text much quoted by Christian writers.

The common belief that God has his dwelling in the heavens goes along with the belief that he has a form like that of a man – a male, of course – which is easily deduced from Genesis 1:26–7, and is implied by numerous references to his 'throne', his 'footstool', his 'face', his 'hands' and the like. In the primitive period this belief is uncomplicated; thus in Genesis 18 three 'men' appear to Abraham: two of them go to Sodom (19:1) while the third remains speaking with Abraham and is identified as Jahweh. The description of God sitting at table with Abraham of course implies that God is – or can appear to be – the same size as a man; though later texts reflecting on God's cosmic power imagine him as enormously large (e.g. Isa. 40:12–15). There are indeed 'aniconic' texts which deny him any form, such as Deuteronomy 4:12, 15, 16: 'you heard a voice speaking [on Sinai], but you saw no figure; . . . therefore do not make any carved figure, whether in human or animal form'. But more generally the idols are condemned, not as *having* hands or mouths, but as unable to use them; the very familiar attack on them in Psalm 115:4 ff. (= Ps. 135:15 ff.) hardly suggests that the true God has no eyes or mouth!

How far these assumptions persisted into New Testament times is a delicate question; much depended on the individual's education and milieu. In rabbinic theology there was certainly a shift of emphasis: just as it was thought irreverent to pronounce the sacred Name, so there was a reluctance to speculate about God's form and appearance; thus only qualified teachers were allowed to expound Ezekiel 1. More attention was given to God's moral attributes; and this seems to be, broadly speaking, the view taken by Jesus, who preaches God's love and forgiveness but whose cosmic vision looks to the future rather than to the present; and even there the details of the Messianic Banquet or the Last Judgement are more clearly pictured than the supreme Judge or Host.

The apocalyptic writers are less restrained; certainly it was admitted that God could not be seen, but this was because he was surrounded by dazzling light which no human vision could bear (cf. 1 Tim. 6:16). The Book of Enoch (14:9–23) describes a heaven all made of fire, and the passage culminates in a description of 'the Great Glory', saying 'None of the angels could enter and behold his face by reason of the magnificence and glory, and no flesh could behold him'; and the New Testament

Apocalypse, drawing on Ezekiel, presents a similar picture. Some allowance should of course be made for the Hebrew custom of describing actions in physical terms; they could certainly speak of 'seeing someone's face' where we might put 'enjoying his favour'; and in Acts 5:9 Peter says 'Behold the feet of the men . . .', meaning little more than 'Look, they are coming'. But the detailed realism of the apocalyptic writers must have passed on to simple people the impression of a God who has 'feet . . . breasts . . . head . . . hair . . . eyes' and a 'right hand' like a man, as we read the description in Revelation 1:13–16.

The Old Testament writers sometimes speak of God as unchanging (Num. 23:19, Isa. 46:11, Mal. 3:6). In Christian writers influenced by Greek philosophy this doctrine is developed in an absolute metaphysical sense. Hebrew writers are more concrete, and their thinking includes two main points: (1) God has the dignity appropriate to old age, but without its disabilities; he does not grow weary or forgetful (Isa. 40:28, cf. Ps. 147:4–5); and (2) God is faithful to his covenant promises, even though men break theirs (Exod. 34:9–10). On the other hand since God directs and controls human history while allowing human beings (in the short run) to act as they will, the Old Testament writers describe God as responding to men's good or evil deeds with emotion as well as with the appropriate action; he is angry, or again restrains his anger; he shows long-suffering; he desires his people's allegiance; he laughs in scorn at the wicked (e.g. Ps. 103:8–9, 78:38–9, Hos. 11:1 ff., cf. 2:14, Ps. 37:13). This thought of a varying play of emotions, as a just response to the variety of human acts, persists for instance in the Book of Wisdom (4:18, 5:17 ff., 11:23–4); on the other hand the notion that God could actually 'repent' (as Gen. 6:6, Exod. 32:14, 1 Sam. 15:11, 2 Sam. 24:16, Joel 2:13, Jonah 3:10) seems to have been criticized (1 Sam. 15:29, Num. 23:19, Ezek. 24:14); it was of course a difficulty to hellenized Jews and later to Christians. Philo wrote a special treatise *Quod Deus sit Immutabilis* to refute the notion that God could change his mind, as Genesis 6:6 could suggest. Already before his time the Greek version had put this more tactfully: 'The Lord considered that he had made man, and took thought': but it does not obscure the threat expressed in the following verse, 6:7, and God still appears as 'repenting' in the Greek version of Joel 2:13 and Jonah 3:10.

Philo is unusual among the Jews of his time in condemning any notion of God in human form (*Plant.* 35, cf. *Opif.* 69, *Leg. All.* 1.36, *Sacr.* 95 etc.). The majority, while no doubt acknowledging the limitations of human language, saw no reason to qualify the sacred texts which pictured God in human form, having emotions and making decisions, and presiding over human affairs with knowledge, sympathy and judgement. But he is now commonly viewed as immobile, seated eternally on his throne of majesty, and fulfilling his will by particular agencies – his Word, his Wisdom, his Law, etc., – or by created subordinates – his angels. Since he has no needs of any kind, there is nothing corresponding to the rhythm of human life in working, eating and sleeping. This makes for some loss of vigour as compared with earlier notions that God could actually visit mankind, lay out a garden (Gen. 2:8) and enjoy innocent pleasures (Gen. 8:21). The vivid language of (e.g.) Ezekiel 16:8 is no doubt symbolic; but the notion that God could actually relax and play is represented by Psalm 104:26 and Proverbs 8:30, and such passages of course continued to be read, alongside the more sober pronouncements of later writers. Hebrew thought thus reaches a position not unlike that of pseudo-Aristotle *De Mundo* in the Greek tradition, where God retains control of the world but acts without effort or anxiety by means of subordinates; though the Hebrews lay far greater stress on God's moral government.

Our account of the Jewish conception of God shows that though there is an underlying unity of thought, there is considerable variation in detail. Among the Greeks there is much more variety and contrast, so that it is best to avoid generalizations and attempt to distinguish the various theologies.

Among the ancient Greeks, polytheism was usual, springing naturally from the great variety of local cults, accentuated by the geography of Greece with its islands and mountain ranges dividing the settled areas. Early attempts to assimilate these cults led to the recognition of an Olympic pantheon of some twelve deities, already prominent in the Homeric poems; but this left out of account numerous local deities, demigods and 'demons', the last-mentioned being not necessarily malevolent, but intermediate between the high gods and mankind, and not controlled by a supreme deity like the Jewish angels. The traditional polytheism had largely lost its hold on the educated classes by early Christian times, and was of course condemned by Jewish apologists; but it still survived in rural communities (Acts 14:11–13).

Among the major philosophical schools only the Epicureans had virtually no influence on Christian theology. As shown in Chapter 5, in a sense they accepted popular polytheism; but they taught that the gods were indifferent to human affairs, and that the wise man should be free from religion, discarding both reliance on divine help and fear of divine punishment. Jewish and Christian apologists condemned the Epicureans, not always justly, as atheists and sensualists.

The Platonists, Stoics and Pythagoreans, however, all made a positive contribution to early Christian theology. Plato himself cannot be described as a consistent theist; in the *Republic* Socrates is shown as criticizing the crude tales of popular mythology and stating some elementary truths about the divine nature; but he does not pronounce clearly in favour of monotheism; he seems to speak of 'God', 'divinity' and 'the gods' without perceptible difference of meaning. Nor does 'divinity' necessarily represent the highest perfection, which Plato can also depict in non-religious terms; the Form of the Good in the *Republic*, transcendent beauty in the *Symposium* (see Chapter 2 above). But in later life he seems to have moved closer to monotheism (see especially *Laws* 10), in contrast to Aristotle, whose religious feeling appears to have weakened with age.

The *Timaeus*, with its picture of a divine Craftsman, was of all the dialogues much the most acceptable to the Jewish–Christian tradition,[1] though it stands a little detached from the main current of Plato's thought. The figure of the Craftsman is not clearly related to the basic contrast between the eternal and the temporal order (27d–28a), so that some scholars regard him as a

---

[1] See especially D. T. Runia, *Philo of Alexandria and the Timaeus of Plato* (Leiden 1986).

mere personification of the active principle which resides in the former (see above, p. 27). There is no mention of his form or appearance, although he is not said to be invisible; he is described in human terms as 'maker' and 'father', and as prompted by a motive of generosity; but the episodes of his work are indicated in curiously indefinite language in which 'begetting' alternates with 'shaping' and 'blending'. Many later Platonists, however, ignored these obscurities and were happy to identify the Craftsman with the ultimate principle of the universe, who produced the Forms from his own mind; though as we have seen, the majority of them agreed that one could not envisage a creation taking place in time.

Plato's own search for an ultimate principle, however, seems to have led him to a concept which is unrelated to religion, though it was fed back into theology by the Platonists of later times. He adopted the Pythagorean method of seeking explanations in mathematical terms; thus the ultimate principle of all order and of all goodness must be found in the origin of all numbers, namely the One. Aristotle is quoted as referring to 'those who heard Plato's discourse "On the Good". For each of them came in expectation that he would obtain one of the commonly recognized human goods like wealth, health, strength; in a word, some marvellous good fortune. But when the arguments turned out to be concerned with mathematics – with numbers and geometry and astronomy – concluding with the dictum that goodness is unity, they thought this quite extraordinary.' No doubt religiously minded enquirers would have been equally bewildered. In later Platonism, however, this concept of 'the One' collected a number of related ideas which will be discussed below, and which were to transform the One into a being who is personal, intelligent and divine.

Stoic theology has been briefly outlined; we have noted that the supreme god is the rational principle of the universe, deployed in that especially pure and powerful entity known as spirit; he does not transcend the universe, except in the rather limited sense that he survives the destruction of each successive world and initiates a new one after the conflagration. The Stoic God also contrasts with Platonic and Christian concepts in that he can change himself into any form at will; this is perhaps a symbolic way of indicating that he is operative at various levels throughout the cosmos.

What is perhaps more important for our purpose is to note two ways in which Stoic theology came to form part of the background of Jewish and Christian thought. First, we have seen that the Stoics explained the lesser gods of polytheism as 'powers' of the supreme God, or Zeus (see above, p. 50). These 'powers' were taken up and developed by Philo in a rich though inconsistent complex of thought which gave a philosophical basis to the Jewish doctrine of angels, linking them on the one hand with the Greek demigods or 'demons' (and even 'heroes'!), on the other with the Platonic Forms in their later guise as intelligent spirits or minds. Secondly, we have noticed the revival of 'dogmatic' Platonism, in which for a time the Platonists were prepared to accept the Stoics as allies. It does not seem that the cosmic deity of Stoicism was ever acknowledged as a true representation of the supreme principle; but he seems to have been given recognition as a 'second God', involved in the detailed administration of the cosmos under the authority of the supreme transcendent Unity. Thus the Logos in Philo is sometimes described in terms which unmistakably recall the Stoic deity. His treatise *On the Cherubim* explains the 'flaming sword' of Genesis 3:24 in various ways, one of which identifies it with the divine Logos, the highest of God's powers, which is most rapid in movement, and hot and fiery (§§ 27, 30); another treatise, *On Sacrifices*, represents the Logos in Stoic terms as 'swift-flowing fire' (§§ 80, 82, 87), though this is oddly combined with a Platonic description of him as 'a fabric of innumerable Ideas' (§ 83) and 'the divider' of them (§§ 82, 85) who gives them order and structure. And the Stoic doctrine that God interpenetrates the world (see p. 48) is recalled when Philo speaks of the Logos as 'extended and drawn out and present everywhere completely' (*Heres* 217), just as gold can be beaten out into the finest possible membrane.

The same Platonic–Stoic amalgam can perhaps be seen in a passage (*Migr.* 182) while Philo comments on the text 'God (is) in heaven above and on the earth below', Deuteronomy 4:39.

This, he says, cannot apply to the supreme being, who is not contained by anything, but rather contains them; it refers to his creative power. And it is this power who is identified with Plato's Craftsman, being described as 'goodness . . . which repels envy', a clear allusion to *Timaeus* 29e. This seems to reflect a Platonic teaching which assigned the supreme place to the One or the Good, and made the Craftsman his imitator and executor.

Such teaching leaves clear traces on the Christian doctrine of the Logos. Christians were concerned to show that the Creator of the world is good, as against Gnostic theories of an ignorant or malicious creator, (p. 70); and again, that the source of all goodness is a loving, personal Father, not a mere static ideal. In making this claim they found natural allies among those Platonists who identified the Craftsman with the supreme creative principle and made him the source of the Ideas (see p. 55). But Christians also adopted the notion of a 'second God', the Logos, who formed the material world according to Ideas received from the Father which expressed his creative will. Thus the word *Demiourgos*, or 'Craftsman', came to mean 'Creator'; in Christian usage it would stand for the Father, as the supreme creative source, or for the Logos, as his executive power, or again for the 'Demiurge', the misguided creator imagined by the Gnostics.

Some Platonists held that the universe derives from three distinct principles, God, the Forms and matter, as explained on p. 55, each of them independent of the others. At the opposite extreme is the doctrine that God is the source, not only of the Forms, but also of matter, as in the Christian doctrine of creation *ex nihilo*. This can perhaps be seen as a synthesis of three elements which had not previously been effectively combined. First, the notion of a once-for-all creative act, the natural reading both of Genesis and of Plato's *Timaeus*, though only a minority of Platonists understood it so. Secondly, the view of Eudorus, that matter derives (though timelessly) from a divine source. Thirdly, the clear definition of *ex nihilo* in a strongly existentialist sense, 'from utter nullity', which so far as we know was first put put by Basilides (p. 68). Eudorus probably influenced Philo, and Christian thinkers through him; but he himself remained firmly in the Platonist tradition. He emends a text in Aristotle's

Metaphysics so as to credit Plato with the doctrine that matter, as
well as the Forms, derives from the One (Alexander, *In Metaph.*
p. 59, ed. Hayduck). Plato's mathematical explanation of the
different forms of matter in Timaeus 53–5 makes this interpretation seem natural enough.

The mathematical approach to theology culminates in the
doctrine that God is not only unchanging and self-consistent,
but also undivided in the most radical sense; he is pure Being; he
has nothing corresponding to distinct organs or faculties,
because his whole being is involved in each perception and
action. It is nevertheless held by many orthodox Christians that
the one God can exercise a variety of powers or energies, and
that these do not compromise his perfect simplicity. Irenaeus
tells us that God is 'wholly mind, wholly spirit, . . . wholly
hearing, wholly seeing, . . . and wholly the source of all good
things' (*A.H.* 2.13.3). But our experience gives no indication
how these distinct functions can be identical with one another
and with God himself. Thus none of them can be used as a
reliable clue to the nature of God himself, which must remain a
mystery; indeed it was sometimes thought that God's pure unity
and completeness is denied if one attaches any particular
description to Him. Such theories have been accepted by
modern thinkers of distinction, among them John Henry New-
man, but I myself cannot see how they can be reconciled with the
biblical presentation of God as the loving Father personally
engaged with his human creatures. I have tried to comment on
them in my book *Divine Substance* (pp. 186–9), and I shall return
to them briefly in Chapter 11.[2]

[2] See pp. 130–4.

CHAPTER 10

Proofs of the existence of God

Two basic issues called for philosophical treatment by Christian writers: the proof of God's existence and the question of his nature. It might seem that such debates were ruled out *ab initio* by the widely accepted principle that we can know that God is, or exists, but can ever know what he is;[1] this appears to make the first exercise unnecessary and the second impossible. But the principle was not consistently followed, even where it was accepted in theory. In the first place, Christian writers appreciated the need to offer some rational justification of their faith; they had to reply to sceptics who denied the possibility of knowledge as such, to propagandists who accused the Christians of unreasoning credulity, and to atheists who denied the existence of any divinity. Secondly, the proposition that God cannot be known was rarely taken in the literal sense it might have for a modern reader; to do so, indeed, would disallow the positive teaching about God which is found in the Bible. It was usually taken to mean that direct or adequate knowledge of God was impossible for men,[2] at least in this life; for the future there was St Paul's promise that we should see him 'face to face'.

We can thus distinguish three philosophical problems:

(1) The rational defence of the doctrines of faith, of belief in authority, and of the general possibility of acquiring knowledge at all.

(2) Proofs of God's existence.

(3) The nature of God.

---

[1] . Very frequent in Philo: *Leg. All.* 3.206, *Post. Cain* 169, *Immut.* 62, *Mut. Nom.* 11, *Somn.* 1.230–1, and especially *Praem.* 39–40. Cf. Augustine, *Trin.* 8.

[2] See my paper 'Die Aufnahme des philosophischen Gottesbegriffes', cited in Bibliography 9.

In treating of faith we can of course offer only an outline of its features, designed to place the philosophical problems in perspective. In Christian usage the Greek word *pistis* is influenced by the associations of Hebrew words deriving from the verbal stem '*mn*, with the root meaning of 'firmness' or 'constancy'; but the Greek word itself derives from the verbal stem *pith-*, with the meaning 'to persuade'. The noun *pistis* thus has the two meanings of 'firm assurance' and 'that which gives firm assurance', whether a personal quality (honesty, trustworthiness) or an impersonal fact (an assurance, guarantee or proof). In practice, several distinct nuances were often combined by Christians speaking of faith. It could be seen both as a gift from God and as a Christian obligation or task; both as a direction of the will and as an operation of the mind; it could be specified as faith in God as such, or in Christ; or more particularly, faith in God's action as seen in Christ's incarnation, death and resurrection. The expression of such faith could be found in the Scriptures, or the tradition of the Church, or the *regula fidei* (a brief statement of belief in roughly, but not completely, fixed form); or again the word *pistis* itself could be used to denote the content of belief or some authorized statement of what should be believed (1 Tim. 4:1, Titus 1:13).

Within this complex of meanings, we are not primarily concerned with *pistis* as the ground for 'justification by faith', but with its essential character as an attitude of belief, and its possible confirmation by argument; and here as elsewhere Christian thinking came to be influenced by the philosophers, especially on the problem already mentioned as to whether certain knowledge is possible at all, and if so, on what conditions.

In the New Testament we find faith treated as an attitude of belief or trust displayed in the face of discouraging circumstances or in the absence of natural, reassuring knowledge; for instance, faith in Christ's power to heal, or to still the storm on the lake. Particularly important was Paul's treatment of Abraham in Romans 4 (especially vv. 17–20), and a similar conception pervades the great hymn in praise of faith in Hebrews 11; faith is trust in God, involving (on its intellectual side) the belief that He will fulfil His promises; it is tested by the refusal to be discouraged (vv. 11–12, 23–7, 29) and by a willingness to perform apparently pointless or harmful actions (vv. 7–8, 17–19) in obedience to his command. Paul similarly draws a contrast between faith and clear vision in 2 Corinthians 5:7; and the contrast between faith and knowledge was later exploited by pagan critics, who complained that the Christians were committing themselves to irrational fancies. Meanwhile *pistis* was also used by pagan writers to indicate a justifiable assurance, or an axiom from which true conclusions could be drawn, or indeed the demonstration itself. Christians could therefore describe the virtue of faith so as to emphasize either the ideal stability of Christian assurance or the element of doubt and insecurity that attaches to human existence, where the believer puts his trust in promises and looks for fulfilments for which our sense-bound experience provides no guarantee. It has to be admitted, moreover, that the complexity of the term *pistis* could easily elude the less reflective and allow them to think that an epistemological problem did not have to be met; in their eyes, faith could be simply demanded, and could be simply produced on demand.

For the defence of Christian faith at least three methods could be used. One was a straightforward acclamation of simple faith, well exemplified by Tertullian,[3] who writes in his *De Carne Christi* 5: 'The Son of God died; it is entirely credible, because it is absurd; and after his burial he rose again; it is certain, because it is impossible'; his words have been paraphrased in the sentence '*credo quia absurdum est*'. Tertullian, however, by no means displayed the simple faith that he praises; his violent paradoxes are the fruit of conscious rhetorical art, and are no doubt a version of the argument that 'no one would dare to invent so improbable a story', for which see Aristotle, *Rhet.* 2.22, 1400a 5 ff. The appeal to simple faith could of course be supplemented by a counter-attack on the philosophers, emphasizing their disagreements, their contentious vanity and their failure to match their principles by their conduct. This type of argument was widely used by Christians, Tertullian among them;[4] though,

---

[3] Cf. Wolfson, *PCF* pp. 102–6.   [4] Tatian, *Or.* 2; Tertullian, *Praescr.* 7.

enterprising and sophisticated advocate that he was, he could move without difficulty to a contrary position and claim the philosophers as allies when it suited his turn.

Secondly, it was possible to argue that Christian faith has analogies with accepted procedures in secular fields. Three forms of this argument may be mentioned. The first, exploited by Clement of Alexandria, was to point out that not everything can be proved by demonstration; if a demonstration is to begin at all, some first principle has to be assumed: 'the whole demonstration is traced back to the undemonstrable assurance' (=*pistis*: *str.* 8.7.2, cf. 2.13.3–15.5). This is clearly indebted to Aristotle, who writes: 'the true and primary [principles] are those which have their *pistis* not from other premises but from themselves'.[5] The second form is to point out that in practical matters complete certainty is often unattainable; one must be content to act on a reasonably trustworthy assurance; this argument, employed by sceptical philosophers, is found in Cicero's *Lucullus* 100 and especially 109, and became a commonplace, with four or five standard examples.[6] A third form stresses the educational value of Christianity, which is not simply a philosophy for the learned, but has the merit of providing for all men and offering instruction suitable for children and women and ignorant men (so Tatian *Or.* 32, Origen *Cels*, 1.9–10, Athanasius *Inc.* 47). This argument of course needed to be balanced by a claim that the difficulties of educated critics could be met, which was taken up, amongst other concerns, by a long series of Christian apologists. One method, employed especially by the Alexandrians Clement and Origen, was to limit the scope of *pistis*, treating it simply as the acceptance of the primary articles of Christian belief, as a foundation on which there could be built a system of rational knowledge or understanding, *gnōsis*.[7] In practice the Alexandrians' *gnōsis* amounted to a synthesis of the Bible, freely interpreted, with an eclectic philosophy based mainly on Platonism. In this way they were able to

---

[5] *Topics* 1.1, 100b 18. Other parallels and full discussion in Lilla, *Clement of Alexandria*, pp. 121–31; cf. also *RAC* 11 col. 90.

[6] Theophilus, *Aut.* 1.18; Origen, *Cels.* 1.11; Arnobius 2.8; Cyril Jerusalem, *catech.* 5.3; Augustine *Conf.* 6.5.7.   [7] See especially Origen, *Princ.*, preface to 1, § 3.

challenge the claims advanced by the Gnostics that their own *gnōsis* was superior to the *pistis*, the uninstructed faith, of the orthodox. Most of the Christian apologists had only a moderate competence in philosophy; but this was more than enough to refute most of the Gnostics.

A third, quite distinct, approach to *pistis* was adopted by Clement, though not I think imitated by other writers (cf. *RAC* 11 col. 102). In some passages at least he interprets *pistis* as the assurance produced by a rational demonstration. In this case the distinction between faith and reason virtually disappears; 'reason' describes the method, 'faith' the resulting conviction or assurance. Indeed this could equally well be called *gnōsis*, though in a rather different sense, emphasizing the rational method applied to the basic problems of theism, rather than an imaginative interpretation of sacred texts to show their coherence in a philosophical scheme.

The principle quoted at the beginning of this chapter might well suggest that the question of God's existence and that of his nature were separable and independent. This of course would be misleading. Even empiricist philosophers who use the term 'existent' with no special implication of quality or value, to mean simply 'actual', 'not fictitious', agree that the statement 'God exists' has no meaning unless there is at least some understanding of what is meant by 'God'. For most ancients the connection of 'existence' and 'nature' was much closer. The same word *ousia* could stand for both; and it often suggested a mode of existence appropriate to the subject in question (and the same was true, in many cases, of the verb *einai*, to be). Accordingly, proving the existence of God might indicate something more concrete than simply showing that there is such a being; it could suggest comprehending the distinctive quality of the divine life; to which it was natural to reply that no God worthy of the name can be comprehended by our limited human intelligence. Ancient theories of knowledge tend to make it an all-or-nothing affair, as if nothing short of perfect comprehension deserves to be called knowledge (cf. pp. 109, 133). This connection of thought may help to explain a fact which we shall shortly encounter; it was the Stoics, who identified God with the rational principle of the universe and appeared to make him wholly immanent, who developed the proofs of God's existence with the greatest enterprise and ingenuity; the Platonists, with a stronger sense of God's transcendence, seldom attempted to prove his existence, and tended to concentrate on the question how God can be known.

For the origin of such proofs, however, we must go back to some earlier Greek philosophers who encountered a sceptical challenge to the traditional beliefs and had the intellectual power to seek for rational answers. It is hardly possible to imagine such proofs being devised except as an answer to scepticism; the Israelites also encountered sceptics (see, e.g., Ps. 14 = 53), but were content with a simpler form of reply.

Anaxagoras explained the world order as proceeding from a divine mind, and we have access to arguments from the regularity and beauty of the cosmos as presented by his pupil Diogenes of Apollonia. The work of Diogenes can also be traced, it seems, in a common pattern of argument preserved in Euripides, in Xenophon's account of Socrates, and in the related but more personal arguments of Plato.[8] Starting from the principle that the soul is prior to the body and is the source of all motion, Plato reasoned that the perfect circular motion of the heavens must be caused by a perfect soul, who is *causa sui* and thus ranks as God; so *Laws* 10, especially 892a, 895a, 896a–897c.

Plato's *Timaeus*, we have seen, presents the world as the product of a divine intelligence, and he goes into some detail in describing the structure of the human body so as to show that each part is appropriately formed to fulfil its function. This type of argument was greatly expanded by Aristotle, who could draw upon a much wider and more accurate knowledge of biology, both human and animal. However the theistic interpretation of this teleology becomes less definite in Aristotle's later works; he can speak of 'God and nature' almost as synonyms to indicate the presumed but unspecified source of the world order.

A second type of argument can be traced in an early work of Aristotle (*De Philosophia*, fr. 16) to the effect that, since there are degrees of goodness, there must be a most perfect being. This

---

[8] Euripides, *Suppl.* 201–10; Xenophon, *Mem.* 1.4.2–14, 4.3.3–12. Both authors emphasize the usefulness of nature to man.

proof he later rejected. He also criticized Plato's argument from motion (*Metaph.* 12.6); nevertheless he himself argued (*ibid.*) that since movement is eternal, and one cannot postulate an infinite series of movers, its origin must be sought in a mover which is itself unmoved; and this must be a conscious being or mind, who initiates movement in the universe through the attractive force of his own perfection. The argument from movement depends, of course, on the assumption that movement requires to be sustained by a continuous force, an assumption first disproved by Isaac Newton. The argument from degrees of being reappears in the handbook of the Platonist Albinus, who incorporates other conceptions drawn from Aristotle.

It was the Stoics, however, who showed the greatest initiative in devising theistic proofs, and a notable conspectus of their arguments is given by Cicero in his *De Natura Deorum* 2.2.4–16.44, though their arrangement and enumeration are not always clear. (A very similar conspectus is given by Sextus Empiricus, *Adv. Math.* 9.49–136, followed, as in Cicero, by counter-arguments.) Among those which passed into later tradition we can note the argument from the beauty and regularity of the heavens (*Nat. Deor.* 2.2.4, 5.15), from the agreement of all mankind (*ibid.* 2.5), from the usefulness of nature to man (5.13), from the fact that rational beings are better than irrational (8.21), so that the world includes a series of beings of increasing goodness which points to a supreme being (12.33–13.36), as claimed by Aristotle and Albinus. The Stoics, however, were arguing for a pantheistic view; they held that the supreme reason is immanent in the world as its directive principle, a view which was unacceptable both to Platonists and to Christians; though some Christians accepted the Stoic and Platonic teaching that the heavenly bodies were intelligent beings (cf. *ibid.* 15.39–43).

How far did the Christians appropriate these philosophical proofs? Within the New Testament the most important text, no doubt, is Romans 1:20. Its rather abstract terminology suggests that Paul is drawing on hellenistic popular theology; but it should be noted that Paul does not introduce this argument in order to strengthen Christian assurance (in which case he might reasonably have developed it further); still less to imply that the mystery of God's being is accessible to human minds; but rather to show that even pagans can know that God exists, and that therefore they have no excuse for their idolatry and immorality. This did not prevent Paul's words from being widely used by later writers as a positive argument for belief in God. This positive approach of a *theologia naturalis* is, however, suggested by two passages in Acts, 14:15–17 and 17:22–9, where Christian missionaries are shown building on their hearers' existing beliefs in order to elicit an active faith in the one God.

The Christian Fathers before Augustine make only a limited use of the theistic proofs. One can indeed trace a certain reluctance to offer proofs at all; even Clement once remarks that only an atheist would ask for them (*Str.* 5.6.1), and we have already noted the conviction that God, because of his incomparable dignity, must be inaccessible to human reason; to say that God cannot be described also suggests that he cannot be inferred. Moreover, where reasons are given for belief in God, these often serve to confirm the faith of those who already believe rather than to convince unbelievers. No new forms of proof emerge in this period; several of the older proofs are discarded; and those that remain are not substantially strengthened or improved, though there are impressive literary enlargements especially of the argument from design.

We can therefore describe the Christian use of these proofs under three headings; (1) The argument from general agreement, *e consensu gentium*; (2) arguments from the regularity and purposiveness of the world order; and (3) the modifications and new arguments introduced by Augustine. Under (2) some authorities (e.g. the *RAC*) distinguish between 'cosmological' arguments, namely those from the order and regularity of the universe, and 'teleological' arguments, those from the usefulness of things for human life; this terminology differs from that of Kant, whose 'cosmological' argument turns on the necessity of there being a first cause, and who includes the whole of (2) in the heading 'teleological'.

The argument *e consensu* might seem difficult to present convincingly, in view of the Christian's concern to combat popular polytheism, which led them to satirize precisely the disagreements among pagans! The argument is sometimes used with the limited aim of condemning mere sensualism and atheism; so Lactantius (*Inst.* 7.9.5) and possibly Hilary (*in Ps. 52, tract.* 1). Where it is maintained that all men believe in *one* God, the claim is sometimes so briefly stated that it hardly amounts to argument; so Irenaeus *A.H.* 2.6.1, Tertullian *Apol.* 17.1 and *Spect.* 2, Clement *Str.* 5.87.88 and Didymus *Trin.* 3.16. Minucius Felix (*Oct.* 19) surprisingly contends that all the Greek philosophers were theists! A more reflective approach is found in Eusebius *Praep. Ev.* 2.6.11 ff.; he claims that all men are taught by nature, indeed by God himself, that the name and nature of God are indicated by a good and useful (sentiment); but only a few have retained the right belief in one God, whereas the majority have relapsed into polytheism. The theory of a primitive belief in a 'high God' has indeed been revived in quite recent times.

The argument from design plays a larger part in early Christian thought; it is sometimes briefly mentioned (Tatian *Or.* 4, Irenaeus *A.H.* 2.9.1, 4.6.6), sometimes developed at length, though few new points are established. Athenagoras (*Leg.* 4–7) claims the support of Greek philosophers in presenting this argument, and Theophilus (*Aut.* 1.5–6) enlarges on it in some detail; though they also criticize the philosophers' disagreements (*Leg.* 7.2, *Aut.* 2.8, 3.7), and Theophilus condemns the common view that the world was made from pre-existing matter (*Aut.* 2.4). Eloquent, though hardly original, statements of the argument can also be found in Minucius Felix (*Oct.* 17–18), Athanasius (*C. Gent.* 34–5), Gregory Nazianzen (*Orat.* 28.6, 22–7) and Gregory of Nyssa (e.g. *Or. Cat.* 12).

Many Christian writers, however, suffered the philosophical disadvantage that their descriptions of the natural world are closely dependent on the narrative of Genesis 1–2, which they treated as a literally exact account of its origin and form (cf. p. 86 above). They thus adopted views which must have seemed naive to many of their pagan contemporaries. An example is Basil's suggestion that the firmament, if it is a solid vault, must include reservoirs which prevent the rain-water from rolling down over the outer surface before it is released to water the earth! To be fair to Basil, this is put forward as an argument *ad hominem*: a solid heaven *need* not be convex on its upper side. But his own concept of the firmament is far from clear; it seems to be both rarefied and dense (*PG* 29, 60B, 68BC, 180C).

Augustine's contribution to natural theology is far richer and more original, even though he allows it only a limited importance. In fact his teaching hardly matches his own experience. In his own development an intellectual conversion to Platonism was a decisive step; his final adherence to Christianity depended mainly on his overcoming emotional and moral objections and reluctance. But he came to regard the latter step as the crucial move towards full understanding and devotion; accordingly he recommends converts to commit themselves first to belief in the Scriptures; rational demonstration can then ensue (*Lib. Arb.* 2.5.13–15).

The argument *e consensu* can be found in Augustine (e.g. *Tract. in Joh.* 106.4), and there are certainly traces of the argument from design; but this is presented in a personal and devotional form that does not attempt to provide a strict demonstration; see for instance *Conf.* 7.10.16, *En. Ps.* 41.7. The same may be said of the argument from degrees of being; Augustine hardly seems concerned to demonstrate that a perfect being exists, but rather to convince his hearers and readers that true and lasting satisfaction can be found nowhere else; see *Conf.* 10.6, 11.4. There is a somewhat closer approach to a formal treatment in *Trin.* 8.3.4–5 and *Civ. Dei* 8.6; and the negative part of the argument, which stresses the mutability of all created things, sometimes foreshadows the later argument – 'cosmological' in the Kantian sense – *e contingentia mundi*; see, for example, *Lib. Arb.* 2.17.45.

The most original and complete demonstration is also to be found in the *De Libero Arbitrio*, 2.3.7–15.39. Augustine makes his interlocutor admit that he himself exists, which indicates that he has being, life and intelligence. Next comes an argument designed to show that intelligence is the best of human attributes. It is then suggested that there is something higher than human intelligence, indeed higher than everything else (2.6.14), a description appropriate only to the eternal and unchangeable God. To prove this case, Augustine argues that human intelligence depends upon a reality which is higher than itself (12.34), namely absolute truth, which must be identified with God, the source of all happiness (13.35) as well as intellectual satisfaction.

CHAPTER 11

God as simple unchanging Being

Christian writers naturally turned to the Bible for their teaching on the nature of God. But their use of it was often influenced by the philosophical thought of their own day. The Hebrews, we saw in Chapter 9, pictured the God whom they worshipped as having a body and mind like our own, though transcending humanity in the splendour of his appearance, in his power, his wisdom, and the constancy of his care for his creatures. Such a conception, set out in the earlier books of the Old Testament, retained its authority despite some later changes of emphasis. But this biblical view, we noted on p. 58, was radically modified in the teaching of Philo of Alexandria. Philo, a devout Jew, does indeed insist on God's moral attributes: his patience, his wisdom and his loving care. But he also presents him as the metaphysical first principal of the universe, without bodily form or human passions, indeed without any sensible qualities: a perfectly simple, unchangeable, unfathomable being, who can only be positively described in the words of Exodus 3:14 as 'He who Is'.

Christian writers developed a broadly similar view, partly because they were influenced by the same philosophical authorities, partly through direct imitation of Philo himself. To this they added their doctrine of the Trinity, which will concern us later; here too their thinking was influenced by Philo, especially in his conception of the divine Logos; but there was less in the way of actual borrowing. The Christian theologians worked out a trinitarian doctrine which has no clear precedent in the Jewish writer, and which developed into something very different from the triadic theologies which emerged about the same time among the Neoplatonists. These acknowledged three levels or stages or grades of divinity; not three coequal Persons united in a single Godhead.

The Greek version used by Philo renders the crucial phrase of Exodus as 'I am He who IS'; it uses the participle phrase '*Ho ōn*', which suggests the present tense. The Hebrew gives no certain warrant for this, but it was chosen long before Philo's time, presumably to emphasize the thought of God's unchanging being.[1]

Why should this extremely abstract phrase be used to describe a God who is the fullness of energy and perfection? The answer depends on the Platonic theory of Forms, already explained in Chapter 2. The theory began as an attempt to account for general descriptions; men are called healthy in relation to a standard to which they conform, and which can be named as 'health'. This need not involve considerations of value, for the same can be said of tallness, or of sickness. Yet Plato came to conceive of the Forms as standards of perfection, a view which works tolerably well with Forms of good qualities or mathematical concepts or animal species, but not with defects like diseases. These two aspects of the theory conflict, and Plato himself admitted the difficulty, but still thought that it could be resolved, allowing for Forms corresponding to every general description. His successors became more cautious; they clung to the Forms as ideal standards, but eliminated the most awkward cases. On the other hand they continued to teach that the Forms could be arranged in an order of increasing generality, which culminated in a single principle, which was both pure Being and pure Goodness.

We might say, then, that the Platonists thought of natural classes or kinds as we would think of the many copies of a single masterpiece. The original stands at the head of the class, but in some sense outside it, since it is not itself a copy. Moreover the variations in the several copies result from their failure to match the original; their individuality goes with their imperfection. We ourselves might think it logically possible that a copy might

---

[1] Contrast the rendering quoted by Hippolytus, *Ref.* 5.7.25, 'I become what I will', which recalls the Stoic doctrine of a self-changing God. Some modern scholars also render: 'I will be what I will be'.

actually improve on the original; but the Platonic theory cannot allow the copies to improve on their Form.

Thus to characterize anything as 'a so-and-so' means that it imitates, or participates in, the appropriate Form. But again, to say 'X is a so-and-so' appears to imply 'X *is*', or as we now phrase it, 'X exists'. What does this mean? Thinkers in the Platonic tradition understand the verb 'to be' much as we commonly understand the verb 'to live'; it has, not sharply distinguishable senses, but a meaning which varies according to the subject with which it is used. Used of a man, 'being' points to the variety and complexity of human life; used of a worm, it signifies the worm's obscure condition.[2] 'The Being of God' therefore designates the inexpressible fullness of God's perfection.

But all this hardly explains why Philo should use 'He who Is' as a preferred designation of God, and not merely an allowable one. We can amplify as follows: If 'X is a so-and-so' means 'X resembles the ideal so-and-so', this ideal represents a limited perfection beyond which X cannot go, so long as it remains a 'so-and-so'. If, however, we represent God, not as being 'so-and-so', but as 'being' pure and simple, we remove any idea of limitation; God is seen as pure goodness which, like Plato's Form of the Good, is the origin from which all the manifold kinds of being derive. And the paradox that we refer to this infinite creative source by the abstract phrase 'pure being' is justified by the limitations of human knowledge; we can only know *that* God is, or exists; we cannot know what he is.

But this time-honoured metaphysics has been challenged by the exponents of modern logic, working mostly within the English-speaking world, though the new developments were largely inspired by the revolutionary ideas of Gottlob Frege at Jena. To appreciate the enormous difference in approach, it is instructive to compare the article on 'Existenz' in Joachim Ritter's *Historisches Wörterbuch der Philosophie* with that on 'Existence' in Paul Edwards' *Encyclopedia of Philosophy*.[3] The former

---

[2] Concentration on human affairs is especially characteristic of the existentialist school; when Paul Tillich wrote on *The Courage to BE*, he was undoubtedly considering the challenges presented by *human* life or existence.

[3] Ritter (Darmstadt 1972), 2.854–60. Edwards (New York 1967), 3.141–7. Ritter does of course deal with Frege under the headings 'Frege' and 'Logik'.

carefully sets out variations on the traditional theme, with no mention of modern symbolic logic, but noticing recent thinkers who understand 'Existenz' as a word applying specifically to human conditions of life. The latter makes an entirely fresh start based on modern logical theory, though the author traces its origin to the British logician John Venn (1834–1923) rather than to Frege.

The limitations of the traditional teaching can be summarized as follows: (1) it invests the verb 'to be' with a coherent philosophical role, whereas modern logic detects a variety of uses which our ordinary language fails to distinguish; (2) it postulates a necessary connection between being and value; and (3) as a consequence, it is committed to the view that disvalue, or evil, is to be explained as absence of being. It will be convenient to review this last point in Chapter 19, in connection with St Augustine. For the moment let us consider the first objection.

Long ago, Aristotle suggested that we should dissociate 'being so-and-so' from 'being' as such; otherwise we could argue 'Not-being is thinkable, therefore not-being *is*' (*Soph. El.* 5, 167a 5ff.). Modern logical theory proposes a new treatment of both types of sentence. Classical theory did of course distinguish between substance and accidents, which enables us to classify sentences of the 'S-is-P' form as either necessary or contingent. Modern logic develops this point; but it also discriminates between several functions which such statements can perform. Simple descriptive statements like 'Socrates is wise' have to be distinguished from those which assign an individual to a class, for example 'Socrates is a man', and these again from those which indicate relations between classes, like 'All men are mortals', or 'Some Greeks are citizens'. Various systems of symbols are used to indicate these distinctions.

More important for our purpose is the new logic of existential statements, since it closely concerns the subject of our last chapter, 'Proofs of the existence of God'. God's existence is certainly debatable; and the atheist will hold that God does not exist, any more than mermaids do. Let us then consider the sentence 'Mermaids do not exist'. It is easy to assume that 'mermaid' should be a name for something; from Plato onwards it was commonly assumed that all nouns are names. But on this assumption we have a paradox; we seem to be implying that there is something which has the name 'mermaid', but also asserting that there is no such thing. The new logic proposes that statements of this type should be reinterpreted, so that the word which appears to name a subject is now seen to have predicative force. The true statement 'pigs exist' is to be understood as saying that 'that is a pig' is applicable to one or more objects; and so again with the statement 'mermaids exist', though that is of course untrue. And the true statement 'mermaids do not exist' denies that 'that is a mermaid' applies to anything. Similar considerations will hold good for classes with a limited number of possible members, or with only one, like 'the King of France', a role which is at present unfilled.

On this view, to say 'X exists' is not to attribute any kind of activity or condition to X; it means that some subject can be supplied for the predicate 'is (an) X'. To put it differently, we assert that the class of X's is not empty: 'To assert existence is simply to deny a nullity' ('Es ist ja Bejahung der Existenz nichts anders als Verneinung der Nullzahl', Frege, *Grundlagen der Arithmetik*, § 53). Taking the traditional view of a proposition like 'mermaids exist', it looks as if the verb takes its meaning from its subject; we seem to suggest that mermaids exist, or live, in a manner appropriate to mermaids, just as eagles fly eagle-fashion. The modern symbolism will make it clear that 'mermaid' is taken as logically predicative, while the symbol corresponding to 'there are' can now be seen to be a perfectly colourless general-purpose expression.

But if this is correct, does the symbol corresponding to 'there are' put forward a claim that something actually exists in the real world? Certainly it can be used to do this; and philosophers have held that this is its proper use, and again, that it offers the only proper way to make such claims. But it should be clear that no system of logic can include the restriction that it applies only to things *in rerum natura*. Thus the logic pioneered by Venn and Frege will apply to abstractions, such as numbers or figures: 'there are just five regular solids'; 'there is no prime number between 31 and 37'; such statements define possibilities, but tell us nothing about the number of actual objects of any kind that can be encountered. Fictions are a very different case; but here too the logic will apply, provided that they are sufficiently well established to provide an agreed context within which predications can be made. Provided that we can enumerate them, two centaurs and two more centaurs are bound to make four.

A well-known essay by Professor Geach suggests that in accepting the new logic we need not abandon the older use of the word 'to be'. He goes back to Frege for the doctrine that we should distinguish between actuality (Wirklichkeit) and the existence expressed by 'there is a . . .' (es gibt ein . . .), which has just been considered. Geach offers 'a provisional explanation of actuality . . . thus: x is actual if and only if x either acts, or undergoes change, or both' (*God and the Soul*, p. 65). We can indeed say 'Joseph is not' (Gen. 42:36), meaning 'Joseph no longer lives'; but in saying this we presume that Joseph *was* an actual person whose activities are partly recorded and who underwent the change of dying. A disbeliever in the biblical narrative could of course use just these phrases; but in so doing he would be accommodating himself to the believer's manner of speech.

There is much to be said for this view. For one thing, it is a desideratum for the historian of ideas; it may help him to distinguish between thinkers who argued correctly within the limits of their own conventions and those who made adventitious errors. But some cautions are needed. Thus if we agree to explain actuality in terms of doing and suffering, we must avoid confusing it with activity; a point at which the existentialists could well mislead us. Leopards are active, and sloths are inactive; but both alike are actual. The same may be said of a thing that is highly resistant to change, like the Koh-i-Noor diamond. Acting and suffering may help us to recognize actuality; but they are not the measure of it.

Moreover we must allow for the inescapable element of convention in our use of language. It seems allowable to say 'Prometheus brought fire from heaven and was tortured by Zeus'; we can ostensibly describe the doings and sufferings of a character who was not actual, because by convention we are not obliged always to specify 'according to the usual Greek mythology'. On the other hand it would be strange to treat 'Prometheus actually existed' in this way, as merely expressing part of the content of the myth, since the normal use of this phrase is precisely to disclaim any resort to fiction. In general, we cannot detect the function of sentences from their form alone; we need to consider their context, and the intentions of their users.

We have argued that the traditional use of the word 'being', which we explained as analogous to 'living', is still intelligible and can be adopted. But it has been used to imply that a qualitative description of God's being, or the intensity of his action, suffices of itself to settle the question of his actuality. This is not necessarily an absurd suggestion; it is in fact the principle underlying the ontological argument, which has been defended in quite recent philosophical writing, though it is too complex a subject to be treated here. But an effective defence of it can only be mounted by thinkers who are prepared to look beyond the traditional understanding of being. Modern treatments of the concept of existence have to be considered; which is one reason why we have discussed them here.

(2) But if it is allowed that a use can still be found for the terms 'is' and 'exists' as indicators of actuality, can they still function as value terms? Let us return to Plato's view that any class of beings whatsoever must be related to their Form which is at once universal and good. We may explain the problem by following his example and drawing an analogy from common utensils. Plato mentions shuttles and their functions; let us consider knives and theirs. On Plato's view there should be an ideal knife, which perfectly fulfils the knife's function. Our trouble is that we use many different kinds of knife which have different functions; a chopping-knife will be different from a paring-knife or a throwing-knife; and one very useful appliance is the all-purpose knife, which will not do any job quite as well as a specialized instrument, but has the advantage of being adaptable. To do every job perfectly, a knife would have to have contrary qualities; it would have to be both heavy and light, both rigid and flexible. To some extent this simple illustration can be paralleled in human life and the possibilities of human goodness. Can we conceive of a perfect man? Not, surely, in the sense of a man who exemplifies every form of human goodness; even Jesus,

it appears, did not claim this for himself; it was not his vocation to be an ascetic (Matt. 11:19, Luke 7:34). We can believe him perfect in the sense of 'faultless' (1 Pet. 2:22), or 'tested and approved' (Heb. 5:7–8), but that is a different matter. Moreover, if it is difficult to conceive of a Form of the species which embodies all the good qualities of its individuals, it is far harder to envisage a genus which does the like; say, the ideal animal-as-such, which combines the good qualities of every species. Yet in Plato's hierarchy of Forms, this passage from species to genus is a necessary step in the ascent to the summum genus, which is pure Goodness.

The doctrine that God is pure being is closely related to the doctrine that God is One, which has been briefly noticed (see pp. 56, 98). Among Christian writers the word 'one' as used in this context came to have several distinguishable senses, which are conveniently summed up in the phrase *unicus, simplex, constans*, and which are not always clearly separated.[4] The claim that there is *only one* God, i.e. only one who really deserves the name, reproduces the biblical tradition represented by Deuteronomy 6:4 and is of course upheld by all Christian writers. It does not exclude the admission that there are other beings who can in a sense be called gods (1 Cor. 8:5); not only the gods of paganism, but angels, or even men inspired by God, see Exodus 7:1, Psalm 82:6.

The doctrines that God is simple, and that he is unchanging, are closely connected, as will soon be explained; but before approaching them we should point out one other implication of the claim that God is One. In ancient number theory, the numbers all derive from unity; thus the statement that God is the One, or the Monad, implies that he is the originative source of all being; just as the phrase 'He Who Is' suggests, though rather less clearly, the pure and originative Form of Being. In practice God was often described as 'unoriginate' or 'ingenerate' (*agenētos*); this term expresses two distinct attributes: (i) not dependent on any other being, sole ultimate cause; (ii) not having a beginning, existing from all eternity. The first point would exclude even the timeless dependence assumed by many Platonists; the second

---

[4] For discussion see my book *Divine Substance* (see Bibliography 12), pp. 180–9.

would be consonant with theories of time which made it depend on God's creative action.

The phrase 'He Who Is', we have seen, suggests unchanging or timeless being. Rather differently the wording of the Apocalypse (1:4 etc.), 'From Him who Is and who Was and who Is to Come' expresses God's perpetuity *within* and throughout all ages. Christian writers almost without exception adopted the doctrine of God's changeless being, often confirming their belief with the argument derived from Plato's *Republic* (2.380–1): God, being all-powerful, cannot suffer change at the hands of any other; he could only change if he were to change himself. But this is impossible; being perfect, he cannot change for the better; and being good, he will not make himself worse; and this seems to exhaust all the possibilities.

This doctrine came to be developed in an absolute sense which goes well beyond anything that we find in the Bible. In the Old Testament God can even be described as changing his mind (see pp. 102–3 above); and where God is described as 'unchanging', this appears to indicate a general constancy and faithfulness to his covenant and purpose which does not exclude appropriately various responses to changing human acts and needs. But a doctrine of changeless being in an absolute sense rules out any experience of change, or response to change; God can experience changing events only through a perfect foreknowledge, or rather extra-temporal knowledge, which implies that the pattern of future events is irrevocably fixed, and seems to leave no scope for human free will. (The word 'seems' should be noted; Origen for one thought that divine foreknowledge was compatible with human freedom; and many modern philosophers, I think wrongly, argue that such freedom can go with determinism.)

The doctrine of God's changeless constancy – or 'identity', or 'sameness' – was often supported by the claim that 'sameness' or 'constancy' is a basic human virtue, contrasted with the inconstancy of the evil-doer. But this claim overlooks obvious objections. Mere 'sameness' could well be sluggish indifference, or indeed obstinate persistence in vice; 'constancy' needs to be understood as 'constancy in virtue'. But even this ignores the good man's duty to suit his acts to their occasions, to make progress in virtue, and to accept new moral responsibilities.

Nothing less could do justice to the Saviour's demand for repentance.

Despite such limitations the doctrine of God's absolute changelessness held the field; there was little sympathy for the Stoic view that God has the power to change himself and manifest his power in any form he wishes; the orthodox view was that God's complex and various energies all proceed from his simple and unchanging being. But something like the Stoic view was acceptable as applied to Christ, or the divine Logos, who appeared to the angels as an angel, to men as man, and so on; it being understood that the divine Word suffered no change in becoming incarnate. Sometimes there are traces of the philosophers' distinction between simple and complex unity (see pp. 56, 153–4); thus Origen explains (*Comm. Joh.* 1.20.119) that God himself is altogether one and simple, but the Saviour 'becomes many things', *polla ginetai*, according to the needs of his creation.

The doctrine of God's absolute changelessness leads naturally to the claim that he is 'impassible', a term which we believe conceals a whole series of pitfalls, some of them connected with a misuse of the term *pathos*, 'passion', some with confusions about the divine will.

(i) *Pathos* in Greek connects with the verb *paschein*, 'to undergo'. It often stands for an emotion, for instance anger or fear, regarded as a condition which one does not choose, but which simply comes upon one. Nominally a distinction is drawn between the morally neutral word *hormē*, impulse, and *pathos*; the latter then comes to stand for a discreditable impulse, for example lust, or indeed actual vice. But the distinction was often disregarded, and the word *pathos* could then suggest that any impulse was blameworthy unless it was explicitly based on a rational decision. Another common assumption was that any powerful impulse was immoderate, and therefore blameworthy.[5] It was only by tacit convention that good impulses like pity were not described as 'passions'.

(ii) The description of God as impassible was based on the

---

[5] See my paper 'The concept of Mind and the concept of God' in *The Philosophical Frontiers of Christian Theology* (Festschrift for D. M. MacKinnon), ed. B. L. Hebblethwaite *et al.* (Cambridge 1982), pp. 41–8; repr. in my *Substance and Illusion in the Christian Fathers* (London 1985).

sound principle that his will is sovereign; he cannot be overcome by any other power, or by an impulse foreign to his nature. But it was often forgotten that God wills to condescend, to attend and respond to human needs and human prayers. The doctrine of God's impassibility, though designed to secure his sovereignty, ran the risk of making him insensitive and imperceptive; much the same drawback, indeed, attaches to 'apathy' as a recipe for human conduct. And when Christian writers are forced to recognize in God something analogous to the emotional warmth of human love, they find themselves using suspect terminology and contravening established teaching. Origen's embarrassment is obvious when he says that 'The Father Himself is not impassible. He has the passion of love.' (*In Ezech. Hom.* 6.6.).

We turn to the doctrine of God's simplicity, which again has become a recognized part of Christian orthodoxy. But as handled by the Fathers it raises problems; the word *haplous*, 'simple', and its equivalents (*amerēs, asunthetos*), are used in different contexts which really call for distinct definitions of the term; though the need for this, it seems, was not remarked. The problem can be traced back to Plato's discussion of the soul. In the *Phaedo* he distinguishes between material things and incorporeal realities, and argues that the soul of man is akin to the latter. These realities are described as pure, changeless and incomposite (*axunthetos*) in contrast to bodies which are composite (*sunthetos*), ever-changing and dissoluble. There is thus a strong suggestion that the soul itself is simple, though Plato does not say this explicitly. Soon afterwards, however, in the *Republic* he contended that the soul has distinguishable functions or 'parts' (*merē*); and this gave rise to a debate, already noticed in Aristotle's *De Anima*,[6] whether it is correct to speak of 'parts' in this connection. The Stoics apparently did so without inhibitions;[7] but the Platonists came to regard the soul as a simple substance, which however is capable of exercising a variety of 'powers', *dunameis*; and a similar doctrine of the divine nature was adopted by many Christian writers.[8]

---

[6] See especially 1.5, 411b 1 ff.   [7] *SVF* 1.143, 2.827–8, 2.830 ff.
[8] See, for example, Gregory Thaumaturgus (?), *PG* 46.1101–2; Basil, *Ep.* 234.

But this position, and the arguments for it, were too simply conceived. The Christian Fathers often argue that God must be simple because he is clearly not composite and therefore dissoluble, like material things. But how much is implied by the word 'simple'? Sometimes at least it suggests a pure mathematical unity which excludes any form of multiplicity. But this leads back to problems we have already considered. The notion that a *purely* simple being could exercise a variety of powers cannot be defended; for God must understand and control each separate power. Nor can one see how a mathematically simple God could direct his love towards a multitude of creatures, or control the events of a changing world. It will not do to argue, with Origen (*Princ.* 3.1.10–11, etc.) that God's action is simple and uniform, but produces different results on different recipients; for this reduces it to something impersonal and mechanical, and again leaves the initiative solely with man, denying prevenient grace. The most intelligible, though unsatisfactory, solution was to say, with Origen again, that God acts through his Logos, who resembles him in being one (unique rather than simple!), but is distinct in that he distributes his power as human needs require.

The problem cannot be solved unless we redefine our terms. An object like a tree, or a human body, it not simple in the strict sense, for it consists of distinguishable parts, a trunk, branches, etc.; but it is not composite either; it is not produced simply by adding one part to another, as a house is built of bricks. And death or destruction is not necessarily brought about by the separation of the component parts, as the ancients commonly assumed. A tree can die without its branches falling apart from the trunk; both may rot together. But if this is allowed, the argument by elimination fails; if a thing is not composite in the crude sense, there is no need to conclude that it is completely simple and undifferentiated. It may embrace many different aspects or functions within an overall unity; and in practice the Christian doctrine of God had to allow this, even though in theory it was committed to the concept of ideal or perfect simplicity. An ambitious treatment of divine unity appears in Christian writers from Irenaeus to Augustine, to the effect that all God's attributes and activities are identical with each other, and with God himself (see p. 108 above); but it is not explained how this is compatible with the well-grounded belief that God deals differently with different people at different times (Rom. 11:32 etc.).

How was the word 'simple' actually understood and used? I have not been able to trace any critical discussion of the term, though the materials for this no doubt existed. Aristotle speaks of the elements as 'simple bodies'; this does not mean 'indivisible', since fire, for instance, appears in innumerable separate fires; it presumably means 'without characteristic parts or structure'. Sextus Empiricus has a quite different concept (*Adv. Math* 8.94); changing his example, we might say that a water molecule is simple, in that it is the simplest form in which water can exist; it has parts; it can be divided; but in that case it is no longer water. Christian writers apparently cannot allow that a thing can be both simple and diversified, or at least will not apply this principle to theology. True, the word can be used in a moral sense, to mean 'honest' or 'unaffected', but this belongs to another realm of discourse; we might perhaps say that the hypocrite has two or more unrelated complexes of behaviour, the 'simple' man has only one such *complex*! Athanasius once argues that the sun's ray is a 'simple and pure offspring from the sun', and so a good analogy for the divine Logos (*Syn* 52); but his normal practice is to treat all material substances as composite, in contrast with the perfect simplicity of the divine. I do not believe this passage rests on any careful analysis of terms; Athanasius has simply adapted his physical view to fit its theological application.

The doctrine of God's perfect simplicity was sometimes taken to imply that he is totally inaccessible to human knowledge, or again devoid of qualities and attributes, 'inasmuch as every attribute is what it is only in distinction from others'.[9] Such claims raise enormous problems if taken literally; but they were not always precisely formulated or understood. Absence of properties in God was sometimes taken to mean merely that he is not subject to accidental qualifications, like sickness and health,

---

[9] W. Pannenberg, 'The appropriation' (see Bibliography 9), p. 167 = 'Die Aufnahme', p. 35: 'insofern jede Eigenschaft nur im Unterschied von andern ist, was sie ist'.

or not endowed with sensible qualities like colour and form. On this view it was still allowable to compare God to the mind and the intelligible world, which Plato had described in positive terms as 'pure, simple and unchanging'. It goes without saying that the description of God as 'formless' expresses a firm opposition to the anthropomorphic picture so easily suggested by a literal reading of the Old Testament, and symbolic interpretations had to be found for the innumerable texts which refer to God's bodily parts and functions, as also for emotions like anger or love.

Much greater difficulties are raised by Clement of Alexandria's claim that God stands outside every category available to human thought (*Str.* 5.81), or by descriptions of God as 'unknowable, incomprehensible, ineffable', and the like. How can such claims be upheld in the face of the traditional and biblical authority for describing him by such well-understood adjectives as 'good', 'righteous' and 'merciful', or again for symbolizing his being in terms of such familiar concepts as 'fire', 'light' and 'love'?

These problems can be mitigated, though possibly not resolved, by attending to the philosophical background of the negative terms. In Greek thought 'knowledge' is commonly taken to imply complete or perfect knowledge. Aristotle defines it as 'the mind's identity with its object';[10] and this interpretation clearly leaves no room for a knowledge which is genuine but incomplete: St Paul's 'I know in part', 1 Corinthians 13:12. But with negative terms the situation is reversed; if 'knowledge' suggests 'complete knowledge', then 'unknowable' can be taken to mean that *complete* knowledge is impossible; it need not exclude every kind of genuine apprehension. Thus to say that God is *akataleptos*, incomprehensible, suggests a comparison with the Stoic *kataleptike phantasia*, the completely certain apprehension of some perceived fact; it is not difficult to admit that God cannot be known in this fashion! Whether the escape-route which I have suggested was actually taken, I cannot say; it seems more probable that the negative adjectives were used in a

---

[10] *De anima* 3.4, 429b 6 ff.; 3.7, 431a 1 ff.; 3.8, 431b 20–432a 1; *Metaph.* 12.7, 1072b 21; 12.9, 1074b 38–1075a 5.

rhetorical, maximizing sense to stress the depth of the divine mystery, without regard for the problems that necessarily followed. Much the same holds good of the term *akhōrētos*, which appears in similar contexts. This embodies a spatial metaphor; in a literal sense it means that there is nothing larger than God which is capable of surrounding or containing him; and this clearly harks back to the Stoic view, still echoed by Tertullian (*Prax.* 16.6), that God is at the outer surface, the extreme bound, of the universe. But more usually it signifies that there is nothing that can 'take in' or 'embrace' (*emperiechein*) the mystery of God's being. Once again it is *complete* knowledge that is excluded. Clement's negative theology is no doubt much more drastic than this; what we have shown is that such 'agnostic' predicates can be used by writers who are much less agnostic than Clement. Terms such as 'unknowable' may point to divine glories beyond our comprehension; they do not forbid us to characterize God by epithets or analogies which express some aspect of his being.

Similar comments apply to the claim that God is indescribable, *arrhētos*. Philo, for example, notes the opinion that the Jewish Law gives 'descriptions which symbolize the indescribable', *sumbola rhēta arrhētōn*, *Spec. Leg.* 3.178. And the doctrine that God cannot be named is at least sometimes based on the view that a name should belong uniquely to one owner, and moreover should express his distinctive characteristics, like 'Triquetria' ('triangular') used as a poetic name for Sicily. But the question of God's name raised difficulties of its own.[11] Exodus 3:14 describes God's response to Moses' request for his name. An answer is given in the enigmatic phrase 'I AM HE WHO IS', according to the Septuagint Greek version; but the next verse contains a declaration which originally revealed a proper name, though it was later disguised as 'the LORD'. So we would naturally describe the passage; but of course *onoma*, *nomen*, which we render by 'name', could mean more generally 'noun', and so 'title' rather than 'proper name'. Scholarly writers such as Eusebius realized that the original Hebrew text of verse 15 contained the sacred unpronounceable name YHVH

---

[11] See my paper 'Logic and the application of names to God', in *El 'Contra Eunomium I'* ed. L. F. Mateo-Seco and J. L. Bastero (Pamplona 1988).

(*Dem. Ev.* 5.11.3 etc., cf. *Praep. Ev.* 11, 6.36 and 12.1–2). But the Greek phrase *egō eimi ho ōn*, with its sequel rendered as 'the LORD', would easily suggest that no proper name was given; so Ambrose, *Explan. Ps. 43*, 20: *non respondit nomen, sed negotium; hoc est, rem expressit, non appellationem*. In general, there was no agreement as to whether God could be named; on the negative side Justin *Apol.* 2.5(6) is often quoted; but Athanasius, *Decr.* 22, asserts that 'God' and 'Father' are themselves names.

CHAPTER 12

How God is described

Gregory of Nazianzus has the confidence to demand 'Are not spirit and fire and light, love and wisdom and righteousness, and mind and reason and the like, names of the First Nature?' (*Orat.* 28.13). He goes on to point out that all these names can convey misleading suggestions. Nevertheless they were firmly rooted in Christian tradition. Hence, as we have shown, the common descriptions of God as 'unknowable' or 'indescribable' are not to be pressed in a literal sense; they do not debar us from shadowing out God's nature by using words drawn from our everyday experience. These words, indeed, could not be avoided, in view of the biblical texts which describe God as Fire, Light, Life, etc. (Deut. 4:24, 1 John 1:5, John 1:4, etc.). But reinterpretation is needed, and the Christian writers tend to refine such bold metaphors; very commonly they retain the notion that God is mind or intelligence, and interpret the other terms as indicating dispositions or activities of the divine mind. At the same time, Neoplatonist philosophers were debating whether or not *nous* was the proper designation of the First Principle.

It is convenient to distinguish the predicates applied to God as metaphysical and natural, the latter group including both physical and moral terms. Within the first group we have dealt briefly with the descriptions of God as Being, as Unity, and as ultimate Source (Jer. 2:13 etc.). We must now consider the attributes of Mind and Spirit.

Mind, *nous*, was of course a key conception in Greek philosophy; living beings are sharply divided into the intelligent and the unintelligent, and it is assumed that the intelligent are better; so Plato, *Tim.* 30b; cf. Aristotle *De Anima* 2.3 etc., Clement of Alexandria *Str.* 2.110–11 = *SVF* 2.714, etc. There was in fact a tendency to idealize the mind; although references to 'a corrupt mind' can be found, it was often supposed that vice proceeds always from the failure of the mind to assert its proper supremacy over the passions, from a defeat of the mind, rather than from its evil designs, which always presuppose some prior defeat. Hence it seemed natural to affirm that 'God is either mind or something better than mind' (Aristotle fr. 46, p. 57 Ross, cf. Origen *Cels.* 7.38, etc.). Many Greek thinkers acccepted *nous* as the proper designation of God; this analogy had the advantage of representing God as both mysterious and powerful; for though the mind is in a sense familiar, it is not visible, and its workings were not understood. Again, we contrast the quickness of thought with the laborious efforts of the body to carry out its decisions – not always justly, of course; one may have to wrestle with a problem. Moreover, our power of imagining distant scenes was often described as the mind's ability to 'go' anywhere it wishes (Philo, *Leg. All* 1.62); though this is misleading, and Athanasius very properly observed that the human mind cannot *act* at a distance (*Inc.* 17).

The designation of God as mind was criticized by some Neoplatonists, who observed that thinking involves an element of plurality; the subject must be distinct from the object of thought; whereas the supreme divinity must exist in perfect simplicity. This was authoritatively laid down by Plotinus (see p. 72 above), for whom the supreme hypostasis was the One, or sometimes the Good; Mind, *Nous*, came next in rank. Some Gnostics took a similar view; but most of the Christian Fathers were content to regard the mind as a simple substance which exercises a variety of powers, and to describe God in these terms.

The Old Testament lacks the clear conceptualization of Greek philosophy; in effect it is clear that God is conceived as a conscious, intelligent being, but there is no biblical warrant for describing him as Mind. Perhaps for this reason, Christian theologians were not wholly agreed on the propriety of this term. Philo had used it with confidence, as do most of the early Christian Apologists, followed by Clement, Origen and Dionysius of Alexandria.[1] Eusebius and Athanasius are somewhat less

---

[1] See my *Divine Substance*, p. 169.

confident, though both of them explain the generation of the divine Logos on the analogy of the word, or thought, proceeding from our mind (Eus. *Eccl. Theol.* 2.21 etc., Ath. *Gent.* 41), and this remains a theological commonplace. But almost all Christian writers accept the Platonic contrast between body and soul, and between perceptible and intelligible realities; and however the latter were conceived in detail – as patterns in God's mind, as his powers, or as angelic intelligences – it was always acceptable to say, as a first approximation, that God belongs to, or is akin to, or is to be sought through, the intelligible realm, and that the first step in man's upward pilgrimage is to turn his attention away from the body and its needs and satisfactions, and focus his thoughts on the ideal world. This doctrine was hardly challenged in cultivated circles until the growth of the monastic movement revived attention to a more naively visualized impression of God and to the duty, within the ascetic life, of mutual service and practical good works.

The words coming nearest to *nous*, mind, in the native Hebrew tradition were *ruach* and *nephesh* (see p. 98), of which the former was usually translated into Greek as *pneuma*, 'spirit'. In Christian thought the biblical concept was affected by Stoic teaching, where *pneuma* plays a part in an elaborate physical and psychological theory (see above, pp. 47, 60). This was largely overlooked by Christian writers with the one certain exception of Tertullian; but it needs to be remembered that 'spirit' remained in use as a fairly general description of divine life, energy and power; its use did not always imply the distinctive Christian doctrine of the Holy Spirit.

Pneuma meant 'wind' or 'breath', and the Old Testament view of spirit rests on the close association of breath with life and thought. Man could live and think, perceive and feel, only when God breathed life into him; when this 'spirit' (*ruach*) was received and assimilated, it took the form of man's *nephesh* or soul, his invisible animating agency. By extension, then, *pneuma* could characterize God himself; but it was also applied to lesser invisible beings both good and bad (the 'unclean spirits'), or to particular human impulses or capabilities, again both good and bad. Nevertheless 'spirit' often stood for a principle which was both superhuman and good; the being of God himself; God-given inspirations in human life; and in Christian teaching, the distinct source of such inspirations, the Holy Spirit. It could also refer to the divine element in Christ. In primitive christology it could be taken for granted that Christ was unique in being 'God according to the Spirit'; this and similar phrases do not necessarily imply what is now known as 'Spirit christology', the doctrine that sees Christ's divinity as a higher degree of that inspiration by the Spirit which is in principle available to all men. Views of this type were certainly held by some second-century Christians, and were often condemned as making Christ no more than an ordinary man; but such views need not be suspected whenever Christ's divinity is defined in terms of 'spirit'.

Gregory's divine names or titles include Reason (Logos) and Sophia (Wisdom). These are not in fact commonly applied to the Father, since from pre-Christian times they had already been appropriated to the second Person, God's principal executive agent. The reasons for this are not quite the same in the two cases. In the hellenistic Judaism of Philo, the sense of *logos* is strongly coloured by his philosophic tradition (see above, pp. 60, 106) rather than by the associations of the Hebrew word *memra*. With the Stoics, *logos* could stand for the supreme divinity in his capacity as a rational, ordering principle; but the Platonists were accustomed to distinguish between *logos* and *nous*; *logos* denoted thought expressed in words, whether uttered or silent; *nous* stood for the intuitive power on which such expressions depend. When the Platonists came to think that the simplicity and purity of the ultimate Godhead were incompatible with a detailed supervision of the world and its inhabitants, it became natural to distinguish between God as ultimate source and God as outgoing power, and it was to the latter that the term Logos was applied. The Christian use of *sophia*, by contrast, is less influenced by a distinct philosophical background and rather more by the associations of the Hebrew word *hokmah*, as transmitted by the Wisdom writer and by St Paul in their use of *sophia*; she is rather more distinctly a personal being, as portrayed in Proverbs 8. The form taken by *sophia* in Philo is very similar to that of his *logos*; no consistent distinction is drawn between them;

both reflect the same need for a mediator; but *sophia* carries less in the way of philosophical apparatus. Here, then, the use of *logos* rests directly on philosophical tradition, that of *sophia* less directly on a similar tradition. Philo even explains that Sophia is a male person, despite the feminine gender of the word (*Fuga* 52). It was not difficult, therefore, for Christian writers to amalgamate the two conceptions as a designation for the heavenly Christ.

God's being is often described or symbolized in terms of light. In the Old Testament this often refers to the terrible splendour of God's appearance, which even the angels dare not behold; cf. p. 101 above. Sometimes it is a metaphor for his kindness and favour (Ps. 67:1, 118:27 etc.), or more generally for relief and deliverance (Ps. 112:4, contrast Amos 5:18). In the Greek tradition there is a close connection between light and understanding or intelligibility; it was a commonplace that sight was the most valuable of the senses; and, as in other languages, 'to see' can mean 'to understand', side by side with the alternative metaphor of 'grasping' or 'comprehending'. Plato referred to the mind as 'the eye of the soul' (*Rep.* 7.533) and the phrase was constantly repeated. 'To see' is an especially appropriate metaphor for those moments of experience when the solution of a problem first comes to us, before we embark on the labour of formulating it; and so also for our unverbalized but discerning apprehension of friendship, of beauty, or of divinity.

In Christian usage the splendour of God's appearance is still recalled in the words of 1 Timothy 6:16, and in the narratives of the Transfiguration and of St Paul's conversion. The notion of 'favour' is much less evident; but new emphasis is given to the idea of honest actions which need no concealment (John 3:19ff., Rom. 13:12–13, etc.). In the Fathers, however, it is the association of light with understanding which becomes the dominant theme. The Alexandrians especially take over the phrase 'intelligible light' and its equivalents, already common in Philo, to denote the intelligence which is communicated to men by the divine Logos, and indeed the divine nature itself, the ultimate source both of the providential ordering of the natural world and of the moral order. These connections of thought can be seen in

Philo, *Opif.* 55 and *Sacr.* 36. In St John a moral sense seems to predominate; but many of the Fathers conceive of the moral life almost entirely in terms of allowing the mind to gain control of the passions (see pp. 129, 137), and spirituality is seen by extension as the unhindered passage of the mind to grasp as much of God's invisible beauty and wisdom as human nature allows.

In the Greek tradition the use of this metaphor is affected by physical theories of light. The maxim 'like is known by like' was widely accepted; hence it was thought that the eye, which perceives light, must be analogous to the sun or some other luminary, which emits it. Light was often conceived as a current or radiation flowing out from the luminous body, and the Platonists supposed that the eye correspondingly emits a 'visual ray', and that vision results from the union of the two. In later Stoicism we find a different theory, in which the eye is supposed to 'contact' or 'touch' the object seen through the medium of the air, as if probing it with a stick! (*SVF* 2.864–7); and similarly the ray of light is conceived as a static extension of the luminous body (Marcus Aurelius 8.57, Tertullian *Apol.* 21, etc.). This makes it natural to say that the ray of light is inseparable from the source of light (Justin, *Dial.* 128); and this dictum is accepted even by those who think of light as an out-flowing current (Plotinus 1.7.1, cf. Athanasius *Syn.* 52, cited p. 132). This notion of inseparability underlies the comparison of the Logos to the radiance (*apaugasma*) flowing from the sun (Heb. 1:3, Origen *Princ.* 1.2.7, Athanasius *Decr.* 24 and *passim*).

Gregory describes God not only as light but also as fire. Fire is of course naturally associated with light, and Stoic theory connects it also with spirit, *pneuma*, though the two notions of light and spirit are not themselves very closely linked. In Greek thought fire is of course an element, and therefore a substance, as opposed to a process of combustion, as we now regard it; this makes it an appropriate symbol for the divine nature, in that one can ignore its dependence on an exhaustible supply of fuel. Indeed fire need not involve combustion; the word could stand more generally for the principle of heat, as we have seen; see p. 46.

In the Old Testament fire, like light, is part of the splendour of God's appearance (Ezek. 1:4 ff., especially 1.27); but there are two further important associations, in which fire is presented first as the instrument of God's wrath, and secondly as a means of purification. Deuteronomy 4:24 sums up a whole series of texts in which lightnings and volcanoes are seen as the weapons of divine vengeance (Ps. 18:8, 2 Kgs 1:10, etc.); more generally 'fire' can stand for God's anger without referring to any definite means of execution (Ps. 79:5, 89:46, Mal. 4:1, etc.). On the other hand fire can be seen as a cleansing agent, consuming impurities and refining base metal (Isa. 6:6–7, Mal. 3:2, etc.). The Fire of the coming judgement contains both motifs, destroying the wicked and purging the just. In the New Testament both these aspects are well represented. On the other hand it does not develop the symbolism of Moses at the burning bush (Exod. 3:2 ff.), which is elaborately worked out by the Fathers.

In fact the Christian use of fire-symbolism is far too rich and complex to be described in this book; it will be enough to note a few points at which it reflects the philosophical tradition. Philo had already observed that fire both burns and gives light (*Decal.* 49), recalling the contrast between destructive and constructive fire *per quem omnia artificiose facta sunt* which we have found in Stoicism (*SVF* 1.120, 2.422, p. 46 above). Here it assists the work of creation; elsewhere it is mentioned as an aid to human constructions (*Vit. Mos.* 219 etc.). Clement's Stoic inspiration is clearly seen in *Ecl.* 25–6, especially 26.3: 'The power of fire is two-fold, one suitable for the creation and the ripening of fruits and the birth and nourishment of animals . . ., the other for destruction'; but this philosophical dictum is merged with biblical motifs, beginning with the Baptist's prophecy that the Saviour will baptize with the Spirit and with fire, and ending with the reminder that fire has both destructive and cleansing power. Origen gives a prominent place to the cleansing fire at the beginning of his *De Principiis*, insisting that the divine fire of Deuteronomy 4:24 does not imply physical destruction, but rather the destruction of wicked thoughts.

Another use of fire-symbolism found in Philo and destined to have a considerable future in Christian writing is that of a torch which loses none of its heat in setting fire to another (*Gig.* 25). Philo compares this process to the activities of a teacher, who does not lessen his own knowledge by passing it on. Justin shows how this metaphor can be applied to explain the generation of the Logos from the divine mind (*Dial.* 61.2, 128.4); and it easily combines with the metaphor of light and its radiance already discussed. It is interesting that Arius himself accepts the principle that the Father loses nothing in generating the Son, although he rejects the comparison of the two torches (Athanasius *Syn.* 16). The Stoic theory of total mixture (p. 48 above) also reappears in Origen's view of the soul of Christ as totally permeated by divinity like iron red-hot in the fire (*Princ.* 2.6.6, cf. *SVF* 2.463 ff.), and the same simile is used of the union of Godhead and Manhood in Christ by later writers, both orthodox and heretical.

The moral attributes of God are briefly noticed by Gregory as 'love and wisdom and righteousness'. Our treatment of them can also be brief, since this part of Christian teaching is largely based on the biblical tradition, and the philosophers are brought in occasionally by way of confirmation rather than serving as principal authorities. There seem to be three points which call for attention: (1) the defence of the Bible, and especially the Old Testament, against the charge of crude or immoral teaching about God; (2) the problem of God's moral attributes as involving something analogous to human emotions; and (3) the notion of divine Providence.

(1) Neither Christian writers nor their pagan opponents were able to regard ancient writings as composite documents, or as limited by the workings of primitive minds; the Bible, like the Homeric poems, was treated as a unity and regarded as equally inspired throughout, in theory though not in practice. Christian writers most naturally and properly accepted the teaching of Jesus as their central norm; and his apprehension of God as a loving Father could to a large extent be confirmed by selected texts drawn from the philosophers: God's truth (Plato, *Rep.* 382e), his goodness (*ibid.* 379c), his generosity (*Tim.* 29e), and his creative wisdom (*Sophist* 265cd). There remained the problem of texts from the Old Testament which depicted God as

jealous, cruel and vengeful (along with other difficulties, such as the immoral behaviour attributed to the patriarchs). Christians had to meet the attacks of Marcionite and Gnostic heretics, for whom the Old Testament simply presented a different God, and of philosophers, including both sceptics like the satirist Lucian and serious-minded Platonists like Celsus. The solution most commonly adopted was in principle that already employed by pagans in defence of the Greek myths in general and the Homeric poems in particular, namely to explain the offensive passages as allegories which when interpreted convey good moral and spiritual teaching. This is already the practice of Philo, who for instance makes Noah's drunkenness (Gen. 9:21) into a symbol of spiritual exaltation (*Plant.* 141, referring forward to his *De Ebrietate*); though he also puts forward other defences: moderate inebriation is acceptable (*Plant.* 144); and Noah's offence was not serious, since it was not public (*Leg. All.* 2.60). The method of allegory was extended and systematized by Origen and other Christian writers, notably Gregory of Nyssa, and was particularly valued as giving a spiritual interpretation to the erotic imagery of the Song of Songs; but the details must be studied elsewhere.

(2) God's moral dispositions have to be conjectured by analogies drawn from human experience, allowing as far as possible for the supreme position which he holds. Clearly it is more natural to invest God with the virtues appropriate to a king than with those acceptable in a wife or a slave. But even with this allowance it seems impossible to conceive of the virtues without referring to human emotions; and in this field, as we have explained (p. 102 above) the biblical writers are fairly uninhibited in investing God with love, longing, anger, repentance and the like. But difficulties are raised by the philosophical tradition, which tends to idealize the human intelligence and to treat the emotions as *pathē*, passions, from which God, as impassible, must be free.

Occasionally, as we noted, this problem is met by a frontal attack, as when Origen declares that God does, in a certain sense, experience passions (p. 130 above). But the problem, though tangled enough, is not quite so crippling as it might appear if we interpreted *nous* simply as intelligence; for the term includes a tacit reference to emotional dispositions that make for intelligence. It is commonly accepted today that intelligence involves a sublimated form of the sexual impulse, expressed in our delight in creating something new, or in appreciating elegant formal structures; and that aggressive impulses underlie our determination to master a problem. Plato's *Symposium* had indicated a continuity between erotic impulse and devotion to the eternal beauty; but the Greeks usually recognized the lower impulses only in their direct and largely irrational manifestations, which they saw as hindrances to the work of intelligence. Thus intellectual delight and intellectual effort were treated simply as functions of the *nous*. God could therefore be represented as taking a rational delight in the structure of his created world as prefigured in his Logos, and as executing rational decisions to punish, or again to postpone punishment, for the good of his creatures. Nevertheless it is hard to deny that the image of God most commonly found in the Fathers is cooler, more austere and more consistent than the rich and conflicting imagery of the Old Testament. A compensating warmth is found mostly in those for whom the concept of divine simplicity provides a focus for mystical devotion.

In the main, therefore, the concept of God's love is linked with a moral tradition that sets little store by the romantic affection so powerfully evoked by Plato's *Phaedrus* and *Symposium*. That such affection existed in Christian circles can hardly be doubted; it can be found, for instance, in the unlikely context of the anecdotes of the Desert Fathers. But it was controlled by a moral tradition in which the only unexceptionable expression of love was to seek the spiritual benefit of one's associate, and in which the special value of human individuality was largely ignored. Christians in fact were moved by warmer and simpler feelings – as indeed is shown by the popularity of the Song of Songs, and its numerous commentaries; shame, relief and gratitude towards their redeemer, no less than protective tenderness towards their spiritual dependents. Again, with their strong sense of hierarchical order in the Church, they could often regard their superiors with a reverence that reflected their self-abasement before the holiness of God; a reverence which could turn to savage hostility when they felt that their ideals had been betrayed. But the official teaching influenced by philosophy commends abstinence, discipline and self-restraint, even when it employs highly emotive oratory to do so.[2]

(3) Christians had already taken a certain departure from human warmth in largely abandoning the Greek concept of *erōs*, with its associations of passionate admiration and possessiveness, in favour of the more dignified *agapē*, the normal word for love in the New Testament; but God's love for man could be further refined into *philanthropia* (represented in English by 'kindness' perhaps better than 'benevolence'). His protective care combined with his wisdom and power find expression in the doctrine of divine providence, *pronoia*. On this subject the philosophers had expressed conflicting views: that there is no providence, the Epicurean view; that it exists, but governs only the heavenly regions, a doctrine commonly attributed to Aristotle; that it regulates only the general course of the universe, as believed by many Stoics; conversely, that it extends to individuals (so Plato, *Laws* 10. 899–903: God cares for small things as well as great). There was considerable support for the view last named, and Christians naturally adopted it on the strength of Jesus' teaching on the hairs of our head, and on God's care even for sparrows (Matt. 10:29–31, Luke 12:6–7).

The belief in God's beneficent providence is of course challenged by the elements of disorder in the world, natural catastrophes, the misfortunes of good men and conversely the prosperity of the wicked. These problems had already been faced in the Old Testament, for instance in Psalm 73 and most impressively in the Book of Job, but without producing an answer convincing to the natural reason. Among the philosophers it was possible for a time to appeal to the recalcitrance of the world's basic matter, not fully mastered by the Craftsman's organizing power; but this resource was lost when matter came to be regarded as itself the product of the Creator's will; though traces of the former view do survive, rather illogically, in Christian

---

[2] Cf. 'The concept of Mind' (see p. 129 n. 5), p. 47.

writers. From the pagan side the most impressive contribution is probably Plutarch's work *De Sera Numinis Vindicta*; the four books *On Providence* by Chrysippus, which were clearly influential, have regrettably been lost. Much early Christian writing was occupied with the rather specialized task of opposing dualism, the doctrine that evil proceeds from a spiritual being whose power rivals that of the beneficent Lord, a view upheld by many Gnostics, Marcionites and Manichees. Against such views Christian writers employed a doctrine foreshadowed by the Stoics, namely that evil is not a positive reality, but rather a deficiency, the absence of some good. Many problems, however, remained to be solved; significant contributions come from Irenaeus, Clement, Origen and Augustine. These cannot be summarized here; we may perhaps remark that Origen's theories, though interesting and acute, depend on assumptions which Christian theology has presumably discarded for good; for instance, that our souls live many lives, both past and future, so that inborn faults can be explained as resulting from past sins, God having originally created all souls equally gifted and equally good; and that our moral education can be completed in a subsequent earthly life, so as to fit us for heaven. In the teaching of Irenaeus and of Augustine it is widely recognized that there are elements of permanent value; for these we may refer the reader to the well-known work of John Hick, *Evil and the God of Love*. I cannot, however, myself accept the negative theory of evil, which plays an important part in Augustine's teaching.[3] Evil, to my mind, can often be seen as the corruption of what is potentially good; but that is not the same thing as the mere absence of goodness.

[3] See below, pp. 231 ff.

CHAPTER 13

Logos and Spirit

Christians came to characterize God as a Trinity of Father, Son and Spirit, three Persons in one substance. We shall have to explain the meaning and background of the technical terms employed here; but some larger questions call for attention. Pure monotheism is commonly thought to be one of the great achievements of Israelite religion. Why then did later Judaism apparently complicate and confuse it with a doctrine of subordinate agencies and powers? And why did Christians pick out just two of these powers, God's Word and his Spirit, connect them with their master Jesus, and associate them with the Father in a triadic or trinitarian theology? We might, perhaps, explain this process theologically, in terms of a divine providence preparing the way for the later Christian doctrine; but this would not answer our perfectly proper historical enquiry into the stages by which the transformation came about and the human reflections which it involved.

The first question could be answered in general terms by saying that the Israelites found it necessary to envisage God both as enthroned in majesty above the heavens and as intervening actively in the affairs of men, to reward, to punish, or to inspire. The early Israelites pictured God as himself coming down and appearing in human form (see p. 100 above); but it was clearly naive to suppose that God could absent himself from heaven and attend exclusively to some particular human crisis. It was then supposed that God acts at a distance through the medium of subordinate spiritual beings, the angels. But this in turn could suggest that what immediately affects the world and man is not God himself, but some deputy, who could act irresponsibly (Job

2:3) or even disobey. Later Judaism came to imagine both wicked angels and 'angels of the nations', a form in which pagan deities could be recognized as tolerated by the Almighty, though not of course as affording their worshippers authentic revelations. There was need, therefore, for a theology which did justice both to the transcendence of God and to the directness of his action on earth; and this was sought by appealing to functions of the divine nature which stood closer to him than mere assistants or subordinates: the Spirit of God, his Word, his Wisdom, and his Law. God's Name and his Glory (the 'Shekinah') may also be mentioned; these were introduced from motives of reverence in order to avoid referring to God directly, whether by name or by a designation like Adonai, 'my Lord'. Philosophical writers used the more abstract notion of God's powers or energies.

However, since the titles mentioned above were used to refer to God's personal action, it was easy to treat them as proper names; no doubt this began as a mere literary device of personification, but it soon came to be taken more seriously. Thus what are nominally God's attributes, agencies or functions, come to be invested with personalities of their own, a process which scholars refer to as 'hypostatization'. It looks as if the wheel has come full circle; will not such beings raise much the same problems as the angels?

We have had to describe this process in general terms; it can be made clearer if we take the example of God's Wisdom, where the transformation is plainly seen. Early Jewish writers had commended the virtue of wisdom in human affairs; hence it was natural to attribute it to God, and to praise the wisdom of God in creation. God 'considered wisdom and searched it out'; so Job 28:27, a text which already sets wisdom at a certain distance from God himself. But Wisdom is also represented as herself speaking to man, describing herself as God's companion and assistant at creation (Prov. 8:30) and speaking of the Almighty as her creator and commander, a being personally distinct from herself (*ibid.* 8:22, Ecclus. 24). Finally, though mainly in Gnostic circles, there emerges the concept of a rash and presumptuous Wisdom who falls and is excluded from the divine presence.

It is interesting that in Ecclesiasticus 24:3 Wisdom identifies herself with God's creative Word, an association that was to have a great future in Christian theology. But Wisdom is also identified with the Holy Spirit, and this even by some second-century Christian writers, at a time when a clear pattern of trinitarian thought was emerging; *a fortiori* it would seem that at the beginning of the Christian era no clear distinctions were made between these principal divine powers. Wisdom was also identified with God's Law; W. D. Davies has shown that Paul's christology in Colossians 1:15–18 is based on Jewish exegesis of the opening words of Genesis; Christ is pictured in terms of a Jewish piety which brings together God's Wisdom, his Law and his Spirit as inspiring the coming age of salvation. In the long run the divine Law, the Torah, did not retain this central role in Christian thought; St Paul himself had clearly given his verdict on its limited and provisional function, and this opinion was readily accepted in a Church which was soon consciously diverging from the thought and institutions of pharisaic Judaism. The future thus lay with God's Wisdom, his Word and his Spirit.

At this point the ground had been prepared by hellenistic Jews like Philo, themselves already influenced by Greek philosophy. We have seen how the concepts of *pneuma*, spirit, and *logos*, word or rationality, were used in Stoicism (pp. 46–8 above). In Philo the Logos is the more important figure, and is sometimes pictured in Stoic terms as fiery, quick-moving and all-pervasive (*Cher.* 28, *Sacr.* 87, *Heres* 217). But the influence of Platonism is much more marked: the Logos for instance is identified with the mind of God in which his creative Ideas or prototypes are assembled, and again presides over the division of things into genera and species, which makes up the permanent structure of the world (e.g. *Heres* 131 ff., and cf. pp. 57–60 above). All this probably shows the endeavours of several generations of Jewish thinkers attempting to adapt contemporary Platonism to the basic postulates of their religion. The Logos acts as a mediator, undertaking tasks for which the Almighty is ultimately responsible, but which could seem to impair his transcendent holiness. Just as the angels deputize for God in creating man, who is liable to moral evil, so it is the Logos who appears to Moses in visible form at the burning bush (*Somn.* 1.231–8) 'to assist the man who cannot yet behold the true God'. Philo can even say that the Logos serves as God for those who are not fully enlightened (so especially *Qu. Gen.* 3.34); although presented in a scriptural context this claim is backed by very typical Greek illustrations, and looks like an attempt to give some relative value to the cosmic deity of Stoicism while maintaining a Platonistic–Jewish insistence on a supreme transcendent Godhead.

By comparison, the figure of God's Wisdom in Philo seems to be coloured rather more by Jewish speculations, perhaps Palestinian. She is seen as God's agent in creation, following Proverbs 8:22 (see *Ebr.* 31, etc.) but Philo reproduces fewer traces of Platonic or Stoic ideas such as appear in Wisdom 7:24. Moreover he has no clear conception of the relation of Wisdom to the Logos. He can indeed identify them (*Leg. All.* 1.65); and where they are distinguished, he can say both that God's Wisdom is the source of his Logos (*Somn.* 1.242) and conversely that God's Logos is the source of his Wisdom (*Fuga* 97). A distinct personality is suggested when Wisdom is described as God's consort (*ibid.* 109); but she is also his daughter, Bathuel (*ibid.* 51), who on account of her dignity is paradoxically declared to be male! Philo's imprecision is well displayed by these inconsistencies within the compass of a single book.

We turn to our second question: why did Christians settle for a doctrine of just two associated powers, which with the Father make up the Trinity? We might of course reply that belief in the Holy Trinity was divinely revealed to the Church by our Lord, as reported in Matthew 28:19 (so J. Lebreton, 1910). But few modern scholars would agree that St Matthew is reporting authentic words of Jesus; what the passage makes clear beyond doubt is that a triadic formula in these terms was accepted and used in an influential Christian community some time before AD 100 (since even if the Gospel were dated somewhat later, the writer could hardly be introducing a novelty). The earlier New Testament writings do not establish that it was usual in apostolic times. St Paul's grace-formula in 2 Corinthians 13:14 was important for later Christians, but it is not entirely typical of his usage, since he much more commonly speaks of 'God the Father and our Lord Jesus Christ' (cf. 1 Cor. 8:6), though sometimes also of Jesus and the Spirit (*ibid.* 6.11). His language seems to reflect the experience of a believer who had not known Jesus in his lifetime. He accepts the common tradition about the life and acts of Jesus, and is also vividly conscious of the inspiration of the Spirit in the Church. But he has no consistent formula to connect them. Christian tradition reminds him that Jesus is a man, an Israelite born under the Law (Rom. 1:4–5); but his exalted status calls for other language; Christ is the power of God and the Wisdom of God (1 Cor. 1:24); he became a life-giving Spirit (*ibid.* 15:45); indeed he can be simply identified with the Spirit (2 Cor. 3:17). But there is no question of the *Spirit* having a human birth, even though it can pervade human life. The Spirit is a gift from God received by Christians at their baptism (1 Cor. 2:12 etc.); yet the Spirit of God is also the Spirit of Christ (Rom. 8:9–11) whose resurrection is re-enacted in the renewed life of his people.

St Paul's language, then, is vivid, but essentially plastic and inventive; it gives us no reason to suppose that there was any stable convention in the Church of his time for grouping together Father, Son and Spirit as a triad; indeed there are scattered references to a quite different triad of Father, Son and the angels (Mark 13:32, Luke 9:26, cf. 1 Tim. 5:21). Evidence of trinitarian thinking may perhaps be found in the Johannine literature; but I would not myself regard the Fourth Gospel as throwing much light on the Christian beliefs of the mid-first century.

Is it possible, then, that the Christian confession of a Trinity was encouraged by developments on the side of Greek philosophy distinct from those already mentioned as current among Greek-speaking Jews? This is not impossible *a priori*; we know that about this time the Platonists were evolving a triadic theology; by the time of Numenius, in the late second century, this had developed a clear structure which could be quoted in support of the Christian doctrine. But to show that it influenced the Christianity of apostolic times we should have to go back to the early first century, within the lifetime of Philo. And our clear evidence does not reach so far back.

A much quoted passage from Porphyry, transmitted in turn by Simplicius (*In Phys.* 230.34 ff. Diels; see *LGP* p. 92) describes the work of Moderatus of Gades in the latter half of the first century. If our informants are to be trusted, Moderatus wrote of a first, a second, and a third One, or Unity. Plato's later mathematical theories (see pp. 27–8) had sought to explain all reality as proceeding from a combination of the One and the 'indefinite Dyad', the 'more and less', or undetermined quantity, which can only be measured and made comprehensible by means of numbers or units. But in what sense of 'numbers'? Plato had based his theory on 'ideal' or 'non-addible' numbers. Thus the pure unity, which he took to be the source of all rational order, had to be distinguished from other forms of unity, including the mere arithmetical number one, which so to speak loses its unity by being repeated or added to another number.

The theory of three Unities was supported by a new interpretation of Plato's *Parmenides* (see pp. 24–5), which understood it not as a logical exercise but as a positive essay in metaphysics. Plato's arguments that 'If there is a One, nothing can be said of it', and conversely, '. . . everything can be said of it', were now explained as indicating two kinds of unity: first, a pure, transcendent, unknowable unity (to know it would be to copy or duplicate it) and secondly, a complex unity-in-multiplicity. A third section of the *Parmenides* was detached and taken to refer to the soul; not of course some individual soul, but the world-soul which Plato had described in the *Timaeus*. Platonists taught that the world is a living, animated being; hence in the Platonic 'Trinities' it makes little difference whether the third member is called 'Soul' or 'the World'.

But could such a doctrine have been current early enough to have influenced the Christian movement in its infancy? It is hard to be sure; we certainly do not find in Philo any passage which resembles our fragment of Moderatus. Henry Chadwick has rightly observed that 'Philo betrays no special interest either in the *Parmenides* or in the passages from the Platonic epistles which were to play so substantial a role in giving authority to the Neoplatonic Triad' (*LGP* p. 145). Philo does indeed show that he knew of various beliefs about the status of the Monad, or One, since he states both that God *is* the Monad and that he is above the Monad; but this is not clear evidence of a theory which places one Monad above another.

Another line of argument might be based on Philo's reflections in *Ebr.* 30–1, where traditional commentary on the *Timaeus* is used to expound the text of Proverbs 8:22. 'We shall properly say at once that the Craftsman who made this universe is identical with the Father of the created order' – and not distinct, as might be inferred from 'Father and Maker' at *Timaeus* 28c – 'and its Mother is its Maker's knowledge, with whom God consorted and sowed the creation, though not as man does. But she, receiving the divine seed . . . brought to birth his only and beloved visible Son, this universe. For Wisdom says of herself [Prov. 8:22]; for it was necessary that everything that comes into being should be junior to the Mother and Nurse of all things' – the last phrase being drawn, not from Scripture but from *Timaeus* 49a, 50d and 51a. In this passage the world is certainly represented as 'God's visible Son', but there is no other indication that it is considered personal or divine. A triad of divinities appears only in a passage which is not further developed, *Fuga* 109, where it is the divine Logos who has God as his Father and Wisdom as his Mother.

Another passage of some interest is *Immut.* 31, where Philo claims that the universe is God's younger son, as being perceptible, in contrast with his elder Son, the Logos. This might conceivably be influenced by the Platonic scheme of three original principles, God, the Ideas and matter (see pp. 55–6 above); for it has been shown that Eudorus of Alexandria, a little earlier than Philo, taught that God is the source of matter as well as the Ideas (cf. p. 68). Philo constantly connects the Logos with the Ideas; and it is not too difficult to pass from 'matter' to 'the material world', perhaps animated by a cosmic soul, which would agree with Philo's image of it as 'son'. But all these suggestions are unproven. Moreover they do not bring us at all close to the thought of the New Testament, where we do find traces of a cosmological principle in St John's Logos and St Paul's Wisdom-christology, but where the third Person is quite differently conceived, being connected with the divine inspiration of Christ and the sense of his presence in the Church. The most we can say is that they illustrate the popularity of triadic schemes in the philosophical theology of the first Christian century.

It seems to follow, then, that the Christian doctrine of the Trinity in its earliest form is not much influenced by non-Christian triadic theologies, whether deriving from the Greek philosophical tradition itself, or from the echoes of it which we have been able to trace in Philo. More probably the doctrine was suggested by a contrast between two ways in which the mission of Jesus was perceived. On the one hand he is seen as a man like ourselves, but a man uniquely beloved and chosen, inspired by the Spirit of God, that Spirit which still inspires his work within the Church. But a contrasting picture emerges very early, when St Paul identifies him with God's pre-existent Wisdom; and this conception is soon developed in the incarnational terms familiar to Greek Platonism: Christ is God's Wisdom or Logos who entered a human body and made it his own, yet even in this life can speak of his pre-cosmic existence with the Father (John 17:5), as well as his future exaltation. To be faithful to its New Testament inheritance the Church could do no less than acknowledge God the Father, his Wisdom–Logos–Son, and the Holy Spirit who inspires both Jesus and his followers.

The later history of the Christian doctrine of the Trinity has been constantly re-examined, and we cannot enter into the details of its development; these will be found in histories of Christian doctrine. But we must give some impression of the influence of philosophy on this process; and here we need to consider three representative groups of thinkers: (1) the Christian Platonists from Justin to Eusebius; (2) Athanasius and the Cappadocian Fathers; and (3) Augustine and his successors.

The first school are much interested in the relationship between God and his Logos, which they interpret with the help of their Platonic studies. This made it natural to bridge the gap between the pure unity of God and the manifold events of the natural world by naming the Logos as its proximate creator and controller. Belief in the Holy Spirit is upheld by Church tradition founded on the Bible; but failing clear guidance from the philosophers, his origin and function are much less clearly worked out, and sometimes He almost disappears behind the Logos, so that historians of doctrine can speak of a 'binitarian' tendency in the second century. Early in the next century both Tertullian and Origen insist on his importance and distinct reality; but a remarkable survival of the older view is found in Athanasius' *De Incarnatione*, no less, where there is no mention of the Holy Spirit until the final doxology.

On this view the divine Persons are clearly distinguished and differ in dignity. The order Father, Word, Spirit is fixed and invariable, as of course it remained for all later Christians. The Logos is pictured in two-fold form, as the Father's immanent Reason and as his outgoing, active and creative Word (cf. Isa. 55:11). But the traditional contrast between the unspoken and the spoken word is also criticized as a false analogy; it does not do justice to the effectual power and permanent existence of the Logos. We thus find Christians arguing that to give effect to God's purposes, the Logos himself must be a substance, having a permanent life of his own, rather than a mere transient utterance. It seems then to follow that, if a substance, he must be a distinct substance; and so also, by analogy, the Holy Spirit. The Trinity, therefore, is seen as a triad of three distinct 'hypostases', as Origen calls them, who necessarily differ both in rank and function. God the Father delegates to his Logos tasks which it would be inappropriate for him to perform in his own Person – a conception which we have already encountered in Philo (see pp. 58–9, 150–1). A picturesque analogy found in Eusebius (*Dem. Ev.* 4.6.4) explains that the Father himself could not become incarnate; his personal presence would be insupportable, just as devastation would result if the sun descended on to the earth. It must be the Logos who comes; he alone can endure the Father's radiance, but transmits it to us in a mild and beneficent form (an echo, perhaps, of the Stoic idea of two kinds of fire, see pp. 46, 141). The Logos might therefore be described as the permanent agent of God's self-limitation and condescension. The Spirit, again, has a more restricted function; a famous and much-criticized passage of Origen (*Princ.* 1.3.5, fr. 9 K.) apparently said that the Father's power extends to every kind of being, but the Son's power only to rational beings, and that of the Spirit only to the 'saints' (i.e. the Christians together with the angels and the faithful departed). Origen, however, gives no consistent teaching on how the unity and distinction of the divine Persons is to be expressed in terms of *ousia*, the technical term for 'substance'.

This hierarchical picture of the Trinity was of course by no means universally accepted. It appealed to well-educated believers; but less thoughtful or less cultivated folk tended to fall for over-simplified views, which were either suspected or denounced as heresies. One such idea was to set aside the Logos doctrine and think of Christ as just a man uniquely inspired by the Spirit. A contrary defect was to conceive him simply as God in human form, suggesting that the Father himself suffered upon earth. The details of such views may be discovered in the text-books under the headings respectively of 'adoptionism' and 'modalism'. But these are modern descriptive terms; the ancients referred to the former group by their leading figures, Theodotus, Artemon, Paul of Samosata; the latter group were known as 'Sabellians' or 'Monarchians', as priding themselves on uphold-ing the Father's 'monarchy', or 'sole rule'. Among the early orthodox writers, Irenaeus and Tertullian were the most important who diverged from the Platonizing tradition men-tioned above. Irenaeus apparently wished to associate the Son and Spirit more closely with the Father, picturesquely describ-ing them as 'the two hands of God' (*A.H.* 5.6.1, etc.). Are these 'hands' supposed to be coequal? Possibly; this idea would come more easily to Irenaeus, in that he identified the Spirit, not the Logos, with Wisdom; and he does not allude to the conventional view that the right hand must be superior. But his image hardly suggests the later view that *all three* Persons are coequal. Irenaeus does indeed say that 'the Son is God, for whatever is begotten of God is God' (*Dem.* 47); and he draws on a philosophical source to attack the Gnostic doctrine of emanations (*A.H.* 2.17.1); but he does not seem to apply this analysis to formulate his concept of the Trinity.

Tertullian is influenced by the Stoic view that nothing can be real unless it is in some sense a body. Thus materializing language comes naturally to him; he is not much concerned either to disguise it or to press it as a matter of controversy. He devised a Latin terminology which came into its own in expressing the Nicene doctrine of the Trinity, describing God as a substance which expanded into three Persons. But it is a mistake to think of him as already formulating Nicene theology, as has sometimes been done. His *una substantia* does not unambiguously stand for 'a single individual being', though it certainly marks out God as qualitatively distinct from all else. And his theory of the Persons retains some primitive traits. They derive from the Father by a process pictured as 'extrusion' or 'shooting out', *probolē*, a term which is not to be condemned for its use by the Gnostics. And they are not fully coeternal, but depend in part on God's creative work. Although the Word exists eternally in God's mind as *ratio*, his distinct existence as spoken Word (*sermo*) or as Son begins only with the creation; a view which has links with Arian theology rather than with Athanasius. And the Spirit is subsequent again.

Athanasius is commonly and rightly regarded as the pioneer of a new theology of the Trinity; but this judgement would certainly have surprised him. He regards himself as upholding the invariable tradition of the Church, and is far less open to suggestions from the philosophers. He was soon involved in opposing the extreme subordinationist views of the Arian party, so that much of his work was written in the heat of controversy. The Arians held that the Logos is – not indeed merely one of the creatures, as their opponents alleged, but nevertheless in some sense a creature, brought into being prior to the world as a preliminary to God's creative work. Athanasius taught that he is fully divine and coeternal with the Father.

Much of Athanasius' theological output was devoted to a defence of the Nicene Creed, which had given formal expression to a high doctrine of the Logos or Son, declaring him 'from the substance (*ousia*) of the Father' and 'consubstantial (*homoousios*) with him'. An informed exposition of these phrases can only be given when the technical terms are understood; but it may be said at once that a serious mistake has been made by those who have assumed that *ousia*, and *homoousios*, must have been understood in terms of Aristotle's distinction of primary and secondary substance (see pp. 37–8). This would present us with the alternatives that *homoousios* must have expressed either the total identity of 'Father' and 'Son', which would render both names inappropriate, or else a mere generic similarity between them. This embarrassing choice has only been obscured by the use of ambiguous phrases like 'numerical identity of substance', an unfortunate legacy of Aristotle. But in any case historical investigation has shown that Christian writers took little notice of Aristotle's *Categories* and its distinctive treatment of substance until at least the late 350s, when it perhaps began to be noticed by Arian logicians. The distinction commonly recognized was that between material and immaterial substance; but the latter, as represented by an Idea, cannot easily be classified either as merely individual or as merely generic (cf. pp. 121–2); still less can the divine essence, which is unique and incomparable. Athanasius means to say, rather, that the Father's essence, with all the goodness, wisdom and power that belongs to it, is necessarily, fully and eternally communicated to the Son. What is reserved to the first Person is his title of Father and his position as the ultimate origin of all things.

Athanasius lived on to see the Arian theology largely discredited, though it met its decisive reverse with the accession of the Emperor Theodosius in 379, six years after his death, and the ensuing Council of Constantinople in 381. Meanwhile the intellectual leadership of the Eastern Church had passed to the 'Cappadocian Fathers', a group headed by Basil of Caesarea (*c.* 330–79), his friend Gregory of Nazianzus, and his younger brother Gregory of Nyssa. The theological priorities of this group were perceptibly different; though strongly opposed to Arianism they disliked any theology which obscured the distinct existence of the three divine Persons; they accepted Origen's concept of three distinct hypostases, regarding them, however, not only as coeternal but as coequal. This doctrine had to be integrated with the Nicene theology of a single divine *ousia*; they thus adopted a formal distinction between *ousia* and hypostasis which became the norm for Eastern theology. This development will be explained in the next chapter.

CHAPTER 14

Unity of substance

We are accustomed to sum up the Christian doctrine of the Trinity in the Latin formula derived from Tertullian, three Persons in one substance. Greek theologians confess three hypostases but one *ousia*. The last two words, whatever their precise meaning, are clearly authorized by the Nicene Creed – both the original version of 325 and the customary version attributed to the Council of 381 – which states that the Son is *homoousios* with the Father; the word can be rendered in Latin form either as 'consubstantial' or as 'coessential'. But problems arise from the fact that the Latin word *essentia*, which is the exact equivalent of *ousia*, fell out of use. Latin theologians therefore translated *ousia* by *substantia*, which is etymologically equivalent to the Greek 'hypostasis'. The Latins thus used *substantia* to express the divine unity; the Greeks used the corresponding word to confess three hypostases: Father, Son and Spirit. Consequently the Greeks were liable to suppose that the Latin *una substantia* (like 'one hypostasis') denies the Trinity. The Latins, conversely, could suspect the Greeks of preaching 'three substances', three distinct or different Godheads. Nor was this merely a difference of technical terms; both sides were to some extent influenced by their own terminology, so that at important moments the Latins were inclined to put their main emphasis on divine unity, the Greeks on a clearly articulated Trinity.

The word *homoousios* has been much discussed; but the traditional explanations are unreliable. We begin by considering its constituent parts. First, the prefix *homo-* suggests unity or togetherness; but its sense is not perfectly constant. Two buildings are *homotoichos* if one and the same wall belongs to both; but two birds are *homopteros* if their plumage is exactly alike; they cannot share any single feather! Sometimes, again, the sense is necessarily indefinite; *homonoia* denotes agreement, and since there is no question of actual telepathy, it does not much matter whether we speak of 'the same mind' or of 'likemindedness'. But this point was often missed in antiquity; Christian theologians came to draw a sharp distinction between *homoousios*, 'of one substance', and *homoiousios*, 'of like substance'; but this could bring no real clarity without a better understanding of the noun *ousia*.

This second element, *ousia*, is a wide-ranging and complex term which till recently has not been sufficiently examined. In common usage it can mean 'property', 'possessions', as in Luke 15:13; but it was also used by almost all the philosophical schools in a variety of senses which are hard to disentangle. (By contrast, its companion term 'hypostasis' has been carefully studied, no doubt because it developed such an intriguing variety of meanings in common usage before being adopted by philosophers and theologians.) In dealing with *ousia* we shall begin by outlining the traditional account which can still be found in old-fashioned text-books; we can then proceed to a corrected explanation.

The traditional view assumes that the sense of *ousia* was fixed by Aristotle's discussion in the *Categories* (see pp. 37–8, 158–9) which distinguished between the individual and the species. As we have explained, this raises a problem; if *homoousios* is understood as implying 'same individual', the Creed seems to be declaring that Father, Son and Spirit are one Person, not three. But if it implies only 'same species', it gives no sufficient expression of divine unity; it does not seem to differ materially from the view that the Persons are *similar* in substance (*homoiousios*), the view held by fourth-century conservatives who objected to the Nicene Creed precisely because it seemed to abolish the personal distinctions. The traditional answer has been to claim that Father, Son and Spirit do indeed differ 'as Persons', but are also conjoined in a 'numerical identity of substance'; though it is often added that we must not expect to understand these divine mysteries.

It is usually admitted, however, that at the time of Nicaea the sense of *ousia* was not fully understood. It was not clearly distinguished from 'hypostasis'; indeed we find orthodox writers, including Athanasius and Jerome, arguing much later that the terms are synonymous (*Tom. ad Ant.* 6, *Ep. ad Afros* 4, Jerome *Ep.* 15.4). Being both of them firmly committed to Nicene doctrine, they meant of course that 'one *ousia*' demanded also 'one hypostasis', but without giving clear definition to the latter phrase. Athanasius had indeed admitted, for the sake of agreement, that 'three hypostases' was not necessarily heretical; it was more important to consider what was believed than to insist on a precise terminology.

Consequently, though perhaps surprisingly, the standard terminology of the orthodox Church was not determined by Athanasius, but by a group whose theological interests were perceptibly different, namely the Cappadocian Fathers. They associated the phrase 'one hypostasis' with Marcellus of Ancyra, who taught a sophisticated version of the modalist theology; in their own view it was vital to uphold the permanent and distinct reality of all three Persons. The solution they found was to restrict the sense of *ousia* to the species; the individual was to be indicated by the word 'hypostasis'. Father, Son and Spirit were therefore compared to three individuals having the same nature or species, all equally divine. Of itself this formulation gave a comparatively weak expression of the divine unity; but the Cappadocians exerted themselves to express this unity by other means. The divine nature, they argue, is essentially simple; the three Persons do not differ in rank or resources, but solely in their 'mode of origination': the Father unoriginate, the Son begotten, the Spirit in some way proceeding or 'breathed out' from the Father. One single divine activity or energy is exercised by the three together.

The Cappadocian theory was in effect revived, without its original counterbalancing features, by Joachim of Flora, whose teaching was condemned at the Fourth Lateran Council of 1215. The Council criticized the comparison of the Holy Trinity with a species containing three members; and this of course provided a reason for interpreting the Nicene definition in the sense that Father, Son and Spirit are *una res*, which suggests a unity comparable to that of a single individual; yet somehow the distinction of the three Persons had to be maintained. This has often been done, as we have noted, by saying that, though distinct 'as Persons', they have a 'numerical unity of substance'.

In my judgement, this is an unhelpful phrase. In theory it is ambiguous; its meaning depends entirely on the sense given to 'substance'. If 'substance' were interpreted to mean 'species', then all members of any species whatsoever, since they belong to exactly the same species, would have 'numerical unity of substance'. But clearly this is not what the phrase intends. In practice 'substance' takes on a sense which is suggested by 'numerical unity'; and if we stick to the 'Aristotelian' doctrine that there are just two possible senses, we are forced to conclude that the three Persons simply are the same individual. There may perhaps be a better exegesis, which takes account of the uniqueness of divine being; but if so, it has not come my way.

Another difficulty results from the fact that the Cappadocian distinction between *ousia* and hypostasis is none the less accepted as normative; so much so, that a term used for an individual is often said to be used 'in the sense of hypostasis'; if used more generally, to be used 'in the sense of *ousia*'. But this seems to conflict with the traditional interpretation just mentioned, which takes the Nicene *ousia* to mean 'individual thing' or 'individual reality'. If this latter usage is indeed correct, how is *ousia* to be distinguished from 'hypostasis'? This question has led to some remarkable speculations, notably in the work of G. L. Prestige, for whom the Godhead is 'one object, regarded as real, in itself, and three objects, regarded as objective, to itself' (*GPT* p. 273; cf. my 'Significance of the Homoousios' p. 399).

I do not believe that Prestige's solution is coherent; but unless some such explanation can be found, we seem to have reached an impasse. An escape can be found, I believe, if we attack the problem from both sides; we need a better historical account of the way these words were actually used, and a clearer analysis of their possible senses, which is necessary for accurate and unambiguous description.

First, then, on the history of the word *ousia*. In my book *Divine Substance* (pp. 113–18) I have shown that the Aristotelian distinction between primary *ousia* and secondary *ousia* seems to have had no influence on the Christian Fathers before Nicaea. I found only one reference to Aristotle's discussion, Hippolytus *Ref.* 7.16–18. Needless to say, Christian writers knew that various terms can be used both generally and with reference to individuals. But they do not apply this distinction specifically to the word *ousia*; still less do they treat *ousia* as the key instance of it. Putting it differently, there are references to *ousiai*, plural, where *we* can conclude that individuals must be intended; but where ancient writers themselves mean to speak of individuals, they call them *ta kata merous*, etc., not (*prōtai*) *ousiai*. Indeed, when Christian writers note that the word *ousia* has different senses, they are usually concerned with the question whether immaterial *ousia* is primary – the *noēta* or Forms as conceived by the Platonists – or whether material *ousia* is the primary reality from which thoughts and concepts are derived, the view taken by the Stoics. Origen's discussion of *ousia* in the *De Oratione* 8 has just this antithesis in mind, and it can easily be paralleled from Philo and from Middle Platonist writers. It is worth noting that in this discussion *ousia* does not have either of the senses commonly attributed to it; it is used as a 'mass term'; one is considering, on the one hand, the realm of intelligible realities taken as a whole, and on the other, corporeal reality, taken again as a whole. But this brings us to the second problem: granted that the Fathers used the word *ousia* loosely and confusedly, can we construct a better analysis of the possibilities which will serve as an instrument of criticism?

I attempted this task in the book just mentioned, which can be consulted for a fuller account. I believe we need, not just a single division of the senses of *ousia*, but two independent divisions, which lead to a cross-classification. An easy first step is to note that the verbal noun *ousia* may be equivalent either to the infinitive of its verb, *to einai*, or to the participle, *to on*. In the first case it will indicate some sort of fact or state of affairs which relates to a subject. Representing *to on*, it most naturally refers directly to the subject itself: 'that which exists, or is so-and-so'. But again, *ousia* may represent, not the infinitive, *to einai*, nor its participle considered as subject (*to on*, that which is . . .), but rather a predicate used with *einai*; not 'that which is . . .' but '*what* something is', its character, species, material or whatever one attributes to it. (For the moment we can disregard the unusual case where the 'is' simply states an identity, so that subject and predicate coincide: Ilium is Troy.)

In my book I have therefore presented four 'modes of reference' as follows:
(1) Infinitive, noting a fact
(2) Predicative
(3) Subjective-general
(4) Subjective-particular
The distinction between (3) and (4) is not necessarily that between species and individual, since (3) has to include not only species, genera, etc., but indeterminate things like 'fire', which cannot be regarded as a species having individual fires as its members. But I prefer not to make the diagram more complicated.

An example may be useful here. Suppose the main nuance of *ousia* be simply 'existence'. This can be interpreted (1) simply as a fact about *x*, which one can assert or deny; (2) as naming the kind of existence which *x* possesses – though I myself would prefer to avoid this usage of 'existence'; or, (3, 4) it can refer directly to *x* itself, either in general ('that which exists') or in particular (some particular existing thing).

But of course the 'main nuance' of *ousia* need not be simply existence; and I came to think that we need to recognize at least seven possibilities:
A Existence
B Category or metaphysical status
C In particular, the category of substance
D Stuff or material
E Form
F Definition
G Truth
Most of the senses are familiar to readers of Aristotle; beginners who are puzzled about B, as compared with the much more familiar C, might consult my book *Divine Substance* at pp. 136–8.

In the *De Oratione* as mentioned above, Origen is contrasting the Stoic sense of *ousia*, D, with the Platonic sense, best classified as E; but he is referring very generally to a kind of reality taken as a whole; we may describe him as contrasting sense D3 with E3.

It must be repeated that this analysis has a strictly limited intention; it is designed solely for critical purposes. There should be no suggestion that the Fathers who used the word *ousia* themselves detected any such multiplicity of senses. What distinctions they did in fact recognize is a separate question, on which we have briefly touched. A writer such as Athanasius often moves from one sense to another without noticing the transition. He does indeed recognize a distinction akin to Origen's; thus he contrasts 'created *ousia*' with 'divine *ousia*' in *C. Ar.* 1.57–9. But we can observe more accurate distinctions; and this will sometimes allow us to decide whether the saint is arguing consistently, or whether he equivocates.

Using such an analysis, we are better able to consider the phrases in the Nicene Creed which involve the word *ousia*; namely that the Son is 'from the Father's *ousia*' (and not from any other); and that he is *homoousios* with the Father. Our judgement will be affected by the view we take of the church-political influences which bore upon the Council. It used to be thought that it was dominated by Western opinions stemming from the Emperor Constantine and from Ossius of Cordoba, his ecclesiastical adviser. More specifically it has been argued (and recently by W. A. Bienert)[1] that the term *homoousios* was already current in the West as an accepted equivalent of Tertullian's *una substantia*. This would make it probable that it took its colouring from the Roman tradition represented by Popes Callistus and Dionysius, which laid strong emphasis on the divine unity and was critical of Origen's insistence on three distinct hypostases.

But there seems by now to be a fair consensus that this 'Western' interpretation of *homoousios* is to be abandoned; in which case it becomes advisable to consider the whole history of the word so far as we can trace it in Greek writers (including Greek-speaking Western writers), as well as paying attention to its controversial possibilities; for it is not improbable that *homoousios* was adopted at Nicaea largely on the ground that Arius had already condemned it.

[1] *ZKG* 90 (1979), pp. 151–75.

Examining the early uses of *homoousios*, one is struck by the extraordinary flexibility of the term. It appears first in Gnostic writers, and in the Christian Fathers who opposed them, generally in one of two contexts: (1) the theory of emanation, turning on the question whether God can actually communicate his divinity to any other being, and (2) the Gnostic scheme of three orders of rational beings, dominated respectively by spirit, soul and matter. Since these three are all conceived in quasi-material 'mass terms', though a moral difference is of course implied, it is a tempting approximation to say that in such contexts *homoousios* is figuratively used, but that the basic meaning is 'made of the same kind of stuff'.

For present purposes, we have to consider its use in trinitarian thought, especially as expressing the relationship of the Son to the Father. There is a faint possibility that it was so used by Clement of Alexandria, who employs roughly equivalent expressions. The case for Origen is rather stronger, though some extremely eminent scholars reject it. It rests largely on a passage translated by Rufinus, whose work is sometimes inaccurate, since he wishes to represent Origen as orthodox by the standards of his own time. And Rufinus' material is taken from an earlier defence of Origen by Pamphilus. Origen is quoted as referring to Wisdom 7:25, which describes Wisdom as 'a breath of the power of God and a pure effluent of the glory of the Almighty'; these descriptions are metaphors, he says, drawn from material processes, but are meant to show that the Son has a community of substance with the Father, for an emanation appears to be *homoousios* (with its source). The context of this pronouncement gives some grounds for suspicion that Rufinus has 'improved' Origen's text. On the other hand this passage does not stand alone; and in one text preserved in Greek (*Comm. Joh.* 2.2.16) Origen criticizes those who 'deny the Godhead of the Son and make his individuality and his *ousia* distinctively separate from the Father'.[2] In the light of this text, it is intelligible that he should have upheld 'of the same *ousia*'; though this cannot have been his usual practice, or the term would not have been so much

---

[2] My interpretation of this passage (*Divine Substance*, pp. 211–14) has been challenged by Dr J. Hammerstaedt, *Jahrbuch für Antike und Christentum* 34 (1991), pp. 14–20, and may need revision.

disliked by later Origenists such as Eusebius. Its meaning was still fairly fluid; at *Princ.* 4.4.9 Origen says that *every* intellectual nature is consubstantial with every other! In his comment on Wisdom it implies some kind of continuity of being, but clearly neither identity nor exact equality, since emanation is a one-way process; both the Gnostics and their orthodox critics had used it of the community between outflow and source.

As relating to the Trinity, the term first appears for certain in a dispute involving Bishop Dionysius of Alexandria and Pope Dionysius of Rome, *c.* 255–60. Sabellian, modalist teaching was established in Libya; Bishop Dionysius' criticisms of it were strongly worded, and a complaint against him was sent to Rome, reporting *inter alia* that he did not teach that the Son was *homoousios* with the Father. It looks as if the complainants were using *homoousios* to condemn the Origenistic doctrine of three distinct hypostases, which we know the Alexandrian held; they may well have taught that God is a single hypostasis, and they clearly expected a sympathetic response from Rome. When challenged to defend himself, Bishop Dionysius pleads that he had used expressions equivalent to *homoousios*, for example the analogy of human generation; but he does not actually adopt the term, and it does not appear that Pope Dionysius required him to do so. The latter criticizes both the Sabellian doctrine and the error of supposing three *separate* hypostases; but he seems to have stopped short of condemning 'three hypostases' absolutely.

A little later we find traces of a more decided opposition to the term *homoousios*; it was rejected by a Council held at Antioch in 268, which condemned the teaching of Paul of Samosata. Paul's critics were certainly Origenists, but we know too little about his own teaching to be certain what use he made of the term.

On the eve of the Nicene Council we find *homoousios* rejected by Arius and criticized by his more cautious sympathizer Eusebius of Caesarea. Arius opposes it on two grounds; it makes the Son equal to the Father, and it suggests a quasi-physical process of generation which would involve the Father in change and partition (*Thalia*, lines 9 and 16, in Athanasius *Syn.* 15). Eusebius has much the same reservations; the Son cannot be equal to the Father, who must be supreme (*Praep. Ev.* 11.21), though it is allowed that the Son is exactly *like* the Father (*Dem. Ev.* 4.2.7) – which Arius of course denied; and the Son's derivation from the Father must not be explained in materializing terms, though in *Dem. Ev.* 5.1 he reluctantly allows the metaphors of sunlight and of fragrance. These are stock examples of emissions which cause no diminution of their source, and were so used by Plotinus (*Enn.* 5.1.6), whom Eusebius quotes at *Praep. Ev.* 11.17.3–6; significantly, Plotinus remarks that the product is less than the souce.

The Nicene Council itself has of course been endlessly discussed. The facts are hard to ascertain, since no official minutes were preserved. Why was *homoousios* introduced into the Creed, and what was it supposed to mean? At present no certain answer can be given. It used to be thought that Constantine, or Ossius, imposed it as a 'Westernizing' term intended to stress the divine unity rather than the distinctness of the Persons (cf. p. 166 above). But we have little evidence of its actual use in the West; and an important objection to this theory is the fact that the later Council of Serdica (342–3), which favoured a monarchian theology, made no mention of *homoousios* but spoke rather of 'one hypostasis'. More probably at Nicaea several different motives were at work. One reason for introducing *homoousios* was the mere fact that Arius himself had rejected it (so N. H. Baynes, following Ambrose *De Fide* 3.15); and Constantine himself may have preferred not to define its meaning too precisely (so E. Schwartz); his aim was not to make victims, but to isolate Arius from his supporters, and attract as many of those as possible on to the winning side. In the short run this policy was vindicated when Eusebius of Caesarea, with other Arian sympathizers, accepted the Creed; but theirs was a reluctant submission, and controversy soon broke out again. Eusebius wrote to his diocese to explain why he had accepted the unpopular term, with the other Nicene clauses. His letter shows how the Council was regarded by conservative Origenist theologians; but it also reveals that acceptance of the Creed was all that was required; no exegesis of it was officially imposed. In effect, then, it declared that Christ was fully divine and coeval with the Father; but it laid no particular emphasis on divine unity.

Athanasius' defence of *homoousios* has generally been accepted as authoritative. But the term was not basic to his theology; he first began to insist on it some twenty-five years after Nicaea, and uses it only in the context of the Creed itself. He came to regard it as essential, though as a rule (we have noted) he is tenacious of his central convictions but fairly flexible as to their formulation. He uses philosophical-sounding phrases; but he is more concerned about their agreement with his Church's tradition than about their internal consistency and logic.

Athanasius' opposition to Arius was absolute from the first. (I myself believe that he drafted his Bishop Alexander's Encyclical Letter *Henos Sōmatos, c.* 318; so J. Möhler, *Athanasius*, p. 174). He held that the Son is in no way inferior to the Father, and exists from eternity with him. But in what form? Athanasius conceives him both as internal to the Father, as his Wisdom, and as intimate with the Father, as a Son 'in his bosom' (John 1:18), who can say 'I and the Father are one', but nevertheless name two distinct subjects (*ibid.* 10:30; *C. Ar.* 3:4). Indeed a contrast can be seen, not simply between God's Wisdom and his Son, but between two distinct conceptions of Wisdom. Sometimes Wisdom is personified, in the tradition of Philo, so that Son, Logos and Wisdom are alternative titles for the same Being. Thus in expounding Proverbs 8:22 Athanasius teaches that God 'established' Wisdom, giving her a distinctive role as 'the beginning of his ways'; and this is nothing else than the Incarnation (*C. Ar.* 2.45, 51–3). But in describing the creation he also insists that Wisdom is not a mere assistant or subordinate whom he could instruct, but a power essentially peculiar to himself (*ibid.* 2.28, 3.64). Here he comes close to denying distinct personality; though he does not argue, like Marcellus, that God and his Logos were, or ever will be, one Person (*prosōpon*). Rather, the Son is eternally generated from the Father by a spiritual outflow like the sun's radiance which implies no division or diminution. The Son is 'proper to his substance', *idios tēs ousias*, but a distinct expression of it; for though existing 'in the bosom of the Father' he can simultaneously permeate the universe and moreover inhabit the human body in which he suffered on the Cross (cf. *Inc.* 17). No complete understanding of the divine mysteries is possible; how indeed can we conceive what constitutes personal identity or distinctness within a life so different from our own? However this may be, it seems that for Athanasius the Father's eternal enjoyment of Wisdom and his eternal generation of the Son are interchangeable expressions of the same inexplicable fact.

Owning these basic convictions, Athanasius was for many years content to affirm that the Son was 'from the substance' of the Father and 'alike in substance', *homoios kat' ousian*. References to his 'sameness' have to be interpreted in this light; indeed 'sameness' in part expresses the unchanging constancy characteristic of the spiritual world. Athanasius himself never (in his genuine works) refers to the Trinity as 'three hypostases';[3] but he may well have been unwilling to offend those of his diocese who did so, remembering that his Bishop Alexander had used almost equivalent expressions; perhaps he recognized that *homoousios* was intended to discourage such a theology. In time, however, expressions that he himself had used – and especially *homoios*, or *homoios kat' ousian* – began to be favoured by those who wished to compromise with the more moderate Arians. It was at this stage that Athanasius spoke up decisively for the Nicene Creed and its key word *homoousios*. His favourite image of the sun and its radiance shows what he had in mind. The Father's whole being and power is communicated to the Son, and through him to the world; yet we cannot say that the Son is less than, or other than, the Father. Yet they are not interchangeable, still less identical as Persons; the Father himself remains the ultimate source from which glory flows out and to which thanksgiving is returned.

The doctrine of the Trinity needs to be completed by a satisfactory theology of the Spirit. In its earlier phases the Arian controversy had focused attention on the status of the Logos; the Holy Spirit was little discussed, though the conservative party in particular insisted on the distinct reality of all three Persons. But controversy was aroused by a small group who were prepared to

---

[3] The last section, 6, of *In Illud, Omnia* is certainly inauthentic; so is the passage assigned to *Festal Letter 36* and printed by L. T. Lefort, *CSCO* 150 p. 70, 9–10 = 151 p. 27, 12–13; see T. D. Barnes, *Athanasius and Constantius* (see Bibliography 20), p. 184 n. 20, and especially A. Camplani, *Le Lettere Festali* (Bibliography 20), pp. 101–3.

concede full divinity to the Logos but not to the Spirit (the 'Pneumatomachoi' and 'Macedonians'). This provoked replies from both Athanasius and Basil, and the revised form of the Nicene Creed attributed to the Council of 381 gave full recognition to the Spirit's divinity. But this controversy hardly falls within the scope of this book, since philosophical arguments played little part in it. The question was settled mainly by an appeal to Scripture and to the established tradition of the Church. Many of the old anti-Arian arguments were simply repeated in the new context; indeed it has been suggested that the whole dispute was settled too quickly; a more prolonged debate might have encouraged more enterprising and constructive thinking on the special function of the Spirit within the divine economy.

CHAPTER 15

Substance and Persons

The previous chapter has alluded to problems which arose from an imperfect understanding of the terms *ousia* and hypostasis. In the West Tertullian's formulation *una substantia, tres personae* was accepted by thinkers whose theological interests were perceptibly different from his own; whereas Tertullian was anxious to uphold the distinct existence of all three Persons, his Roman contemporaries and successors laid more stress on the divine unity. In the East there was no agreed formula, and tensions were sharper. Many Easterners reacted strongly against modalist teaching. Origen spoke of three hypostases, partly in order to maintain the substantial reality of Son and Spirit; but the phrase came to suggest his distinctive trinitarian teaching which ranked the three Persons in a descending scale of dignity and power. Some Easterners, either to avoid this implication or in imitation of Western usage, spoke of 'one hypostasis'; but this again could suggest that only the Father is substantially real, the others being only his energies or functions. In the heat of theological debate there was little concern for reflection on the terms employed. Theologians drew no clear distinction between hypostasis and *ousia*, though there was some difference of nuance. Origen's use of the latter term was not clear-cut. Later Origenists thus disliked the term *homoousios*, which seemed uncomfortably close to the much-detested 'one hypostasis'; but they were not unalterably opposed to it; a hard-line insistence on three *ousiai* remained a rarity.

As is well known a solution was ultimately found by the Cappadocian Fathers, who drew a clear distinction between *ousia* and hypostasis. But the importance of this development has given the impression that before it occurred, *ousia* and hypostasis were used interchangeably (which is hardly accurate), and that each word was capable of two possible meanings, namely those finally distinguished by the Cappadocians. This latter suggestion is very far from the truth; we have already shown that *ousia* displays a whole complex of different meanings (pp. 161–6); hypostasis, we shall find, despite its very different history and philosophical associations, developed a complex of senses which mirror those of *ousia* pretty closely. Different writers, of course, had strongly marked preferences, depending on the theological context; but otherwise the difference is mainly one of frequency; in some of the possible senses, one term is very much more common than the other.

Hypostasis is a verbal noun; the verb is generally cited by its present form '*huphistēmi*'; but its root form involves the stem *sta-*, cf. the Latin *sta-re*, which yields the compound *substantia*. The Greek verb means, in its transitive forms 'to place beneath', in its middle and intransitive forms 'to stand beneath'; and there has been some disagreement as to which forms underlie the word 'hypostasis'. G. L. Prestige argued that a substantial minority of its uses derive from the active verb, and this view is reflected in the article in the *Patristic Greek Lexicon*. H. Dörrie, however, showed that almost always it is the middle verb, *huphistasthai*, that occurs in conjunction with the noun in the earlier texts. Prestige's view must therefore be abandoned when discussing the formative stage of the term's development; some later writers do indeed connect hypostasis with the active form *hupostēsai*, 'to produce', but this may well be a product of scholarly ingenuity.

Although the verb *huphistēmi* turns up fairly commonly in classical writers, the noun *hupostasis* is rare in poetry and stylish prose; it is found more commonly in scientific and medical writers. I would distinguish three basic senses:

(1) What settles at the bottom; sometimes of urine, but mostly of some solid deposit, a sediment, or the excreta.

(2) What lies below, in concealment; an ambush (so Sophocles once; here note that the verb is used both transitively, 'to post an ambush', and intransitively, 'to lie in ambush'). More generally, a military post (1 Sam. 13:23, 14:4); or

again, adapted from 'concealment', a refuge (Ps. 38:8 LXX; Jer. 23:22).

(3) What stands below, as a support; most obviously in the literal sense, a causeway, firm ground (Ps. 68:3 LXX); the substructure of a building; the limbs of an animal.

From this basic notion of 'support' there derives an amazing variety of senses:

(a) Resistance.

(b) Resources, possessions.

(c) A promise (the verb can mean 'to promise', sc. to provide resources). Hence, a lease (sc. the document that guarantees tenure, in return for a promise of service).

(d) An undertaking, i.e. a task undertaken.

(e) Hopes, prospects; the confidence based on them; so Ruth 1:12 LXX.

(f) A plan, whether of something concrete (a temple) or otherwise (a book). (Possibly the former sense is original; the foundations of a temple indicate its plan.)

(g) In astrological writers, the position of the stars at the moment of one's birth, supposed to determine the course of one's life.

Often these senses are difficult to discriminate; thus at Hebrews 3:14 and 11:1 it is debatable whether the writer is thinking primarily of 'confidence' or of the reality on which confidence might be based. H. Dörrie has argued[1] that 'hypostasis' can mean simply 'a situation', even where it is unsatisfactory or disquieting, as at 2 Corinthians 9:4; but the sense of (misplaced) confidence seems very natural.

However the most important senses for theology derive, not from (3), but from (1), through the medium of Stoic philosophy. The verb was so used by Chrysippus, the noun first appears for us in this context with Posidonius. The Stoics taught that nothing is real unless it is embodied in matter (see pp. 48–9 above). But the most obvious example of this is solid matter; hence the verb, which originally meant 'settling, precipitating, solidifying', came to suggest 'acquiring solid reality'; and the noun, which

[1] "Ὑπόστασις, Wort und Bedeutungsgeschichte', *Nachr. Akad. Göttingen* 3 (1955) pp. 35–92 = *Platonica Minora* 12–69; here see p. 39 (16).

already meant 'solid matter', as opposed to liquid or vapour, came to mean 'something actually existing'. This sense appears clearly in a distinction drawn by Posidonius between *hupostasis* and *emphasis*; lightning exists 'as a hypostasis', even though it is not a solid object; but a rainbow is only an *emphasis*, a phenomenon, even though everyone sees it.

However, there is confusion in the Stoic theory. The metaphor of solidifying is appropriate enough as applied to the cosmological process by which the original world-stuff, fire or *pneuma*, produced the heavier elements and acquired a semipermanent pattern and structure to form the world as we know it (see p. 46 above). But the same metaphor was reapplied to describe something quite different: a supposed process by which pure matter acquires qualities and relations so as to form the objects with which we are familiar. But this is not a process which has ever actually happened, or could happen, since 'pure matter' is no more than an aspect of reality which we distinguish in thought; we conceive it as 'logically prior', we imagine it as existing on its own, and then 'add' qualities to it by simply reversing a previous process of thought. Posidonius explains that pure matter as such has no form or quality, but that it always exists *in* some form and quality; what exists 'in hypostasis' differs only conceptually from (pure) matter: *diapherein de tēn ousian tēs hulēs tēn ousan kata tēn hupostasin epinoiāi monon*, Arius Didymus fr. 20, in Diels *DG* p. 458. The last clause implies that whatever is an example of the one is an example of the other; pure matter is a necessary constituent of things, but is never found in isolation.

In the light of this somewhat misleading theory, the verb is used in a double sense; sometimes of what is presupposed as 'underlying', or theoretically prior; sometimes of what 'emerges' as an actual reality. And 'hypostasis' can mean both 'underlying reality', pictured rather like the base metal of a counterfeit coin, and 'what actually exists'. Sometimes again it retains a verbal sense of 'existence', i.e. 'the fact of existing'; it can also mean 'the act of bringing into being', '*Realizierung*'. Arius Didymus says that matter and form must combine 'for the production of body', *pros tēn tou somatos hupostasin* (*ibid.* fr. 2, *DG* p. 448), where a transitive sense is perhaps detectable; here the 'combination' is a purely theoretical process, but the word is also used for things that really do come into being; Diodorus uses 'hypostasis' for the execution of a plan, and Christian writers apply it to the origination of the divine Persons. Alexander of Alexandria, for instance, interprets Isaiah 53:8 by saying that the hypostasis, i.e. generation, of the Son is inexplicable, like the mystery of the Father's 'theogony' or generative process (Theodoret *H.E.* 1.4.46). Alexander no doubt regards this as a real action; by 'mystery' he means only that its nature is unknown to us.

On the account we have given, 'hypostasis' developed its remarkable range of meanings in the context of Stoic philosophy, in which reality presupposes matter. But it soon escaped from this philosophical setting, and retained these meanings more or less unaltered both in ordinary usage and among Platonist philosophers. These argued, against the Stoics, that intelligible principles 'possess reality' (hypostasis) or 'are realities' (hypostases), and defended the reality of the immaterial soul in similar terms. Mind and soul were of course regarded as substances, independent entities which retain their individuality in spite of change; thus Albinus refers to the soul as 'an intelligible reality which is unchangeable as regards its hypostasis', *ousia noētē ametablētos tēn hupostasin*, *Did.* 14.3, where the last two words suggest 'substance' or 'nature', and one could substitute *ten ousian* or *tēn phusin*. The culmination of this process was reached when Porphyry, as it seems, gave the name 'hypostasis' to Plotinus' three primary forms of beings, the One, Mind and Soul, although they were for him at the furthest remove from matter.

In contrast with their insistence on the permanence and reality of the intelligible world as against perceptible things, it does not seem that the Platonists were equally concerned to represent the Forms as each of them 'one over many', stressing their unity as opposed to the multiplicity of their perceptible copies; Plotinus indeed taught that there are Forms of individuals. At all events they did not normally present such a contrast in terms of a distinction between *ousia* and hypostasis; this clear theoretical distinction, deriving perhaps from the hint thrown out by Porphyry, was first widely expounded by the Cappadocian Fathers. In earlier literature the contrast, then, is largely one of frequency. We have listed the basic senses of *ousia* under seven headings: A, existence; B, category; C, the category of substance; D, stuff or material; E, form; F, definition; and G, truth. It seems to me that 'hypostasis' can be an exact equivalent of *ousia* in senses A and D, and sometimes comes close to it in senses B and E; senses C and F are only occasionally represented by 'hypostasis', but it is nearly equivalent in a few phrases assignable to G.

Let us give some examples. Origen challenges Celsus to prove the 'existence and reality', *hupostasin kai ousian*, of Greek gods like Mnemosyne and Themis, *Cels.* 1.23. In theory, of course, the two words might have different senses, but I cannot see a distinction; when the same two words appear together in the Nicene Creed, most scholars now take them as synonyms. Athanasius also couples them together in *C. Gent.* 6; some Greeks falsely believe that evil 'has existence and reality' in its own right. Here again I think they are equivalent, but the sense is rather different; Athanasius clearly does not mean that there is no such thing as evil (cf. *ibid.* 2), but rather that it has no positive reality; it is a lack of positive goodness (*Inc.* 4). A good instance where 'hypostasis' does mean simply 'existence' occurs in Clement, *Str.* 2.35.1: 'It is knowledge of sin that was revealed by the Law; it did not gain existence thereby'; this corresponds to the previous sentence: 'the Law did not make sin, but showed it'. A related use of 'hypostasis', less easy to classify, is that which contrasts reality with thought or description; thus Origen suggests that the 'water' of John 3:5 may be identical with the 'spirit'; there is a difference of *epinoia* (concept) but not of hypostasis (*Comm. Joh.* fr. 36).

Under heading B I have considered *ousia* as the most general qualitative term. Thus Chrysippus is said to have discussed the *ousia* of the soul, what sort of thing it is (*SVF* 2.885, p. 239 l. 19; N.B. that *ousia* cannot mean 'definition' here, since this has already been stated, *ibid.* p. 238 l. 32, whereas the 'discussion' extends over the first half of the book). Cyril of Jerusalem expresses much the same idea with reference to the Church's faith in the Trinity (*cat.* 16.24); 'It is enough for us to know these things; do not enquire into their nature (physis) or hypostasis'.

Thirdly, could 'hypostasis' mean, not just 'category' but precisely the category of substance? This seems unlikely; the normal term is Aristotle's own word *ousia*. But a passage cited by H. Dörrie suggests that 'hypostasis' is occasionally used in its place ('Hypostasis' (see n. 1), p. 64). The Theaetetus Commentary states that individual things have no reality, hypostasis, contrasting them of course with intelligible realities; but this is associated with a list of Aristotelian categories in which the first item, namely substance, is lacking; it looks as if hypostasis = substance. Tertullian uses *substantia* to mean material reality, but he also connects it with accidents; this looks like an amalgam of Stoic and Aristotelian thinking.

Hypostasis meaning 'stuff' is commonly recognized, and few examples are needed. In this case, again, its equivalence with *ousia* is fairly clear. The *Epistle to Diognetus* (2.1) uses 'hypostasis' to refer to the materials, stone, bronze or wood, from which the heathen gods are made. The contrasting sense of 'immaterial stuff' appears in Origen, *De Oratione* 27.8; discussing the senses of *ousia*, he refers to 'those who maintain that the hypostasis of incorporeal things is primary'. In both these cases 'hypostasis' is used in a generalized sense, for the stuff which is common to a group of idols, or to all incorporeal things; but we also find it meaning 'an individual material thing'; so Cyril of Jerusalem (*Cat.* 9.5) states that God 'raised the sky like a dome and formed the stable hypostasis of heaven out of the fluid nature of the primordial waters'.

The sense of a class or species is commonly expressed by *ousia*, with *physis* as a rather less technical equivalent. 'Hypostasis' in this sense is much less common; however we can cite Tatian *Or.* 15.4: 'the hypostasis of the demons has no opportunity for repentance'; here 'race' or 'species' seems a natural rendering. On the other hand, where *ousia* means an individual member of a species – Aristotle's 'primary substance' – conventional wisdom would suggest that hypostasis is a common equivalent. But it is often hard to determine whether it means the individual member of a species or uses the image of an individual bit of stuff (i.e. senses D_4 or E_4). The difficulty is neatly illustrated by a passage in Origen (*Princ.* 3.1.22) where the two ideas are conjoined: 'one nature of every soul and one material [literally 'lump', *phurama*] of the rational hypostases'. And when he argues that Father and Son are two hypostases, two distinct existents (*pragmata*), their contrasting unity is not traced to a common spiritual stuff or to a common divine nature, but to their 'unanimity and agreement and identity of will'.

The last two senses assigned to *ousia* are (F) definition, and (G) truth. The claim that 'hypostasis' can mean 'definition' looks improbable; however, this is a possible interpretation of Gregory of Nyssa, *Comm. Cant. Or.* 2: 'There is no other hypostasis of evil except separation from what is better'. Gregory is not discussing the existence of evil, or crediting it with some degree of substantial reality; it is a definition that he is proposing. As to truth, I do not think that 'hypostasis' by itself ever reproduces the peculiar Platonic use of *ousia* without qualification to denote supersensible reality; but this is quite often indicated in general terms as 'intelligible hypostasis'; and for a more specific example, see Gregory of Nyssa *C. Eun.* 3.5.63: the definition given of soul will hold good 'of every intelligent hypostasis', *peri pasēs noeras hupostaseōs*. Finally, the adverbial use of *ousiāi* (dative singular) meaning 'in fact', 'in reality', is closely paralleled by phrases like *hupostasei* and *kath' hupostasin*, though the latter at least is apt to suggest material reality.

We have suggested that 'hypostasis' duplicates all the 'main nuances' of *ousia*; though it should be repeated that some such uses are extremely common, others are rarities. There is, then, a basis for contrast. It should be clear, also, from the examples we have given, that 'hypostasis' has varying 'modes of reference' just like *ousia*. Sometimes it stands for the mere existence of something; or again for a character distinguishable from its possessor (the positive reality of evil, the nature of the Trinity). Sometimes no distinction is suggested; Father and Son simply *are* two hypostases, or two realities (*pragmata*) and the 'stable hypostasis of heaven', although a genitive is used, is nothing else than heaven itself, described under one of its aspects.

We do not suggest, of course, that the Fathers who used such expressions were aware of such a complex pattern of usage; explicit observation and analysis of usage is a sophisticated business, the concern of lexicographers. In antiquity, that science was still undeveloped. Once again, we do not claim any monopoly for the scheme suggested. Our business has been to try to bring out certain distinctions of logic; writers of dictionaries are entitled to pass over this arrangement if they think best, and arrange their material in accordance with the various contexts and theological applications of such terms.

As is well known, the Cappadocian Fathers put forward a distinction between *ousia* and hypostasis in terms of the species and the individual. It appears that they were not quite the first to do so; the same distinction was made in an unknown Greek source used by Marius Victorinus *c.* 358 (unless, which seems unlikely, Gregory of Nyssa's work *Against Arius and Sabellius* can be dated early enough to give him the priority).[2] Before this time it seems that no formal distinction was made; but we can observe unformulated preferences. Both terms are about equally common in the very general sense of 'existence' (as fact) or 'existent thing'; both are commonly used to mean 'materiality', 'material stuff', 'material thing'; but *ousia* is much the commoner in the categorial sense of 'substance', indicating either a species or a member of a species, Aristotle's 'primary substance', but *not* referring formally to his distinction. For 'intelligible reality' the usage varies; many Platonists preferred to call this *ousia*, following Plato's own usage; it was the Neoplatonists who introduced 'hypostasis' as a *terminus technicus*.

Can we nevertheless trace the 'Cappadocian' distinction to any earlier source? G. L. Prestige and H. A. Wolfson have both suggested that it goes back to Origen (*GPT* pp. 188–9, *PCF* p. 337), but without offering satisfactory proofs. Indeed it seems incredible that an explicit distinction, if made by Origen, could have been overlooked in the anxious debates about *ousia* and hypostasis in the 340s and 350s. But there may be some residue of truth in the suggestion. In general, of course, Origen's use of 'hypostasis' is extremely flexible. Thus in the Commentary on St John 32.16.192–3 it stands first for the 'concrete reality' of the human nature assumed by the Logos, then for the 'existence' of

---

[2] See F. Dinsen, *Homoousios* (see Bibliography 14), pp. 347–8. M. Simonetti identifies the source in Porphyry: 'All'origine' (see Bibliography 20), pp. 173–5. But Victorinus need not be the only channel of transmission.

the Logos himself; whereas in 20.22.182 'our better hypostasis' seems to mean 'our spiritual nature', and is used in parallel with 'our superior *ousia*'. But in Trinitarian contexts there is a perceptible difference of usage. Origen regularly teaches that there are three divine hypostases, but he makes no consistent use of *ousia*. It may sometimes stand for the common 'substance' of divinity; see pp. 167–8 above. More commonly it denotes a Person, either God's Wisdom or the Holy Spirit (see respectively *Exp. in Prov.* 8:22 and fr. 37 *in Jo.*). It does not appear that Origen actually spoke of the Trinity as 'three *ousiai*'; but he uses the word adverbially to express the personal distinction of Father and Son (*Orat.* 15, the Son is other than the Father in *ousia* and *hupokeimenon*, 'subject'), and criticizes the opposing view (*Comm. Joh.* 2.23.149). In a puzzling passage, *ibid.* 10.37.246, he attacks those modalists who teach that the Son is numerically the same as the Father, so that they are 'one not only in *ousia* but in *hupokeimenon*'; here it is possible that a distinction is intended; 'one in subject' is clearly false, 'one in *ousia*' need not be so. This would square with the evidence given on p. 167, that 'one in *ousia*' is occasionally approved. In the light of such passages it seems very possible that some conservative Origenist of the 350s, pondering whether to come to terms with the Nicene party, should hark back to previously disregarded texts of Origen as evidence that acceptance of 'one *ousia*' need not entail a denial of 'three hypostases'.

This whole discussion assumes that Aristotle's distinction between two senses of *ousia* was unfamiliar to fourth-century Christians. I see no problem here. The principal exponent of Aristotle's logic was Porphyry, who wrote against the Christians and had his writings condemned to the flames by Constantine. Even if they were recovered and read by Christians, as Simonetti has argued, it is unlikely that his writings on logic would have attracted their interest. Basil admittedly seems to have read the *Categories* (*c. Eun.* 1.15), but ignores the early chapters; moreover he tends to think of *ousia* in Stoic terms (*ibid.* 2.1, 2.19), and Stoic theory could accommodate the obvious distinction between the species and the individual (see p. 49) – but in terms of 'quality' (*poion*), not *ousia*. Gregory of Nyssa is harder to interpret. He seems to have a general acquaintance with Aristotelian logic, most probably drawn from text-books. He speaks quite conventionally of species, differentia and individuals, using a variety of terms, but insists that *ousia* should only be used to designate the species. Phrases like *merikē* or *idikē ousia* – 'partitive' or 'individual substance' – used to designate the individual, are misleading; Aristotle's 'primary substance' is I think ignored. But Gregory perversely insists that general terms like 'man' should be reserved for the species; it is incorrect to speak of 'many men' or 'a certain man', even though the Bible condescends to such improper usage. There is no reference to Aristotle in this discussion.[3] In any case, dependence on Aristotle's logic was a reproach levelled against the Arians; moreover an explicit recourse to Aristotle's terminology of 'primary substance' would have had the awkward result of countenancing the description of the divine Persons as three *ousiai*.

Before closing this chapter we must find some space to comment more generally on the Cappadocian theology of the Trinity. It has often been claimed that the Cappadocians abandoned the pure Nicene position, introducing what has been called a 'neo-Nicene' orthodoxy, content to affirm the total similarity of the divine Persons rather than an integral divine unity. This I think is largely an illusion encouraged by the mistaken view that Nicaea declared for the 'numerical unity' of substance in the three Persons. On a realistic estimate of Nicaea the Cappadocians were faithful to its intentions, though their methods and terminology were sufficiently original to mark them off as a distinct group. We have already noted their genuine concern to uphold the divine unity (see p. 162 above)

But there are other objections to their theology which are less easily met; though considering its importance in the Christian tradition, I regret having to expound them so briefly.

We may begin with the comparison of the Trinity with three members of a single species. How seriously is this intended? The Cappadocian Fathers have reservations; they often affirm that the indivisible divine nature is not comparable to the unity of the

[3] See his *Ad Graecos Ex Communibus Notionibus, Opera* 3.1, pp. 28 ff. ed. Jaeger.

human race; for men can be separated in time and place, and by moral differences.[4] Yet Gregory of Nyssa contends, in his much quoted *Quod Non Tres Dii*, that the analogy holds, since three human individuals are in some real sense 'one man'. (Aristotle would have called them 'one in species'.) This attempt must be pronounced a failure. Even if we are 'members one of another' in ways not commonly recognized, yet the physical and moral differences between men cannot be argued away. Gregory takes the example of Peter, James and John. But this is special pleading. His argument is perfectly general, and if it holds at all, it should hold in the most unlikely cases. Gregory needs to convince us that Moses, Eunomius and Cleopatra are 'all one man'!

Secondly, the Cappadocian Trinity shares in some drawbacks inherent in the 'homoiousian' position from which it developed. Reacting against the Arian teaching that the Son and Spirit are 'unlike' the Father, being subordinate or inferior, the Cappadocians pronounced them alike in all respects. There must, then, be some distinction which makes it possible to distinguish three Persons; and this is seen in their 'mode of origination', *tropos huparxeōs*; the Father is the unoriginate source, the Son begotten from the Father, the Spirit in some way proceeding or 'breathed out' from the Father (*not*, of course, 'from the Father and the Son', as the Latin Church was later to assert). Each Person is thus described as a combination of a common substance with an individualizing property, pictured, as we have seen, by the analogy of three men. But this is a logician's view of human beings. One cannot gain any real impression of a human individual by seeing him simply as an example of the species, man, on which distinguishing features are superimposed; why then should this inadequate formula be thought appropriate to the divine nature?[5]

One may then reply: yes, admittedly this is a crude parallel. In the case of the Trinity, the personal distinctions are not really

---

[4] See Dinsen, *Homoousios*, pp. 156–60, especially p. 157 n. 4.
[5] I have developed these two comments in my paper 'Individual personality in Origen and the Cappadocian Fathers' (see Bibliography 20). For a more detailed critique, see my 'Why Not Three Gods?' (Bibliography 20).

mere external distinguishing marks; each Person has his *tropos huparxeōs*, a perpetual fact rather than an initial episode, and one which is integral to his being. But in this case we can no longer regard the common substance as something which is simply repeated with a minimal difference; it is reconstituted in the begetting of the Son and the 'out-breathing' of the Spirit. But how can these processes reproduce the common substance *without change*, if they are distinguishable one from another, and also result in beings distinguishable as Son and Spirit?

Suppose, then, that we say that the whole analogy so far describes the Persons' origin *humano modo*, whereas in reality the one divine substance contains in itself the reasons why it must manifest itself in three forms? This reminds one of Hegel's theory of the 'concrete universal', conceived as dynamic and self-differentiating; but whether that is defensible or not, it requires that the one substance manifests itself 'Fatherwise', and also 'Sonwise' and 'Spiritwise'. If so, it would differentiate itself, a fact which would nullify the professed insistence on the perfect simplicity of the divine nature. To speak simply, the Son must know that he is begotten from the Father, and respond in love to this unique privilege. His love for the Father will thus be a distinctively filial love; and since love is an essential feature of the Godhead, there will be distinction along with unity within the divine essence.

A third criticism turns on the claim that the activity of all three Persons is one and undivided. The dilemma can be put very crudely: should we think of it as an activity to which each Person contributes, or one which each Person completes? In the former case, it seems that the contribution of each Person is incomplete without the others; in the latter, that three Persons are engaged where one would suffice. One would like to believe that the Cappadocian theology is proof against so crude an objection; but I am not entirely convinced that this is so.

On the face of it, one can find suggestions of both the possibilities I have mentioned. Gregory of Nyssa, for instance, speaks of 'a single activity of Father, Son, and Holy Spirit, in no respect different in the case of any' as proof of their unity of nature ([Basil], *Ep.* 189.6), which suggests that 'single' refers to a *type* of activity three times repeated, or perhaps rather, done concurrently in triplicate. But he also speaks of a power which 'issues from the Father, as from a spring; is actualized by the Son; and its grace is perfected by the power of the Holy Spirit' (*Quod non tres dii* p. 41 J., *LCC* 3, p. 263). He continues, indeed, precisely by disowning both the 'repetitive' and the 'contributory' view: 'No activity is distinguished among the Persons, as if it were completed individually by each of them, or separately apart from their joint supervision'. But the latter is not a serious possibility. No one would think of divine Persons as ignorant of each others' activities; so there is not much force in Gregory's denial; and there is no positive proposal for avoiding the dilemma.

Assuming a Trinity of the Cappadocian type, I think myself that the 'contributory' option is to be preferred; its apparent drawbacks can be avoided if one holds that the divine Persons are perfectly united in will and knowledge, as indeed the Cappadocians affirmed. If it seems that the work of each Person, taken singly, is incomplete, one can reply that the Father's actions performed through the Son (for instance) are truly his own no less than those enacted in his own Person. What is required is to eliminate any notion of exclusiveness, misunderstanding or internal friction from the divine Tri-unity. But this is clearly a minimum requirement; it is not intended to suggest that no mysteries remain.

As a more general judgement, the Cappadocian Trinity has at least the advantage of presenting a clearly articulated doctrine from which possible advances may be projected. And it has the outstanding merit of discarding for good one fundamental defect of subordinationist theologies, as expounded both by Arian Christians and by Neoplatonists; namely the thought that God's power is necessarily reduced and obscured in its contact with inferior spirits or with the material world. Limitation there must be: every gift must conform to the measure of its recipient. But the orthodox theologians could explain this better in personalistic terms, as a divine self-limitation and condescension to the needs of created beings.

CHAPTER 16

Christ as God and Man

Christology can be defined as 'The study of the Person of Christ, and in particular of the union in Him of the divine and human natures'. This definition relies on philosophical concepts as employed in the debates about Christ which led up to the Council of Chalcedon in 451. The 'christology' of the New Testament is far less formal and unified; there is no mention of a union of natures, and the key-word *prosōpon* usually means 'face' or 'appearance', sometimes 'dignity' (Matt. 22:16 etc.) but never 'person', except perhaps at 2 Corinthians 2:10. Our present task is to explain how the philosophical concepts were introduced, what they meant, and whether their use is justified. For this purpose we need some account of the actual development of the doctrine of Christ; but this can be reduced to a mere outline, which can easily be filled in from the standard text-books.

The New Testament embodies two contrasted pictures of Christ. In the Synoptic Gospels he is unquestionably a man. He is set apart from other men by the authority with which he spoke, his miraculous powers, the prophecies which he fulfilled, his dispensation of the Spirit, his declared fellowship with the Father, his virginal conception, and above all by his rising from the dead. But he remains a Jewish teacher, a carpenter by trade, the son of Mary, along with his brothers and sisters. By contrast, the Fourth Gospel presents him as a heavenly being come down to earth, who can speak of 'the glory which he had with his Father before the world existed' (John 17:5). In his earthly life that glory is not surrendered, though it is hidden from unbelievers. His 'becoming flesh' is seen as an entry into our world, not as a transformation, divine into human, or a new beginning; but it is not explained how this view is to be squared with the acknowledged facts of his birth and his human parentage. Much the same comments could be made about the pre-existent Christ as pictured in St Paul and Hebrews (e.g. Col. 1:15–17, Heb. 1:1–6).

The first readers of these books were not faced with a problem of combining two different impressions of Christ. They did not find these books assembled in an authoritative collection; and the many rather simple-minded Christians of the second century could easily treat St Matthew's Gospel as their principal authority for the life of Christ, accept the Pauline letters mainly as a source of practical guidance for Church life, and relegate the Fourth Gospel to the margin of their interests – or alternatively, revere it as expounding a mystery into which it would impertinent to enquire. Problems arose, however, when the balance of power in the Church came to rest irrevocably with Gentile Christianity. In a Palestinian milieu it was still possible to picture the heavenly Father in human form and to see the contrast between heaven and earth as one of light and glory against relative darkness and indignity. But even Jews, when hellenized, had come to treat anthropomorphic views of God as a mark of paganism (see Philo, *Opif.* 69, *Post. Cain* 1–4, etc.), and to conceive the Almighty, and also the divine Logos, in the forms presented by Middle Platonist philosophers. God is seen as formless, imperceptible, a changeless unity; human beings, whatever divine aspirations they may have, are confined within a corruptible body and captivated by sensual inclinations.

How could the Church's inherited faith in Jesus be reconciled with this theology? Inevitably, many Christians were led to emphasize one pole or the other in their traditional scheme. Some found it natural to insist on the human elements in the Gospel story, and picture Jesus' link with the Father in terms of election, foretold destiny, and exceptional gifts of the Spirit, a divine 'Sonship' by adoption (cf. Ps. 2:7), confirmed perhaps by the Virgin birth. Others held fast to their faith in Christ's pre-existent divinity, persisting unaltered through the course of his earthly life; he thus remained, despite all appearances, impassible; he only seemed to suffer on the Cross (or, in some versions, his place there was taken by another, perhaps by a human Jesus distinct from the true heavenly Christ). Clement of Alexandria is instructive as showing the force of this persuasion. His intentions were orthodox enough; he could write 'Now this Logos himself has appeared [epephanē] to men, He who alone is both, both God and man' (*Protr.* 7.1). Yet he teaches that Christ had no physical desires, and ate and drank only to demonstrate that he was no mere phantom (*Str.* 6.71); he did not digest his food (*ibid.* 3.59). And much later orthodox writers, who insist that he acted throughout in human fashion, even while displaying divine power, are apt to represent him as doing so in order to confirm or refute some belief, rather than satisfying natural human needs; see for instance Athanasius, *Inc.* 18.

These deviations need not be described in detail; the first can be traced under the headings Ebionism, Psilanthropism, Adoptionism, upheld by teachers such as Theodotus, Artemon, and Paul of Samosata; the second under Docetism and Modalism. Rather misleadingly, some modern scholars have included both groups under the title of 'Monarchianism', which properly belongs to the second. Teachers of this school obscured the personal distinctions of Father and Son, and could be condemned either as Docetists (the Son did not really suffer) or as Patripassians (the Father did suffer). Varieties of such modalist teaching are represented by Praxeas, Noetus, and the little-known Sabellius. Both docetist and adoptionist tendencies are found among the second-century Gnostics; the former is fairly common; some systems, again, distinguished sharply between a divine impassible Christ and a human Jesus; but others pictured the Lord simply as a man uniquely endowed with the Spirit; so Basilides, according to Hippolytus, *Ref.* 7.26.8.

In the end it became clear that the 'Synoptic' picture of Christ could not be accepted to the exclusion of the other view; the Church came to affirm his pre-existence, endeavouring to combine with it as much of the former picture as it could accommodate. The simplest solution was to adopt the incarnational model already provided by Platonism. For the Platonist, of course, every human being was composed of a pre-existent soul introduced into a human body at conception or at birth or intermediately; Porphyry's *Ad Gaurum* describes the mechanics of the process.[1] For a time Christians were willing to accept this Platonist view as applying to men in general (so, notably, Origen); after it was displaced by rival opinions (each soul derived from the parents' souls, and so ultimately from Adam; or, each soul individually created as required) it remained familiar and was in practice retained in the special case of the Logos. (Even fairly sophisticated writers could treat the union of the created soul with its body as a good *analogy* for the incarnation of the uncreated Logos.) Pagan Platonists sometimes objected that a descent from heaven to earth could only be inspired by unworthy, sensual motives; but the Platonic tradition itself had suggested other possibilities.[2]

This account is admittedly much over-simplified. Origen's view is complex, and possibly changed over the years; but a well-known version presents the soul of Christ as a pre-existent being, created before the world began along with all other rational beings, but distinguished from the rest by the intense love which inspired him to fuse with the Logos to make 'one spirit', like iron combining with fire (*Princ.* 2.6.3–6; cf. 1 Cor. 6:17, *SVF* 2.471). The Incarnation of the Logos is thus effected by a *normal* incarnation of this exceptional soul. Origen's view could be criticized, however, as making the divinization of this soul – and consequently the Incarnation of the Logos – depend upon its own resolve in place of a divine initiative; indeed he could appear to be teaching two Christs, like those Gnostics who distinguished between Christ and Jesus. At all events his followers during the next century think of the Logos *replacing* a human soul in Jesus, lodging in his body 'in the manner of a soul' (Eusebius *C. Marc.* 2.4.24) or as his 'inner man'. This conception was not effectively challenged by Athanasius, and it was not until Apollinaris presented lucid arguments to suggest that Christ had no human soul that such views were condemned. A telling argument against them had already been stated by

---

[1] French version in A. J. Festugière, *La Révélation d'Hermès Trismégiste* 3 (see Bibliography 20), pp. 265 ff.   [2] *Ibid.*, pp. 219–22.

Origen; the human soul needs redemption no less than the flesh; and 'what was not assumed could not be redeemed'.[3]

Arius appears to have taken the same view as Eusebius; he argued that the Logos himself experienced the emotions of dismay and terror at the time of the Passion, and therefore fell short of the serene impassibility of the Father. He taught that the Logos was in some sense a creature, though unique in status and the foremost among God's works. In reply, the orthodox ignored his qualifications and condemned him for regarding the Logos as merely 'one of the creatures'. And the desire to exhibit Arian teaching in the worst possible light often led them to emphasize the transience and imperfection of the whole created order.[4] The Incarnation in any case raised the problem of seeing two natures contrasted as finite and infinite conjoined in a single being; the lower estimate of creation, however, sharpened the contrast.

From the later fourth century onwards this problem was encountered in two sharply opposed theologies. The Alexandrian school remained within the general perspective established by Athanasius. True, they disowned Apollinaris; for them, the Logos assumed human flesh 'ensouled with a rational soul'; this improves on Athanasius, who treats our Lord's human psychology by taking 'flesh' in the broad sense of 'human nature', including its liability to desire and fear. Cyril, whose recognition of a soul in Christ was initially not much more than a formality, gradually came to see it in more concrete terms as the natural locus of suffering. But neither the sanctified 'flesh' of the Logos nor his rational soul play any directive part in the incarnate Life; as with Athanasius, all decision rests with the Logos himself, who on occasions will allow human emotions to come into play in order to display his sovereignty over them and his solidarity with mankind, for whom he is the appointed pattern, so that they too by controlling their passions may finally be 'divinized'. It is implied, moreover, that the human nature assumed by the Logos must be ideal humanity, and therefore impersonal; the Logos assumed human nature as such; he could not take to himself a man.

[3] Origen, *Dial. Heracl.* 7; the classic statement is in Gregory Nazianzen, *Ep.* 101.7.
[4] For example, Athanasius, *Inc.* 11; contrast *C. Gent.* 2.

The opposing school, centred on Antioch, had drawn attention to the Arians' failure to recognize a human soul in Christ. The Arians, they claimed, had degraded the divine Logos by attaching to him the emotions and the limitations which properly belong to our human nature. They themselves conceived this human nature in concrete and personal terms; the function of Christ was not merely to bring divinity into a human setting, but to exhibit human nature perfected by total obedience to God through his Logos; Christ was thus 'the new Adam', the pattern and inspiration of the new race of the redeemed. In this scheme, the divine nature of the Logos and the perfected human nature of Christ were distinguished by an ontological divide, infinite against finite. But the Antiochene theologians resisted the charge that they were teaching two Christs. Two beings there necessarily were, since Christ was both God and man; two *prosōpa*, maybe, or two hypostases; there was no established convention to govern the use of such phrases, which had already appeared in both orthodox and heretical contexts; Irenaeus attacked the Gnostics' theory of a partnership between the divine Word and the human Jesus as implying two substances – *ex altera et altera substantia dicentes eum factum*, *A.H.* 3.16.5 – whereas Tertullian speaks of two substances in Christ, *Prax.* 27. For the Antiochenes, however, the gap between the two elements was closed by the perfect obedience of the perfect man in response to God's choice of him; indeed the same word *eudokia* stood both for the divine favour which Jesus merited through his obedience and for God's 'good pleasure' which had summoned him into the world.

The tension between the opposing schools came to a head during the 420s, when a violent quarrel broke out between Nestorius, the new Patriarch of Constantinople, and Cyril of Alexandria; the former, sincere but inexperienced, aggressive and inflexible; the latter, devoted but devious, masterful and unscrupulous. Cyril secured the condemnation of Nestorius at the Council of Ephesus in 431, largely by corrupt means, though the part played by Rome was decisive and deplorable; Pope Celestine blindly accepted Cyril's portrayal of Nestorius as an adoptionist and (perhaps more excusably) took offence at

Nestorius' assumption of dignity as Bishop of 'New Rome'. In reality Nestorius had merely reformulated the teaching of accepted Antiochene theologians; Cyril, though rightly arguing for a clearer statement of the unity of Christ, was the less consistent thinker, and laid up trouble for the Church by deliberately expressing the Alexandrian position in an indiscrete statement which Nestorius was bound to reject and which remained as an embarrassment and cause of division.

The controversy brought new formulations into play; in particular Cyril stood by the phrase 'one nature of the divine Logos made flesh', which he believed to have come from Athanasius, though in fact it was coined by Apollinaris. The Antiochenes argued for 'two natures', Godhead and manhood. A compromise formula was eventually found, namely that a union of the two natures had taken place. The Alexandrian party were willing to concede that Christ was (derived) 'from two natures', but insisted on 'one nature after the union'. But a partial reaction against Alexandrian extremists at the Council of Chalcedon in 451 resulted in a formula more acceptable to the Antiochenes and approved at Rome, namely that Christ was to be worshipped 'in two natures'. These, it was stated, had come together in a perfect unity. On the other hand the union was said to be 'unconfused'; the distinction of the natures was not abolished. The Alexandrian party accepted this formula with reluctance; their preference for the 'one nature' formula was still unshaken, and the tension soon led to a disastrous schism between the Chalcedonian party, imperialist and pro-Roman, and the devotional and nationalist appeal of the Monophysites.

This story has often been retold, though I may perhaps have taken the modern tendency to uphold Nestorius further than many scholars would allow. We now need to bring out some of the philosophical problems involved. In the main, I take the view that the Chalcedonian definition was a fairly limited achievement; it was a statement of the conditions that needed to be met, within a given horizon of thought, for a satisfactory doctrine of Christ; it did not amount to a positive solution. I shall not attempt to argue that, within that horizon of thought, the problem was insoluble; nor, conversely, that a solution had been found and can now be produced. My case is rather, that the problem could not then be solved because too many issues were simultaneously in question, some of them matters of open controversy, some of them undetected assumptions and inconsistencies. We shall try to bring some of this complexity to light.

We begin by considering some of the technical terms involved, the most important of which are 'hypostasis', already noticed in connection with the Trinity; *prosōpon*, the Greek word normally translated by 'person'; and *phusis*, rendered as 'nature'. The usage of these terms is often prefigured by earlier statements framed in non-technical language. Thus the concept of Christ as a unity combining two *phuseis* is already suggested in Irenaeus *A.H.* 3.16.2: 'John knows one and the same Word of God; it is he that is only-begotten, and it is he that was incarnate for our salvation'.

We turn then to 'hypostasis'. As already explained, it reproduces all the main senses of *ousia*, though some of these occur much more commonly than others. It often stands for 'existence', regarded as a fact or state; more commonly, it can denote the totality, or some undefined amount, of existing things. Its best-known use is to denote an individual existent, or an individual substance as opposed to a mere action; it is in this sense that Origen insists on three hypostases in the Trinity. It can, like *ousia*, refer to the spiritual stuff or substance of the Godhead; it is in this sense that the words were equated at Nicaea.

It is important to note that 'hypostasis' can indicate a species, referring either to its members taken collectively, or to the attributes which they have in common. It is sometimes suggested that this usage is a Latinism, derived by imitation from *substantia*; but there are texts which this theory will hardly explain. Thus Origen, *Comm. Joh.* 20.22.182, contrasts 'our better hypostasis', conforming to the image of God, with 'our culpable' (one), which resides in the moulded matter taken from the earth. 'Our better nature' seems the right equivalent, rather than 'our better material'; it contrasts with the culpable element which 'resides in' (*estin en*) the earthy material. Origen also speaks of 'the better hypostasis of Christ' (*ibid.* 2.35.215), which I think refers personally to the divine Logos, not to the Godhead as such, since it is said to permeate the whole cosmos; it is not just 'divinity', but 'his divinity', contrasted, as 'better', with his humanity. Origen often mentions two elements or 'natures' in Christ (so Kelly, *ECD* (1977) p. 155); I cannot say whether he calls them 'two hypostases'.

Fourth-century usage was of course influenced by discussions of the Trinity, and by the language of the Nicene Creed. In particular the 'Old Nicene' party at Antioch, who confessed 'one hypostasis' in the Trinity, became disposed to gloss over the very clear-cut conception of the Godhead as a single *prosōpon* or personality, as formulated by Marcellus of Ancyra, and to modify the sense of 'hypostasis' to bring it closer to the Nicene 'one *ousia*'; this seems to be the position in which Athanasius found himself in agreement with Paulinus. The Cappadocians, we have seen, took a different line, attempting to clarify the doctrine of the Trinity by explaining 'hypostasis' as 'individual person'; but they themselves often ignore this rule.[5] Thus in his *ad Graecos*, where he tries to write carefully, Gregory of Nyssa first distinguishes carefully between *ousia* and hypostasis, as species and individual; but a dozen lines further on (*GNO* 3.1, p. 31 l.18) he seems to treat hypostasis as a common principle within which we distinguish individuals. His intention, I think, is to say that 'hypostasis' indicates an individual as such, whereas 'Paul', for example, names a particular individual.

Thus a generalized sense of 'hypostasis' remained common, and can be found when the word was rather gradually introduced into christology, a development examined by M. Richard.[6] Apollinaris often speaks of one *phusis*, occasionally of one hypostasis (four instances, according to Richard). 'One *phusis*', we shall find, has for Apollinaris a distinctive meaning, which the alternative phrase perhaps leaves unexpressed. Cyril also held to one *phusis*, but (surprisingly) at one time allowed himself to speak of two hypostases; obviously it is a generalizing sense that he adopts; he certainly could not allow two distinct individual beings. The Antiochenes confessed two hypostases,

[5] See my *Substance and Illusion* (see p. 129 n. 5), no. IX, pp. 117–19.
[6] 'L'introduction du mot "hypostase"', *MSR* 2 (1945), pp. 5–32, 243–70.

but rejected the complaint that this meant two individuals, two Christs. Nestorius himself apparently preferred to use 'hypostasis' in a generalized sense; he speaks of the Trinity as three *prosōpa* but one hypostasis. But it is only fair to acknowledge the extreme difficulty of devising unambiguous language at this time, seeing that the three key-words *ousia*, *phusis* and hypostasis had all of them a wide spectrum of senses.[7] Not, we repeat, just two senses each, though the distinction between individual and inclusive senses was of course important. Thus the phrase 'hypostatic union' covers three possibilities at least: (1) a 'real' as opposed to a 'notional' union (*kath' hupostasin* contrasted with *kat' epinoian*); (2) a union of natures, a complex notion which we have still to consider; and (3) the distinctively Chalcedonian concept that two disparate natures are instantiated in a single individual. This, presumably, would always involve some element of paradox, as with the phoenix, if the creature can be seen as both a bird and an immortal; it would involve a contradiction in the case that the two natures had contrary qualities.

We move on to the word *prosōpon*, which corresponds to the Latin *persona*, and serves as an alternative to 'hypostasis' to denote a Person of the Trinity. *Prosōpon* literally means 'face'; but it came to denote the characters in a play, *ta tou dramatos prosōpa*, corresponding to *dramatis personae*. An important paper by C. Andresen has shown that its theological use arises out of biblical study;[8] in many passages the exegete has to decide who is the speaker; for instance in the Psalms, where the writer alternates between expressing his own words and those of the Lord. Similar questions could arise – as we should now say – with regard to the divine Persons; as in Exodus 3:14: is it the Father who names himself Being, or is it the divine Word who speaks? It may be noted that, for some authors at least, the 'person' speaking need not be an individual; thus Origen, commenting on the Song of Songs, distinguishes four 'persons', two individuals and two groups: the bride, the bridegroom, his friends, her friends (*Comm.*

---

[7] *Prosōpon*, we shall find, was somewhat easier; it commonly, though not invariably, signified an individual, and so could be used as a control.

[8] 'Zur Entstehung und Geschichte des trinitarischen Personbegriffes', *Zeitschr. für die Neutest. Wissensch.* 52 (1961), pp. 1–39.

Cant., *Prol.*, p. 61; *Hom. Cant.* 1.1). Again, *prosōpon* can indicate a group of persons addressed rather than speaking, as when Eusebius mentions words addressed 'to the *prosōpon* of the Assyrians', *Dem. Ev.* 7.1.68; other examples appear in the *PGL* article *VI.A*, where the heading 'individual self' is of course misleading. Nevertheless the suggestion of a single individual came to predominate; in this sense Marcellus taught that God and his Logos are one *prosōpon*, the Logos being a function or energy of the one Godhead rather than personally distinct.

It used to be thought that *prosōpon* was an unorthodox term for a Person of the Trinity, suggesting a mere temporary role assumed by the one God, a conception peculiar to Modalism. G. L. Prestige showed that this view is unfounded (*GPT* pp. 113, 160, 187); the word is occasionally used to make this point by fourth-century *critics* of Sabellius and other modalists, but is not so attested in our meagre remains of those writers themselves. *Tria prosōpa* became a perfectly acceptable equivalent of *treis hupostaseis* with the Cappadocians, especially Gregory of Nyssa. It may indeed betoken a measure of sympathy with the Old Nicene party, though it clearly conflicts with the usage of Marcellus. For the Old Nicenes remained firmly attached to the confession of 'one hypostasis', for which they could claim Western support; to speak of 'three *prosōpa*' would then be a tactful way of avoiding the more provocative 'three hypostases'.

It is sometimes said that the modern word 'person' is a poor translation of *prosōpon*, because 'the Greeks had no true concept of personality'. Certainly the abstract noun 'personality' has collected some striking associations which are not suggested by *prosōpon*, for example 'force of character', 'dominance', 'charisma'. But these are much less strongly suggested by the simple word 'person'; so the criticism is perhaps misplaced.

In the fifth century *prosōpon* retained the meaning of 'outward appearance' as well as 'person'. It plays an important part in the christology of Nestorius; and some modern scholars, even those relatively sympathetic towards the unfortunate patriarch, admit that he was sincere in insisting on the unity of the divine and human elements in Christ, but object that he conceived this unity in terms of outward appearance and had no true concept of personality which would give real substance to his doctrine of a single *prosōpon*; so, for example, Kelly, *ECD* (1977) p. 315.

Nestorius' theology certainly suffered from some awkward limitations. He held that when Scripture speaks of the Logos, it refers to the divine Word; when of Jesus, to the man; whereas the words 'Christ' or 'Son' or 'Lord' denote the union of both natures. And he is set firmly in the Antiochene, dualist tradition in using *ousia, phusis, hupostasis* and *prosōpon* alternatively to indicate the duality of divine and human; whereas *prosōpon* alone sustains the task of indicating their unity in Christ. Nestorius came to think that, while divinity and humanity have each their own *prosōpon*, a common *prosōpon* of the unity is created by exchange, in which the Logos takes the *prosōpon* of the manhood, most clearly at the Nativity or the Passion, whereas the *prosōpon* of the manhood is glorified at the Ascension.

My own study suggests that the term 'appearance' can be misleading unless we remember that there is no *necessary* contrast between appearance and reality. If I am a hypocrite, my public behaviour conceals my real intentions; if I am sincere, it accords with them. Nestorius, then, was in no sense a docetist; Christ suffered in truth, not merely in appearance. His critics' objection was rather that, in his view, the real sufferer was the human Jesus, to whom the divine Word was connected only by an external 'conjunction' (*sunapheia*); his supposed '*prosōpon* of the unity' merely glossed over an unbridgeable division.

In my view, Nestorius' *prosōpon* is ambiguous; it resembles the English phrase 'individual character', which can mean either 'individual person' or his 'individual characteristics'. The background here is a Platonic metaphysics, in which the universal or ideal nature has the priority. When some person or thing comes into being, the Platonist sees a pre-existing Form acquiring a temporal 'representation'; but this can be either the individual himself, or his individual characteristics. In Nestorius, the sense of 'individual' is uppermost when he talks of 'one *prosōpon* and one Son' (cited by Cyril, *Apol. Thdt.* 3); whereas 'being God the Word I have assumed the *prosōpon* of a beggar for your sakes' (cited Cyril *c. Nest.* 5.2) need not mean 'adopting a beggar', still less 'adopting the disguise of a beggar', but 'adopting the role of a beggar', in which real humiliations are undergone, so far as the impassible nature of the Word allows; in Platonic metaphysics, as we have suggested, *every* corporeal being is in some sense a role assumed by a longer-lasting entity, the Form or the soul, or in this case the Word. The contrast between 'nature' and 'instance' is always understood (cf. the dictum 'every *phusis/hupostasis* must have its *hupostasis/prosōpon*', cited by Loofs, *Nestorius* pp. 71, 72, 78); but the contrast of universal with individual can be suppressed; the Word is in some sense comparable both to a universal and to an individual Form; universal in scope and power, but incarnate once for all in *this* human life. We shall have to consider whether all this amounts to an adequate christology.

Phusis in turn is of pre-eminent importance in the Alexandrian tradition. The word has been extensively discussed from Aristotle onwards (see *Metaph.* Delta 4, 1014b 16 ff.); a good introductory account is given by H. Dörrie in the *Kleine Pauly*. Aristotle observes its connection with the word *phuein*, to grow, and makes it stand for a principle of growth and development, however that is to be identified. *Hē phusis*, like *hē ousia*, can refer to the universe as such, though retaining some suggestion of 'the way things go' rather than merely 'the things that are there'; cf. our modern word 'nature'. Clement, fr. 37, distinguishes *phusis* from *ousia* along these lines. *Phusis* can also refer to the nature of particular things, or the way they behave, much as *ousia* can refer to the species or Form. It can denote some particular thing itself, corresponding with *ousia* taken as 'primary substance'. This usage is rare in classical literature, at least it is hard to find certain examples, for when the plural *phuseis* is used, one can seldom exclude the possibility that it means 'kinds of things'. So far as I can discover, no ancient author points out the distinction between *phusis* as individual and *phusis* as common nature, as Aristotle does in the case of *ousia*.

The individualized sense is however required in Plato *Republic* 9, 588c, where the *phuseis* described in ancient fables are specified as 'the Chimera, Scylla and Cerberus', each of which is unique, the only example of its kind. But it is hardly probable that Plato noticed any distinctive sense of the word; and other supposed examples are unconvincing (e.g. *Politicus* 272c, 306e). Philo applies the term *phusis* to 'heaven', i.e. the ideal world, the source of *logoi* in the soul (*Leg. All.* 3.162), and describes a grafting operation which results in 'one unified *phusis* of a tree' (*Det.* 108). But such relatively clear cases are the exception.

In Christian literature the individualized sense appears in Origen (*Comm. Joh.* 20.22.184) and in the Apocryphal Acts; while Heracleon seems to use *phusis* for the individual nature or moral disposition of the Samaritan woman (*ibid.* 13.15.92). *Phusis* as 'individual' reappears distinctly when Alexander of Alexandria describes the Logos as 'an unique mediating *phusis*' (*mesiteuousa phusis monogenēs*), and again refers to the Father and the Son as 'two substantially real *phuseis*' (*Ep. Alex.* 9 and 11). Pierius also is said to have described them as 'two *phuseis*' and 'two *ousiai*'; but this usage remained exceptional, and *phusis* was normally used, like *ousia*, to express the one substance or nature of the Godhead.

It was then something of an innovation when Apollinaris boldly claimed that Christ is a single *phusis* – though indeed the roughly contemporary Creed of Eudoxius makes the same claim. Apollinaris associates the teaching of two *phuseis* with the school of Paul of Samosata, and claims that some potentially orthodox Christians fall in with them: 'for these too, I hear, speak of two *phuseis*; although John clearly showed that the Lord is one, by saying "The Word became flesh"; and Paul, by saying "One Lord Jesus Christ, through whom are all things". For if the offspring of the holy Virgin is called "one", . . . he is one *phusis*; for he is one *prosōpon* with no division into two, since neither the body is a separate *phusis*, nor is the Godhead as incarnate (*kata tēn sarkōsin*)', *Ep. Dion.* 2. It would be naive to claim that the whole subsequent controversy about the 'one *phusis*' arose from a failure to appreciate the relatively novel sense that Apollinaris was giving to *phusis*. I suggest, instead, that like so many philosophers before and since, he is putting forward two distinct theses in the guise of one. The first is an irrefutable claim advanced in slightly unusual terms; Christ is one *phusis* merely because he is one *prosōpon*, one individual. The second is a disputable claim relying on accepted terminology; Christ is one *phusis* because his flesh is no longer normal human flesh; it has been wholly assimilated by the Logos. Thus in Christ there is only one *phusis*, one active principle, namely the *phusis* of the Logos.

The attachment to the phrase 'one *phusis* of the Logos incarnate' remained a notable feature of the Alexandrian school, and persisted along with a general willingness to use *phusis* in a wide spectrum of different senses; it could be used both 'abstractly', as we should say, for 'nature' (remembering that for the Platonists the universal nature was more real and richer in content than its individual instances), and concretely, for these instances; and moreover, at every level of generality – mortal *phusis*, human *phusis*, individual *phusis* – often with some suggestion of a behaviour-pattern or activating principle; an individual *phusis* is thus an organism, a 'going concern'. The generalized sense is seen persisting among the Monophysites when they agree that there were 'two *phuseis* before the union'; the lower *phusis* here cannot refer to a man; nor to the Lord's human nature as preformed or prefigured in heaven, since this would remain in being 'after the union'; most probably it means simply 'common human nature'.

Our next chapter will seek to use the information collected here in making its assessment of Chalcedon.

CHAPTER 17

Two natures united

The Chalcedonian Definition presents Christ as a union of two disparate natures, divine and human. We move now towards critical discussion, and identify three problems to be considered. First, are the two natures themselves compatible, or do they have to be considered as polar opposites, so that their union is in logic ruled out as self-contradictory? Secondly, what is the value of the terms and analogies in which their union has been conceived? Thirdly, what is meant by the claim that the Lord's humanity was 'anhypostatic' or impersonal? We shall try to deal with these problems in order; but it will not be possible to separate them completely.

(1) We may take the natures in turn. On the divine nature there is a large measure of agreement, inspired in the main by Platonic theology. God is incorporeal, good and wise. Gregory of Nyssa no doubt introduced a new factor by describing God as infinite; but this is a natural extension of the common belief in God's total transcendence of the created order. What concerns us now is the doctrine that God is strictly impassible and immutable (see pp. 128–30). How then can he relate himself to events in time? The difficulty is perhaps avoidable in the case of the Creation, since this can be viewed as the beginning of time; but the Incarnation implies that God took action at a moment in history. This raises two distinct problems: first the general problem, how can God act on the world at all without acquiring new, and therefore changed, perceptions and relationships? Secondly, the specific problem, how can a divine being enter human life without himself suffering a change?

The two problems were soon associated, and the Incarnation

was commonly described in metaphors intended to suggest that the divine element in Christ suffered no change. Tertullian argued that the Word's becoming flesh did not mean that the Logos was converted into flesh, but rather clothed himself with flesh (*Prax.* 27–8; cf., e.g., Athanasius *Epict.* 4, Theodore of Mopsuestia *In Ps.* 44.9). Again it was said that the Word assumed human nature as a man assumes an office, or lodged himself in a body as in a house or temple; in which case the Platonic model of the soul entering the body is close at hand.

All these analogies presuppose that God does something at a moment in time; they cannot secure God's immutability so long as this is interpreted in absolute metaphysical terms. *That* condition could only be met by interpreting all God's actions as new relationships which result from changes in other beings; to use Plato's illustration (*Theaet.* 155c), Socrates can remain unchanged and yet become smaller than Theaetetus because the young man outgrows him. This model is occasionally used by Christian writers; Origen sees the severity and the kindness of God as a single activity which produces different effects on different recipients, just as the sun's heat both hardens mud and softens wax (*Princ.* 3.1.11). But this analogy deprives God's action of any personal character. It seems more sensible, and certainly more biblical, to understand God as 'unchanging' in a broader, moral sense; in this sense, a man may occupy a house or change his clothes without changing himself. In practice, I think all schools interpret the Incarnation as an act of condescension, following Phil. 2:7; so, for instance, Origen *Cels.* 4.14, Athanasius *C. Ar.* 2.78, and other examples in *PGL* under *sunkatabainō*, *sunkatabasis*.[1]

On the human side there are several different problems to be distinguished. First, there are problems of description. Many of the terms used for the human element are imprecise; they waver between a general and an individualized sense. Thus for *anthrōpos* we have the alternative translations 'manhood', 'man' and 'a man'. The first is attractive if one wishes to bring out the universal significance of the Incarnation: Christ brought div-

---

[1] Note also Leo, *Tome* 4, § 92, Silva-Tarouca, *PL* 54.767: *Deus non mutatur miseratione.*

inity into union with our race. The third is appropriate as pointing to the uniqueness of the Saviour born of Mary; but it adds an indefinite article which is lacking in Greek. The simple rendering 'man' perhaps functions as a sedative compromise: 'He became man' does not seem to be normal English. One can say, 'He became King', of a unique position; but not 'he became priest' or 'he became soldier'.

Now a generalizing description will suggest that the Logos united himself with something already existing – human nature, manhood, flesh; whether these are understood concretely to mean 'the human race', or assimilated to the pre-existent Platonic Form of manhood. But from this perspective, all talk of a particular man will suggest that the Logos simply attached himself to an already existing individual. It was on such grounds that Cyril could represent his opponents as adoptionists: 'For it was not that an ordinary man was born first of the holy Virgin, and then the Logos descended upon him' (*Ep. ad Nest.* 2). Cyril is simply giving a clear statement of objections which already attached to the controversial phrase *homo assumptus*, and largely depend on the ambiguity of the former word.

Clearly this is an avoidable misunderstanding. If a description of Christ's human element is interpreted in particularizing terms, one must represent it as beginning in time, and proceeding from the action of the Logos. But this could be done, and was done. We read that the Saviour fashioned for himself flesh, or a body, in the womb of the Virgin, to be put on like a garment. The metaphor of a house or a temple can be similarly protected; for obviously a man may build himself a house, rather than occupying a house already built; and this point is made by the christological use of Proverbs 9:1, 'Wisdom hath builded her house', for instance by Leo, *Tome* § 51 (*PL* 54. 763), and earlier by Athanasius, *C. Ar.* 2.44; though admittedly the metaphor is strained when we read of the 'house' making moral progress!

But a more serious difficulty crops up when we pass from pure metaphor and describe the human element as *anthrōpos*; for there seems to be no good philosophical model for a personal being who is assumed as a mere adjunct or expression of another person. The notion of a working partnership leads to well-known difficulties; how can there be any partnership between things so different as God and man? – while even the most perfect partnership could hardly represent the unity which we claim to find in Christ. Ancient writers could perhaps have developed the analogy of master and slave; for the slave is in some sense a personal being, and yet has no power of acting in his own person, so long as he strictly conforms to his status; yet his master may freely place him in a position of trust. The prophet, again, may speak and act – though intermittently – in the name of the Lord. But these ideas, I think, were not very fruitfully exploited, and the latter is often condemned as inadequate. A commoner analogy is that of soul and body. But this again is not easy to apply. In ordinary men, the soul was thought to enter the body as its active principle. By analogy, then, at the Incarnation the Logos enters into the man Jesus as his active principle. But Jesus' manhood cannot be defective; presumably, he is body and soul. Nor can his soul be inactive; it must function, then, both as animating the flesh and as taking moral decisions. But in that case it seems to be exercising just those functions which we have already attributed to the Logos. We seem to have two directive principles, not one; at the very least, their unity is so far unexplained.

In crude terms, three answers to this problem were suggested. Apollinaris boldly denied that Christ had a human soul; the Logos was both his animating and his directive principle. Cyril dissociated himself from this position, but initially his recognition of a soul in Christ was largely formal (see p. 191), and though he later came to take a more realistic view, he possibly never advanced beyond seeing the soul of Christ as passively involved in his suffering and his obedience.[2] The Antiochenes at their best held that Jesus did possess both a human soul and human freedom of action, but that he so perfectly surrendered his own will to the indwelling Logos that for practical purposes it was the Logos who was directive of his soul and body together. This answer, however, puts constraints upon the Logos which could not have been to the taste of the Alexandrian school; it

[2] A sympathetic estimate of Cyril is given by Kelly, *ECD* (1977), p. 323.

represents him as acting, not only from the standpoint of a particular body at a particular time and place, which Athanasius and indeed Apollinaris could admit, but in terms of a particular mentality and the limitations of its culture. But this is a difficulty which the Fathers had hardly perceived. They had indeed considered the question of Christ's human limitations in relation to his infancy and his subsequent ignorance of particular facts; and Christian apologists had represented Christ as a man without formal education confounding the philosophers;[3] but in their christology the Alexandrians at least were far more willing to see Jesus speaking as a man than speaking as a Jew, to say nothing of one particular Jew.

A third problem about the human nature raises less intricate points of principle, but nevertheless produced awkward misunderstandings. It results from the contrasting ways in which the created order was regarded, and the apparent failure of the Fathers to recognize this contrast. On the one hand it could be praised as displaying the Creator's wisdom (see pp. 115–17). Yet it was not to be worshipped; one must recognize the disparity between God and his creatures; and there is some residue of the old Platonic assumption that even God's power is restricted by the inherent limitations of his medium; thus Athanasius often asserts that things made from nothing, *genēta*, are inherently weak and unstable (e.g. *Inc.* 4, 10, 11). In due course this tendency was enhanced by the reaction against Arianism described above; the orthodox Fathers argued that Arius reduced the Logos to the status of a creature *tout court*, and sought to maximize his offence by further depreciating the created order.

In this way words referring to the created order came to acquire a pejorative sense. 'Man', 'flesh' and 'body', amongst others, could be used so as to emphasize their negative aspects, or the weakness which contrasts them with divine perfection. Thus Origen can say that the Lord is 'both man and not man' (*Comm. Joh.* 10.6.23); 'man as being liable to death; not man as being more divine than man'. Athanasius, writing in this tradition, can declare both that the Lord was not *merely* man, and that he

---

[3] See, for example, Athanasius *Inc.* 47; more explicitly Eusebius, *Dem Ev.* 3.6.26–7.

was *not* man at all. (The *PGL*, I think, ignores this usage, for which see *Inc.* 14, 18, etc., and Kannengiesser, *SC* 199, pp. 49–50.) Other examples could no doubt be found.

'Flesh' again often expresses man's liability to sin and corruption, despite the persisting influence of John 1:14. Its ambivalence can be seen in Athanasius' teaching on salvation. On the one hand, the Logos sanctifies the flesh which he assumes, and through the solidarity of the human race, or perhaps of the Church, communicates a salutary wholeness to our flesh (see, e.g., *C. Ar.* 3.34). Conversely, the flesh remains, even for the Logos, the locus of weakness and fear, and so, the means by which he can suffer and yield himself as a sacrifice. Apollinaris takes up the former perspective and almost entirely neglects the latter; indeed he has some reluctance to admit that Christ assumed ordinary flesh at all, and obliquely commends the view that the Lord's flesh was prepared in heaven (*Anaceph.* 12), though on reflection he withdraws this idea (*To Jovian* 3, etc). In the case of *nous* Apollinaris notoriously takes a negative view; the human mind is inherently sinful and cannot have been assumed by the Saviour. Even Athanasius hardly gives the mind of Christ any part in his work of salvation; apart from a passing reference to 1 Corinthians 2:16 in *Ad Serap.* 1.9, there is no suggestion of the human *mind* being penetrated and transformed by the presence of the Logos in Jesus, though a positive view of *nous* might seem to follow from its treatment in the *Contra Gentes*.

If then 'man', 'body', 'flesh' and 'mind' can be used to signify the limited and corruptible aspects of human nature, it is understandable that some theologians thought that these created elements were simply absorbed by the presence of the Logos in Christ. Gregory of Nyssa provides an extreme instance of this view: like a drop of wine swallowed up by the sea (see pp. 48, 209) the flesh (of Christ) is wholly assimilated to the divine nature, and retains none of its natural characteristics: 'no weight, form, colour, firmness, softness nor spatial extent, nor any other of the (properties) then visible; since the fusion with the divine assimilates the poverty of the fleshly nature to the divine characteristics' (*Antirrh.*, *GNO* 3.1, p. 201; cf. *ibid.* p. 126). No doubt Gregory is thinking of Christ's condition after the

Ascension, as opposed to what was 'then visible' in his incarnate life; even so his language seems extravagant.

But the prevailing tendency was to see the human elements as present along with the divine; they had to be present if they were to be sanctified by their coexistence with the divine Logos. And this coexistence or union of the two elements imposed problems which do not result simply from the pessimistic view of humanity. All schools at this time saw divinity and humanity as sharply contrasted; immortal with mortal, pure with corruptible, infinite with finite. One might have expected the Antiochenes to reduce the contrast, in view of their more positive estimate of Christ's humanity. Yet Theodore, for instance, asserts that there is no natural kinship between God and man (*De Inc.* 2, Swete 2.291 ff.).

(2) We therefore have to consider the various ways of conceiving a union in which two elements are combined, either on equal terms, or conversely with one element predominating or absorbing the other. The Definition itself speaks of an 'unconfused union', *asunchutos henōsis*. This seems to have been a comparatively unfamiliar phrase, to judge from Gregory of Nyssa's remarks on *henōsis* in his *Antirrheticus* (*GNO* 3.1, p. 184). A source for it can apparently be found in Neoplatonist writers;[4] but the notion expressed is much older, and all the essentials can be found in the Stoic teaching on mixtures, even though the term *krasis* itself is rejected in the Definition. Its context in Stoic physics has already been outlined on pp. 47–8.

Our evidence for the theory comes largely from three texts (*SVF* 2.471–3). They agree in recognizing three possible forms of mixture. The first is *parathesis*, mere juxtaposition, as when peas and beans are mixed in a heap. The second is *krasis* proper, where two substances are combined, but retain their distinctive properties, and can be separated again; iron remains iron even when it is wholly penetrated by fire, and is still iron when it cools; wine mixed with water can be separated by means of an oiled sponge.[5] Total interpenetration, *krasis di' holou*, is required by the

---

[4] See E. L. Fortin 'The Definitio Fidei', p. 493, and brief references in *LGP* pp. 489, 357.
[5] Nemesius, *Nat. Hom.* 2.19; the English version, *LCC* 4, p. 294, has a note on the indifferent success of this experiment.

Stoic theory that matter is continuous, or non-atomic; the atomists could explain all mixtures as *parathesis*. Third comes *sunchusis*, where the combining substances amalgamate and lose their distinctive properties. So far, our authorities are agreed; they differ in their treatment of a fourth term, *mixis*. Arius Didymus makes this a fourth class, analogous to *krasis*, for the special case of solid bodies (e.g. iron and fire); Philo seems to use it as a synonym for *parathesis*; Alexander treats it as a general term which includes the other three.

Two other details of Stoic physics are worth recalling. First, the descriptions we have given suggest a mixture of more or less equal amounts; but what happens with markedly unequal mixtures, as of a drop of wine in a large mass of water? Here the Stoics held that the wine never wholly loses its properties, as Aristotle had suggested (*Gen. et Corr.* 1.10, 328a 27 ff.); it becomes gradually weaker until it is no longer noticeable, but it extends itself through the whole mass. This is hardly a point of practical importance, even if correct as a physical theory; a drop of wine could not noticeably affect the Aegean Sea. But the example was well known, and was used by theologians to suggest complete absorption.

Another sort of absorption was discussed by the Stoics. We have seen that they regarded fire as the source of the other three elements (p. 46); conversely, these would all be resolved into fire at the final conflagration. This doctrine was evidently known to Philo, since he uses the technical term *anastoicheioun*, literally 'to change back into its original element', giving it a spiritual sense: at the end of Moses' life 'God resolved him from a duality of body and soul to the nature of a unity (monad), as he was wholly refashioned into a mind, in form like the sun' (*Vit. Mos.* 2.288). Origen also uses the term for the 'gradual refining' or reversion of the Logos from his incarnate condition to his original existence with the Father (*Comm. Joh.* 1.37.276), as well as for the transformation of the human soul after repentance (*Princ.* 3.1.13); and Gregory of Nyssa puts the analogous term *metastoicheioun* to a directly christological use; the divine power resolved the form of a servant, which came into being through the Virgin, into a divine and uncompounded nature (*Antirrheticus* p. 170

Jaeger); again, the Saviour resolved our nature into his divine power, and preserved it spotless and whole in himself (*Ep.* 3). The last example suggests that what is 'resolved' is transformed, but not lost.

A new point is also suggested here. For the Stoics, the fire itself takes the initiative in resolving the other elements; and Gregory's last example makes the Saviour himself the agent of transformation. But our other parallels from the Stoics present a symmetrical picture of two inactive elements which need some external agency to combine them. The same limitation applies to the phrase 'union of natures', *henōsis tōn phuseōn*, or indeed to *henōsis* itself, to which we now return; it does not of itself suggest a conjunction in which one element is active. And it has two further drawbacks, which demand some care in preventing mistakes. First, the phrase 'union of natures' too easily suggests a mere coalescence into one nature, a *sunchusis*, in which the properties of both are lost; the Definition meets this point by insisting on an 'unconfused union'. The Antiochene party clearly disliked Cyril's phrases 'natural union' (*henōsis phusikē*) and 'substantial union' (*henōsis kath' hupostasin*), which for them suggested a coalescence in which the purity of the Godhead was contaminated by its amalgamation with the corruptible flesh. But Cyril himself could rebut this objection, since in his thinking the Logos remains as the personal subject and directive principle; the soul of Christ hardly retains all its natural powers (see p. 205 above); still less does the flesh, for the Cyrilline Christ does not suffer, in the sense of being truly passive, but 'adopts' or 'appropriates' suffering to fulfil his purposes.

A second drawback is that the phrase easily suggests a union of natures as such. Clearly this is not what Christian doctrine requires; it is not the divine nature as such that becomes incarnate, but one Person, the Word; and one man only, Jesus, unites with divinity. By speaking of iron and fire combining, one does not mean that all the iron in the universe becomes red-hot, and all its fire migrates into red-hot iron. The Fathers do indeed teach that our universal human nature is 'divinized' through its union with Christ. But they insist on his unique function and achievement, which can be obscured if we talk too lightly of a 'union of natures'.

Of these two drawbacks the first is I think the more important. Apollinaris at one time stated that 'in Christ there is a mean between God and man; so he is neither entirely man (*anthrōpos holŏs*) nor God, but a mixture of God and man', just as grey is intermediate between black and white (*Syll.*, fr. 113). The phrase we have given as 'not entirely man' is awkward and ambiguous; it could mean either 'not just a man' (correct!), or 'not a complete man', as Apollinaris unfortunately came to believe. The metaphor of grey colouring is much worse; it suggests a mere demigod, which even Arians could have denied; and Apollinaris himself seems to have abandoned it, adopting an asymmetrical picture in which the divine element clearly takes the lead: 'We worship him not as coming to be in the body like two equals, one in another, but as a master assuming the form of a servant' (*Kata meros pistis* 29). But the problem remains: given two sharply contrasting elements, can we ever truly say that each maintains *all* its distinctive properties when combined with the other? We may have overworked the Stoic analogy with which we began. In red-hot iron, the fire does indeed retain its distinctive quality of heat, but it loses its lightness and its upward-moving tendency; and the iron, as we all know, loses some of its hardness.

This last paragraph explains the objection made by the Antiochene school against Cyril's theology. To some extent it rests on a misunderstanding. Cyril was not thinking of an amalgamation of Godhead and manhood, in the style of Apollinaris; in his more conciliatory moods he could recognize two elements in Christ, describing them as 'facts' and 'substances' (*pragmata, hupostaseis*), and their 'combination' (*sunodos*). But he insists on the phrase 'one *phusis*'; there must be a single 'operative principle', which could only result from a perfect synthesis of the two elements. But the later debates leading up to Chalcedon introduced further complications, which we can only outline, especially those bound up with the phrase that Christ is 'of two natures', *ek duo phuseōn*. In its original setting the phrase is unemphatic; Christ is 'of two natures' just as a coin is 'of gold'. But the monophysite party took it up and altered its meaning.[6]

---

[6] See A. Grillmeier, *Christ in Christian Tradition* (see Bibliography 16), 1st edn p. 458 = 2nd edn p. 524-5.

Eutyches had protested 'I acknowledge that the Lord was "of two natures" before the union, but after the union I acknowledge only one nature' (*Acta Conciliorum Oecumenicorum* ed. E. Schwartz, 2.1.1, 143.10–11). Thus the phrase came to suggest '*from* two natures', as if Christ had formerly existed in two natures, which were then combined. The word *phusis*, 'nature', is so confusing that it is extremely difficult to see what this could mean. Clearly Christ did not share our human *limitations* before becoming incarnate; nor could he have had any *individual* humanity; this would imply that the human Jesus existed before he was conceived, rather like Apollinaris' notion of divine flesh already prepared in heaven (see p. 207). Perhaps what is implied is the Platonic ideal of perfect humanity.

The reply to Eutyches asserted that 'Christ was of two natures (even) after the Incarnation', or again 'acknowledged *in* two natures'. But this does not dispel the troublesome suggestion of two natures before the Incarnation, which lingers on even in the Chalcedonian definition itself. This counts against the undoubted advantage of its clear statement that the two natures came together 'in one *prosōpon* and one hypostasis'.

(3) Finally, we need to comment on the doctrines that the Lord's humanity was impersonal, that it was not personalized apart from the Logos, that the Logos became its hypostasis, and so on. We begin with three preliminary points:

(i) Modern commentators on the debate are liable to translate the word 'hypostasis' as 'person', and to interpret ancient texts in the light of their own, modern, theories of personality. The second step is an anachronism; the first also may be mistaken, since our previous survey of the senses of 'hypostasis' has shown that the translation 'person' is often misleading.

(ii) The whole debate takes place within a Platonic tradition which makes it natural to think of the 'nature' or 'substance' as prior to *any* individual. This way of thinking persists among theologians who have no clear grasp of the conceptual possibilities from which to choose. We can distinguish five at least: (a) a nature as such exists only in the mind; a view held by some Stoics (*SVF* 1.65, 2.360, etc.) and attributed to Cyril by Nestorius (*Bazaar* p. 284 Nau); (b) it exists, though not in our world, as a transcendent Platonic Form; (c) it exists as a formative principle in living species, or in the mind of a craftsman (Aristotle's view); (d) the less familiar 'idealist' view: a nature, i.e. the appropriate assemblage of qualities, is of itself sufficient to constitute a real being;[7] (e) the word *phusis*, 'nature', understood in an individualized sense, simply refers to a real being. The last view, of course, excludes the possibility of a 'nature' being prior to the individual; the others interpret it in very different ways.

(iii) *Phusis* is often contrasted with 'hypostasis' or *prosōpon* without any clear indication of a contrast between a universal and its many possible instances. If we encounter the saying 'Every *phusis* must have its hypostasis' or '*prosōpon*', it is natural to object that the latter nouns should stand in the plural; human nature, for example, is actualized in an enormous number of men. It is only by way of exception that *phusis* might indicate an individual species, or *prosōpon* denote a plurality.

We can now return to the subject proposed.

(1) It is commonly said that Cyril, and other Alexandrian theologians after him, taught the 'impersonal humanity' of Christ. But the word 'impersonal' represents terms which in this context cannot be traced back further than Leontius of Byzantium, if the *PGL* is to be trusted. Leontius encountered the view that the Lord's manhood was 'without hypostasis', *anhupostatos*, which could mean 'non-existent', as well as 'not individually distinct'. Leontius replied that it was *ENhupostatos*, with the supposed meaning that it acquired hypostasis, or was realized, *in* the Logos. The Latin word 'impersonal' of course obscures this point, for its first syllable could represent either a negative (cf. 'insane') or the preposition 'in' (cf. 'innate'); but its usual meaning is 'not personal', corresponding to *anhupostatos*. Moreover *enhupostatos* originally meant simply 'hypostatic', i.e. 'real' or 'existent', just as *enousios* means 'substantial' and *entimos* means 'honourable'; to make it imply reality acquired *in some other being* is a play upon words. However, assuming option (a) above, a nature can be real only if it has instances; and

---

[7] See my 'Individual personality' (Bibliography 20), pp. 292–4, with n. 24; also R. Sorabji, *Time, Creation and the Continuum* (Bibliography 19), pp. 292–4, with n. 21.

'hypostasis' means both 'reality' and 'instance'; so the transition is easily made.

(2) We therefore need to consider how far the debate really was concerned with *individualized* humanity, as opposed to the perfectly straightforward point that Christ's manhood had no *existence* apart from the Logos; He did not simply adopt an already existing man. The Monophysites, I suspect, confused the two possibilities. Leontius of Jerusalem seems clearer: 'We do not wish to show that the Lord's manhood was without reality [*anhupostaton*]; but it was not a distinct reality [*idiohupostaton*] separate from the Logos' (*Nest* 2.10). And a reference to individuality clearly appears in his phrase 'substantially *qua* generally, and "enhypostatically" *qua* particularly' (*enousiōs te kata to koinon, kai enhupostatōs kata to idikon*), *ibid.* 7.1; and John Damascene clearly states that the flesh of the divine Logos is *enhupostatos* as existing *in* the hypostasis of the Logos (*Fid. Orthod.* 3.9: *ou gar idiosustatōs hupestē hē tou theou logou sarx, oude hetera hupostasis gegone para tēn tou theou logou hupostasin, all' en autēi hupostasa, enhupostatos mallon*).

Cyril did not use these technical terms. He taught, correctly, that the Lord's humanity was real, and that it existed only in the Logos incarnate. Nevertheless there are texts in Cyril which are fairly characterized by the phrase 'impersonal humanity'; for instance, that at the Incarnation the Logos assumes human nature, but remains what he was. Does Cyril, and do his modern exponents, really defend the doctrine that the Lord's manhood was 'impersonal' in the sense of 'not individualized'? If so, then Christ was a man without being any particular kind of man. This might seem to be an advantage; a Christ endowed with a purely generalized humanity would be equally related to all men. But in fact it is clear that this condition cannot possibly be fulfilled. Generalized humanity is precluded from the outset by the fact that Jesus was male, not female. And surely, to be a man at all, he must have had a specific psychology, no less than a specific height and weight; indeed the New Testament shows him comparing himself as man with another man (Matt. 11:18–19 = Luke 7: 33–4). His universal appeal, we would think, rests on a blend of divine dispensation and human achievement,

issuing in love and imaginative sympathy. And these are transcendent virtues, not qualities which are found to be present in all
men.

(3) A more considered theory builds on the dictum that the
Logos is the personal subject in Christ, and links this with the
view that human personality requires an 'ultimate metaphysical
subject'.[8] There are theological objections to this view. If such a
subject is required as a component of every normal human
being, and if the Logos takes the place of this component, then
we have simply a refined form of Apollinarian theology; the
Lord's manhood is not in all respects complete. But why should
theologians commit themselves to such a theory of personality?
Two points, I think, can be made. First, we may think of
personality as a characteristic variety of dispositions. It is found,
then, in all normal human beings; but we may be making a
category-mistake if we regard it as a component of them; just as
it is a category-mistake to think that the layout of a garden, or
indeed its beauty, is one of its *components*, like the various trees,
lawns and shrubs. Secondly, we may think of the personality, not
simply as the characteristic pattern of our behaviour, but as its
directive principle, much as the ancients thought of the soul; but
it does not follow that the personality itself is organized by some
further directive principle, the 'ultimate metaphysical subject'.
Of course, if we take this view, we are bound to think of the Logos
in Christ as displacing this subject from its position of authority.
But if, as I am inclined to do, we regard the ego as analogous, not
to a monarchy but to a democracy, as a complex of mutually
supporting dispositions, then their control by the Logos can be
viewed as a special case of the fact that we continually respond to
suggestions coming from outside ourselves. A human friend can
influence, or even dominate, us by the choice of suggestions that
he makes, assuming that there is some basic agreement on
projects and values; and if we share the Fathers' assumption that
the divine Logos can act in this way, there is no theoretical

[8] Kelly criticizes Nestorius for failing to 'explain what constituted His Person, the
metaphysical subject of his being' (*ECD* (1977), p. 317); whereas Cyril taught 'the
identity of the Person of the God-man with that of the Logos' (*ibid.* 342); cf. *ibid.* 311:
'His Person was constituted by the Word'.

difficulty in seeing a human mind becoming perfectly attuned to an influence accepted as divine, who thus becomes its directive principle.

(4) Human personality needs time and experience to attain the mature form that we have been considering. In the first place, we could suppose that 'Wisdom builds herself a house', bringing into existence a human being within the particular moment of history and cultural milieu that she has chosen for her self-disclosure, and acting with that foresight into human affairs which divinity can exercise.[9] In virtue of his human personality, Jesus is acknowledged to have developed over the years, acquiring self-consciousness and freedom of choice. If we think it right, we can believe with the Fathers that the divine Wisdom foresaw that this man would always act out his appointed part, acquiring liberty to choose, but choosing right without constraint, in an exercise of freedom which knows no sin.

In this way we might hope to reach a synthesis of Alexandrian and Antiochene insights; the Logos takes the initiative, and retains it; yet human obedience is also manifested to be our example and inspiration.

---

[9] I would not myself attempt to reconcile *total* divine foreknowledge with human freedom.

PART III

Augustine

CHAPTER 18

Philosophy, faith and knowledge

Augustine is by far the ablest philosopher of late antiquity. He is also one of its best-known characters; he reveals his inmost thoughts at many points in his voluminous writings, but particularly in the *Confessions*, which recalls his early life and his conversion, and in the *Retractations*, one of his last productions, in which he gives a chronological survey of his written work and explains the corrections which he now wishes to establish. More than most ancient writers, his thought underwent a development which is closely related to his changing occupations and concerns. This makes it difficult to capture in a brief account; all its phases are interesting and worthy of note. And there is a particular difficulty in treating of Augustine as a philosopher. The enormous literature he has inspired of course includes examinations of his philosophical thought; but the great majority of these are written by admirers, who moreover share the basic assumptions of his metaphysics. Many modern philosophers, at least in the Anglo-Saxon tradition, reject these assumptions altogether, or in large part, as I am impelled to do myself, and are thus bound to be handicapped in providing a survey which is at once appreciative, scholarly and critical.

Augustine was born in 354 at Tagaste in North Africa, about 200 km west of Carthage and some 700 km south-west of Rome. His father Patricius was a pagan till late in life, his mother Monica a Christian. The parents were proud of their gifted son and made sacrifices to secure his education at the University of Carthage, where he studied law, enjoying his growing success and the diversions of student life, and took a mistress with whom he lived for fifteen years. At the age of nineteen he read Cicero's

Hortensius and was decisively influenced towards philosophy, the pursuit of wisdom; but almost simultaneously he joined the Manichaean sect, which seemed to combine spiritual teaching with a rational justification, as against the Catholics' appeal to faith. Turning from law to literature he taught mainly at Carthage until the age of twenty-nine, when he went to Rome and soon afterwards obtained a professorship at Milan.

The next three years were decisive. He attended the sermons of Bishop Ambrose and was attracted by his intellectual presentation of Christianity. He became disillusioned with Manichaeism; his reading of Platonist philosophy had induced a period of scepticism, which however soon changed to a passionate admiration for its positive teaching and a longing to devote himself to the philosophic life. Meanwhile his reading of the Scriptures gradually convinced him that the revelation through Christ supplied a necessary complement to Platonic philosophy. He was inspired by the conversion of the eminent Neoplatonist Marius Victorinus, as related to him by Simplicianus thirty years after the event. Finally all intellectual obstacles were removed; he was restrained only by his conviction that full adherence to Christianity demanded a celibate life. His resistance ended with his conversion in September 386.

Augustine was baptized on Easter Eve, 387. He determined to live in retirement and pursue the study of philosophy, and his writings during these years are still mainly influenced by Platonism. But with his growing concern for the study of Scripture, the little group of philosophy students he had assembled soon transformed itself into a monastic community at his native town of Tagaste. In 391, however, while on a visit to Hippo, he was induced to accept ordination as a priest, and became the trusted assistant of the aged Bishop Valerius. He was consecrated as coadjutor bishop in 395 and succeeded Valerius on his death in the next year.

From then onwards, although Augustine retained a lively concern with philosophy, a great part of his immense energy was devoted to distinctly Christian scholarship, in the exposition of the Bible and the discussion of theological problems; many of his concerns also crossed and recrossed the boundaries between philosophy, theology and practical Church politics. To the group of writings directed against the Manichees he added another concerned with the Donatist schism, and a third was elicited by controversy with Pelagius, who in Augustine's view took too sanguine a view of the possibilities of a sinless life and emphasized the importance of human effort at the expense of divine grace. This controversy raised some major philosophical issues; notably the nature of human free will in relation to man's inherited depravity, to divine grace, and to God's foreknowledge and determination of all events in time.

Besides these, there are three works of outstanding interest and importance in their own right, which also incorporate original pieces of philosophical reflection. These are:

(1) The *Confessions* (397–401). After describing his early life and conversion in Books 1–9, Augustine turns to consider the wonders of God's creation. Book 10 contains a searching examination of the mysteries of human consciousness, drawing of course on his own experience; Book 11 has an important and original discussion of the nature of time.

(2) The *De Trinitate* (399–419). Augustine accepts the doctrine of one God in three Persons, interpreting it in a typically Western fashion which sets the one immutable divine essence in the foreground. The unity is so strongly stressed that the doctrine of three Persons presents a problem, which Augustine attempts to solve in two distinct ways. One is by saying that the three Persons are defined by their mutual relations, not by any distinction of substance or of accidents. This is sometimes described as a doctrine of 'subsistent relations', a phrase which can lead to unnecessary puzzlement unless one remembers that the term 'relation' is ambiguous; one can talk of 'friends and relations', all of them real subsistent beings. Augustine, then, does not mean that God makes the mere fact of 'being Father of ...' into a real being; on the other hand, God is 'Fatherhood itself', the ideal pattern of all paternity; and so with the other Persons. Augustine's other expedient is to claim that God's being is reflected, though dimly, throughout his creation, and most clearly in mankind. The three divine Persons are thus reproduced in triadic patterns within our mind, based on the triad of

'being, knowing and willing' which psychology reveals, and which had already been identified in the *Confessions*. Augustine thus moves from the triad of the mind's understanding, knowledge and love of itself to its remembrance, knowledge and love of God. His discussion of self-consciousness is unrivalled in ancient literature.

(3) *The City of God* (413–27). As originally conceived, this work had the fairly limited purpose of countering the shock produced by Alaric's conquest of Rome in 410, and explaining that such a disaster was no disproof of divine providence. Over many years it expanded into twenty-two books comprising a major work of political philosophy. Its main theme is the contrast between the two 'cities' or states, the *civitas terrena* represented in his time by the Roman Empire, and the City of God, to which belong the righteous men of every age. The two 'cities' are mutually entangled in this present world, but are in principle separable, and will be distinguished at the Last Judgement. The *City of God* equipped the Western world of the Middle Ages with its political philosophy, and provided the justification for giving the Church a role in social and political affairs parallel to that exercised by the civil power. It had an influence which its author could not have expected, and would not have fully approved.

Augustine's conversion has given rise to controversy. Most readers of the *Confessions* assume that his self-portrait is accurate; the issue before him was the abandonment of worldly ambitions and a commitment to the spiritual life under the guidance of the Catholic Church. But a different impression is conveyed by the writings which he produced immediately after the event; these are edited versions of conversations with his friends, and show him discussing problems in Platonic philosophy. Some scholars have suggested, accordingly, that it was to philosophy that he was really converted; the narrative of the *Confessions* is coloured by a fuller acquaintance with Scripture and with Church life that was only acquired over the next few years.

But this debate assumes that religion and philosophy can be sharply contrasted. Most probably Augustine saw the matter differently. The study of Platonism had helped him on his way to

Christianity. He had, no doubt, encountered it in a form which was already partly Christianized, so that, for example, the impersonal nature of Plotinus' first principle was little emphasized, whereas the system of three hypostases was welcomed and approved. Platonic philosophy, like Catholic Christianity, summoned its adepts to the ascetic life; its dialectical exercises were warmed by a reverence for the master's writings not wholly unlike the Christian reverence for Scripture. It is entirely probable that Augustine saw no contradiction in continuing his study of Platonism as an intellectual substructure for his Christian faith and obedience.

At all events his debt to the Platonists is unmistakable. It was from them that he learned to conceive of God as a simple, transcendent and ineffable source of all beauty and intellectual light, discarding his earlier, Stoicizing, conception of God as a pure but extended substance diffused through the world (*Conf.* 7.5.7). He could approve the Neoplatonic Trinity as an approximation to the truth; it gave some idea of the divine Logos, though the Holy Spirit was either misrepresented or omitted; and of course, for the Neoplatonists, only the third hypostasis, Soul, was a creative principle, and the creation flowed out by necessity rather than by an act of will. But Augustine pictured the cosmos in Platonic terms, as reproducing the pattern of ideas in the divine mind, and controlled in its development by seminal reasons (see pp. 47, 55). He also accepted that all true being is good, and that evil only arises from lack of such being. He believed that true happiness is only to be found in the contemplation of God and in the wisdom which discerns eternal truths; though his Platonic intellectualism was a good deal modified by his pastoral care for simple believers, and most interestingly he came to reject the view commonly held by Platonists and Christian intellectuals alike, that all vices in the soul could be traced to the influence of the body (*Civ. Dei* 14.5). For Augustine the root of sin is pride, and this includes pride in one's own intelligence.

He can thus describe Christian faith as an exercise in humility, contrasted with the philosophers' pride in their own achievements. This judgement was not new (Col. 2:8!); but it was

attractive to Augustine for personal reasons. He had been told of
the distinguished orator Marius Victorinus presenting himself
for baptism among a crowd of unlearned converts; he himself in
turn had sacrificed his prospects of fame and fortune without
fully understanding what his new calling would entail. Faith for
Augustine implied acceptance of beliefs, which of course can
only be accepted if they are understood in some measure, but
have to be accepted in default of full rational insight. He
reformulates familiar arguments which justify such acceptance
by analogies from secular life (see pp. 111–13; *De Ut. Cred.*
12.26, *Trin.* 15.12.21, etc.). Faith is in principle an inferior form
of cognition; but Christian faith has authority because of its
source in divine revelation. Philosophy must therefore yield
precedence to Scripture and Christian tradition, though it can
still be justified as an auxiliary to faith by the time-honoured
analogy of the Israelites 'spoiling the Egyptians' (Exod. 11:2,
12:35–6; see Origen *Philoc.* 13 and note in *SC* 148, p. 90).
Augustine's originality shows up more distinctly in his claim that
faith itself contributes to understanding: 'No one could believe
in God without some understanding; nevertheless that same
faith by which he believes brings healing, so that he can
understand more' (*En. Ps.* 118, *PL* 37, 1552).[1]

One of Augustine's first concerns was to establish the general
possibility of human knowledge by refuting scepticism, which
we have noted as one variant of the Platonic tradition (pp. 63–4)
and which had in fact assisted him to escape from the grip of
Manichaeism. Two arguments are set out in his *Contra Academicos*
of 386–7, and recur at intervals in his later works. First, some
propositions cannot be false; for instance, one or other of two
contradictory statements; or again, some propositions of mathematics and of logic (3.10.23, 11.25 and 29). Secondly, some can
be certainly known. Augustine appeals to the knowledge of one's
own mind; even when in doubt, I can know that I am doubting,
and therefore know that I exist. This claim is tersely stated in the
City of God, 11.26: *Si fallor, sum* – a phrase which foreshadows

---

[1] E. Portalié, *A Guide*, pp. 114–18, shows in a useful discussion how Augustine can say,
quoad verbum, both that faith precedes reason and that reason precedes faith.

Descartes' *Je pense, donc je suis*. But Augustine's deduction from it is quite different from Descartes'; he takes it as confirming the whole structure of Platonic rationalism, arguing that relations between concepts can be known by an intellectual intuition akin to sight. Moreover he identifies the 'intelligible world' of Platonism with 'the eternal and unchanging Reason whereby God made the (created) world (*Retr.* 1.3.2; cf. p. 55 above). This enables him to frame a largely original proof of the existence of God, which we have already considered (pp. 118–19). It is only in his later works that we find a theory of knowledge which comes closer to modern thought by recognizing the role of experience in enabling us to organize our sense-perceptions through memory and the framing of concepts.

Augustine of course recognizes that much of our knowledge is based on sense-perception. He follows the Neoplatonists in observing that 'sensing' (*sentire*) 'is not a function of the body, but of the soul by means of the body' (*Gen. ad Litt.* 3.5.7). We could put his point more clearly by attending to the distinction between sensation and perception. The body and its sense-organs are affected by the objects they encounter, and in that respect are passive; but we quite properly speak of *perception* as an active process in which the mind makes use of the body; so *Quant. An.* 24.45, *Gen. ad Litt.* 12.16.33, cf. Plotinus *Enn.* 4.6.2 etc. We could fill in the gaps in Augustine's account by reflecting on our powers of directing our sense-organs, the eyes in particular, of focusing our attention and picking out significant forms; perception is something that has to be learnt, and in which our mind is engaged.

But Augustine's account of sensation, and sight in particular, shows that he has not fully appreciated the distinction. He tells us repeatedly that the sense-organs are passive; yet he still countenances theories which conceive them as actively initiating a physical process. He alludes to the old Platonic view that our eyes emit a 'visual ray' which goes out to meet the light reflected from the object: *emisso visu per oculos video*; *Quant. An.* 23.43. He also tries to explain how our eyes can see things at a distance from themselves by saying that it is like feeling for something with a rod; this clearly recalls the Stoic theory mentioned on p. 141 above, in which the eye compresses the surrounding air and makes it grope for the object as with a stick (*SVF* 2.864–7).

How does the mind register these sensations? Augustine fails to give a clear account; and I am inclined to suggest two reasons in explanation. First, the whole discussion turns upon the sense of sight; all five senses are quite often mentioned, but important points are made in connection with vision alone, and it is not made clear how far they can be generalized. Much worse, Augustine brings together accounts of ordinary bodily sight, and other operations which at least involve visual imagery, with remarks about the mind which is said to 'see' in a purely metaphorical sense. In his commentary on Genesis he distinguishes three kinds of sight. One such discussion begins from the text 'Thou shalt love thy neighbour as thyself (*Gen. ad Litt.* 12.11.22). Augustine comments: 'The (written) letters are seen with the body, one's neighbour is recalled by the spirit, love is observed (!) by the intellect': *corporaliter litterae videntur, spiritaliter proximus cogitatur, intellectualiter dilectio conspicitur.* 'Spirit' is here understood as something inferior to mind, following 1 Corinthians 14:15; it is misleading to associate it with 'spiritual vision'. In Augustine's usage it seems to include the three possibilities of recalling what we have seen, imagining what we have not seen (by making new combinations of visual images) and thirdly dreaming (*ibid.* 12.6.15, 9.20); it also seems to include our ability to recognize that we are seeing, not imagining, or the converse case; and even the curious possibility that, while dreaming, we can be aware that we are dreaming (*ibid.* 12.2.3).

On the other hand it does not seem possible to make sense of Augustine's description of the mind in terms of vision. How is love 'observed' by the mind? We might be said to know what love is if we can remember examples of loving conduct; but this would seem to be a function of 'spirit', Augustine's intermediate faculty. Certainly we need also to apply the name 'love' to the right examples; but this in itself seems hardly an august enough task to allot to our highest mental power. No doubt Augustine thinks that we do this by appealing to love as a Platonic ideal, the pure form of love which is only accessible in mystical experience (*ibid.* 12.3.6). But he brings us down to earth again when he ascribes to the intellect the power of interpreting visions and dreams; Joseph's interpretation of Pharaoh's dream is a case in point (*ibid.* 12.9.20).

A second reason for Augustine's difficulties about the mind is that he follows the Neoplatonists in thinking that it cannot be affected by the body, which belongs to a lower order of reality. This of course seems to conflict with our common experience of having our judgement overborne by intense physical sensations and the passion that accompanies them; Augustine himself seems to admit that the mind can be overcome in the special case of delusions (*ibid.* 12.12.25); and he has a long discussion of prophetic ecstasy. But he tries to maintain the supremacy of the mind by holding that, residing in the soul, it is diffused through-out the body; it apprehends the data of the senses by a quasi-visual process: *nuntiat enim aliquid lux incorporea, ibid.* 7.19.25.

Underlying this theory is the assumption that action and passivity are two opposed categories which do not admit of combination or intermediate conditions; the mind, then, can only be active if every element of passivity is excluded. But the general assumption is false, and indeed examples of intermediate conditions were known in antiquity; I do in a sense take action if I present myself to the barber or the doctor; what they do to me is what I intend should be done. And one cannot explain human knowledge as a purely active process; it always involves atten-tion to data which are not of our own making, apart from the exceptional case where we attend to our own creative thoughts or fantasies. Augustine often seems to see this clearly enough; but he does not take the decisive step of abandoning the will-o'-the-wisp of a purely active intellect, and the artificial theories to which it leads.

Augustine has another, and perhaps more characteristic, way of moving from sense-perception to the higher forms of knowl-edge, namely his concept of memory. In the *Confessions* Book 10 he describes our ability to recall sense-qualities and the complex patterns they compose; when we remember people or places, we summon up their images as if from some underground store-house or cave. The memory also includes our power of making imaginative pictures, and generally of representing to ourselves possible events, as we do when we plan or hope or fear; in such cases we are freely recombining the images we derive from the senses. But Augustine notes two other cases; with abstract problems or principles we are not dealing with images, but with the things themselves; these have not come to us through the senses, or been told us: 'I found them in my own heart and approved them as true, and committed them to memory to produce when required' (*ibid.* 10.10.17). And there is a problem with our memory of our own mental states; we can remember joys when we are not rejoicing; we can remember what it is to forget. Clearly, then, memory is more than a simple representation of past states; it must involve some form of direct awareness. We count by numbers, not by images of numbers; we speak of images, and know what they are; but this cannot mean that we have images of images. Finally, if we lose something, we must remember it, or we should not recognize it when we find it; but if we forget something, we must still in some sense remember it, or we should not know what it is that we are trying to recall. Similarly (*ibid.* 10.20.29) we must have at least some partial knowledge of the happy life, which all men seek, but which Augustine identifies with God.

We cannot give further space to the details of this fascinating discussion; two brief comments alone may be allowed. First: Augustine's extended use of the term 'memory' has puzzled many readers. It seems that his argument moves from a narrower to a more inclusive sense of the term. In the narrower sense, memory is merely the power of reproducing *sensibilia* by means of images; but Augustine moves from this, by various stages which we have partly noted, to an inclusive sense in which any form of knowledge is assigned to memory simply on the ground that it is available to us to produce when required. Secondly, his discussion is still influenced by the Platonic theory of reminiscence, *anamnesis* (see p. 23 above). True, he explicitly rejects the view that where we have knowledge that is not derived from the senses, this is a gradual and partial recalling of truths we have known in a former life. But he retains the idea that we know some things by an intellectual intuition because they were already stored deep down in our memory (*ibid.* 10.10.17): 'Where were they, and how did I recognize them when they were mentioned . . . unless they were already in the memory, but so remote and tucked away in its hidden recesses that unless they were dug out by someone's admonition, I might have been unable to think of them'. In the end, our primary knowledge of God is explained along these lines; God's being is reflected in some degree throughout the universe he has created, and takes the form of knowledge hidden in the depths of the human mind.

CHAPTER 19

Freedom and goodness

Augustine's three books *On Free Will* have a controversial purpose and are mainly aimed against Manichaeism; his central concern is the problem of evil, which the Manichees regarded as a cosmic principle comparable in power with God himself. Augustine has two distinguishable forms of reply, neither of them wholly original, but both developed with persuasive skill. In the first, he claims that our main concern is with moral evil. Like other thinkers, Augustine distinguishes two forms of evil, sin and suffering; but suffering, he claims, is the just punishment for the sin which man has committed at and after the Fall. Was it right, then, for God to create a world in which men could sin? Augustine answers that sin is a misuse of free will, and without free will there can be no virtuous conduct; God did right, therefore, in creating man free. Embedded in this argument is the claim that sin consists in the choice of lesser goods when greater ones should have been preferred; in particular, of course, bodily pleasures rather than spiritual benefits (*op. cit.* 2.48–54). Evil of this kind can arise in a world which is wholly good, as befits God's creation; no blame attaches to God for creating a world where there are different *degrees* of goodness; indeed such variety enhances its perfection as a whole.[1] It is men who are to blame for choosing the lesser goods (3.5.12–3.6.18; cf. *Civ. Dei* 11.16–18, 12.4–5, etc.).

Two criticisms may be suggested. First, it seems that God might still be blamed for putting temptation in people's way, just as if we left unwholesome sweets lying about where children could find them. And secondly, the argument so far presented is

[1] Cf. R. T. Wallis, *Neoplatonism* (see Bibliography 7), p. 65.

230

weakened by Augustine's later reconsideration of free will. He has so far presented it simply as *liberum arbitrium*, the power to choose either good or evil. He later comes to frame a distinct concept of *libertas*, which he defines as 'inability to sin', *non posse peccare* (so, e.g. *C. 2 Ep. Pel.* 1.5).[2] The paradoxical definition suggests that the really good man loses his freedom of choice; a better formula would indicate that he chooses freely, but all his choices are good.[3] But if this is admitted, why did not God equip Adam with this kind of freedom?[4] There is in fact a contradiction in Augustine's view of Adam; on the one hand, following christianized Jewish traditions, Augustine exhibits him as wise, virtuous and spiritually minded; on the other, he makes him perpetrate a disastrous and irredeemable offence; indeed a dramatic contrast between his unfallen and his fallen state is needed to account for the miseries which Augustine thinks were introduced into the world by this single act. This not only puts a strain upon belief, but also conveys the alarming suggestion that even the most exalted virtue is not proof against temptation in its simplest form. But in practice we all recognize that there are men whose goodness is at least relatively trustworthy. It is ironical that Origen was accused of teaching that there is no security even in our final salvation, although he himself suggests that a really good man will not commit grievous sins and will quickly correct his own minor aberrations; see *Princ.* 1.4.1.

A second form of reply to the Manichees was to formulate a different concept of evil, which plays a comparatively minor part in the treatise *On Free Will*, but is recalled in several other works, and has been widely acclaimed as authoritative, namely the so-called negative theory of evil. It will be convenient to discuss this later, in the context of Augustine's conceptions of being and goodness. For the present we may revert to the subject of free will, which arose in a more pressing form in the encounter with Pelagius and his supporters, p. 221 above.

Augustine's own experience of temptation had convinced him

---

[2] Cf. Plotinus, 6.8.21.1–7.
[3] For a fuller discussion, see my *Substance and Illusion*, no. xvi, pp. 248–53.
[4] Cf. *Gen. ad Litt.* 11.4–11. Augustine's defence is invalid; it makes Adam both weak and presumptuous (§ 5) and presupposes the existence of other sinners, who *ex hypothesi* need not have existed. Augustine claims that the existence of sinners brings the benefit of variety (§ 8); but this could have been secured by varieties of goodness; cf. p. 126.

that man is powerless to achieve any good result without divine aid; indeed, God's grace is needed, not only to assist a man's good resolves, which the Pelagians could admit, but to elicit them by implanting good impulses; there must be 'prevenient' grace. He expressed this conviction in the prayer 'Give what thou commandest, and command what thou wilt' (*Conf.* 10.29.40). But his keen perception of human weakness, coupled with an extreme reaction against the strenuous self-reliance of the Pelagians, led him gradually to take up a position in which the grace of God becomes the sole's determinant of our actions. He saw, most rightly, that God must be the ultimate source and inspiration of our good deeds; but for all his concern to uphold our moral freedom, he could not in the end concede that God had given man an absolute power to choose between alternatives, for this seemed to imply that a man could choose rightly by his own unaided effort. He came to think, then, that God not only offers us the means of grace, but gives, *or withholds*, the ability to use them. The inevitable result of this view is that on God devolves the whole responsibility, not only for the salvation of the elect, but for the failure and damnation of the rest. It must have been possible for God to save them; but in fact he withheld from them the ability to use his grace.

As has long been observed, Augustine appears to convict God of inhuman cruelty and injustice. His own reply was that nobody deserved to be saved; where indeed one could quote Luke 13:1–5 to support him. He saw the human race as tainted, not only by vicious dispositions, but by inherited guilt which went back to Adam, 'in whom all sinned', as he interpreted the Latin version of Romans 5:12. Whatever merits there may be in recognizing that men are corrupted by inherited defects and a sinful environment, there can be no excuse for the theory of inherited guilt, which makes even new-born infants into detested sinners in the eyes of God; nor is there any coherent defence of the view that we ourselves somehow participated in a sin committed by Adam many centuries before our birth.

Augustine was led to these horrifying conclusions, partly by deductions drawn from his insistence on the absolute necessity of God's grace, but partly by the theory that there is a predetermined number of God's elect (Rev. 7:4); the number of redeemed human souls must therefore precisely make up for the angels who fell by disobedience (and so, one would think, deserve our heartfelt gratitude!). Augustine therefore has to find an artificial explanation for 1 Timothy 2:4, 'God wills all men to be saved'; see *Ench.* 27.103, *C. Iul.* 4.8.44, as against *Sp. et Litt.* 33.58. In the end, then, he praises a God who has brought the human race into existence in the full knowledge that the great majority of men are destined to everlasting torment.

Within this deterministic framework, Augustine attempts to preserve human free will, though not to make it an ultimate determinant; indeed he accepts the traditional view that apart from free will there is no place for praise or blame. In the *City of God* 5.9 he insists that God knows all future events, but argues that this does not compromise human freedom; God simply foreknows what in fact we shall freely choose, just as he knows what we have done. A similar theory had already been suggested by Origen (*Princ.* 3.1, especially 12–13). However, Augustine is already moving towards the view that God not only foreknows, but controls, what we shall freely do; he 'orders all wills, granting the power of achievement to some and denying it to others'. He has an extremely ingenious and largely original explanation of this claim, which is clearly set out in the *De Spiritu et Littera* 34.60. He notes that all our decisions have to be taken in the light of impulses which strike us largely at random; now, for example, we hear a hymn being sung, now we encounter a voluptuous-looking prostitute; and there is an immediate involuntary response, which the Stoics call a *propatheia*, before we can recognize and control our thoughts. Augustine holds that God can contrive what impulses shall strike a man at any moment, knowing how he will respond; and so can bring him to the action which is foreordained without infringing his free will. God does not interfere with any movement of the will that we knowingly control; he simply controls what appear to us to be random events.[5]

This theory has a philosophical interest in that Augustine

---

[5] Origen also uses the concept of pre-rational impulses (*Princ.* 3.1.2–4), by which indeed God can lead us to sin (3.1.7–13). But he differs radically (1) in teaching that God will finally save all (3.6.6); and (2) in attributing to God simply the larger *share* in the work of salvation (3.1.19).

adopts what some philosophers have called a 'compatibilist' position; human freedom, in some sense, is compatible with a completely determined course of events. And its theological impact is that the future, including our own personal destiny, is not only foreknown but foreordained. Whatever verbal qualifications one may introduce, in all essentials this amounts to the 'double predestination' taught by Calvin. We act freely in the sense that we are at least partly free of external constraints; within limits, we can do what we want. But we are mistaken if we think that each decision helps to determine a future which was not fully determined before it was made.

Augustine's teaching on the vital necessity of divine grace has generally been accepted as a decisive service to Christian theology (which I would myself endorse); though there is much less agreement about its corollaries of election and predestination. I myself believe that the predestinarian system is wholly incompatible with a doctrine of God's love and mercy; moreover I think that in arguing for it Augustine was the victim of an avoidable mistake. The mistake was to regard divine grace and human effort as competing alternatives in the work of our salvation, so that by emphasizing one one has to minimize the other; such competition is suggested when Augustine says (*Retr.* 2.1) 'I laboured on behalf of free choice, but the grace of God won the day'. Now if there is a limited task on hand – say, to saw up a given quantity of wood – and two partners are at work, then of course more work performed by one partner means less remaining for the other. But a better analogy would be the relation between teacher and pupil, where there may be no thought of a particular goal, such as the passing of a particular examination. It then by no means follows that the pupil who learns quickly makes less demands upon his teacher; his quickness may mean that he proposes more advanced problems for discussion. And the converse holds. We might say that it is God's intention to train our wills, but not to train us to do without him; this is nonsense if we believe that God is himself the source of all wisdom. Hence there is no reason to assume that a man of strong moral fibre will necessarily neglect the means of grace; he may put his moral effort precisely into the task of invoking God's help by constant prayer. And it would be strange if the man who turned towards God confessing his weakness were not rewarded by any increase in fortitude and commitment. Provided, that is, the confession be genuine; it is all too easy to make prayers of contrition into a form of self-indulgence; one dramatizes one's unremarkable vices by proclaiming oneself a 'miserable sinner', and comes to enjoy the role. But this is a mistake of which we can be warned by wise direction.

This seen, we can readily acknowledge that different men have differently proportioned gifts. Some are natural 'achievers', others learn from their own failures to be more sympathetic to the difficulties of their fellows. One of Augustine's failings was that he was apt to read off lessons from his own experience and erect them into principles equally applicable to all mankind.

The discussion of free will, therefore, turns on the question what interaction there can be between infinite and finite beings; in principle, we have suggested, one aspect of God's work of creation is that he really does delegate responsibility to human agents, though himself maintaining an overall control. Augustine's discussion of time in *Confessions* Book 11 has a rather similar theological setting. Having told the story of his life and conversion (Books 1–9) he presents himself as desirous of finding God, yet continually distracted, both by temptations and by the calls of practical service. Christ is the only true mediator, God's Word, by whom all things were made (10.43.68, 11.2.4). He seeks then to understand the creation, in which (we have seen) the traces of God's own being are to be found.

How then did God make heaven and earth, making them out of nothing? And again, if God's will to create was eternal, why was not the creation eternal? (This question, I think, is prompted by the Aristotelian view that the world existed from all eternity; it might seem illogical that the created world should not share God's eternity, but have a beginning). Two difficulties arise in this connection. First, the pagan may say, What was God doing before he made the world? (11.10.12, 12.14). This is an old objection to creation theories which Augustine may have learnt from Cicero (*Nat. Deor.* 1.9.21). Augustine sets aside the easy answer, 'preparing hells for the inquisitive', and replies that time itself is God's creation (11.14.17); and it is only within the time-series that we can speak of 'then' or 'before' (11.13.15). We have already considered some previous attempts at a similar theory (pp. 66–7). A second point, considered elsewhere, is the specifically Jewish and Christian problem of reconciling the biblical narrative of six days of creation with the long-standing tradition that God's will must have been instantly fulfilled. Augustine answers that God did indeed create everything 'in the beginning'; but he invokes the Stoic doctrine of 'seminal principles' (see p. 47) to show that his creatures had potentialities which developed over a space of time.

Augustine next develops the contrast between eternity and time in such a way as to suggest that in some sense time is unreal. We speak of a long time or a short time, which must refer either to the past or to the future. But how can a thing be long or short when it does not exist? The past has gone by, the future has not yet come into being; and as for the present, it seems impossible to identify it. If we speak of 'the present year', not all of it is present; but if we look for something that is wholly present, we have to imagine progressively shorter spaces of time (11.15.20), and finally are driven back to the fleeting moment, which is merely a perpetually shifting boundary between the past and the future, and has of itself no reality. A little later he adds the point that 'we measure passing times by our consciousness' (*sentiendo*); but the past and the future are not there (or, 'do not exist'), so how can they be measured? (16.21). This leads in due course to a distinctive theory of time defined purely in terms of our consciousness.

Before considering this, however, we may comment on the background and the validity of the points made so far. First, one can see why Augustine is prompted to argue for the unreality of time; he thinks of all temporal being as unreal compared with God's eternity. But he is also captivated by a paradox which was mentioned already by Aristotle (*Physics* 4.10, 217b 29 ff.) and was later exploited by the Sceptics. Time must be unreal, because the past had gone by and the future is not yet in being; as for the present, it is a mere instant, not a part, or space, of time;

just as a point is not part of a line, say a quarter of it, or any smaller fraction. Chrysippus is said to have formulated a view which looks rather like this, but perhaps had no sceptical intention; he seems to have said that the past and the future are real (*huphestanai*) but only the present is actual (*huparchein*) – *SVF* 2.509, 518. On the other hand a later Stoic, Apollodorus, challenged the view that the present must be regarded as an instant; for we can speak of the present year (Arius Didymus fr. 26, in Diels *DG* p. 461). Apollodorus appears to conclude that we could mention a longer period, and so by extension describe all time as present. Here we might reasonably demur; to speak of *all* time as present would leave no work for the words 'past' and 'future'.

This account is of course very much simplified; a much better and fuller treatment can be found in Richard Sorabji, *Time, Creation & the Continuum*. But we must turn to a brief criticism; and we can observe, first, that Augustine's problem is bound up with the conception of the present as a 'moving instant'. This seems to involve two separable problems. First, we have already seen that 'the present' can stand for a vaguely defined stretch of time, as opposed to a mere instant. A crude analogy in spatial terms can be found by considering A. N. Whitehead's revised definition of a point, which has 'position but no magnitude'. Whitehead interpreted the last phrase to mean 'no specified magnitude, whether large, small, or zero'; his definition could be satisfied, therefore, by a series of concentric spheres. We can widen or restrict the stretch at will. But secondly, the notion of the present as moving along some sort of scale is only a metaphor. On the one hand, we conceive of time as a series of dates or periods; on the other, we are aware of events as expected, as occurring, and as past. These two series change in relation to one another; but there is no need to introduce the idea of *local* change, under the name of 'movement'. The situation can be simply illustrated by considering a mistake I once made; in my very early years I thought that 'tomorrow' must be the name of one of the days of the week; I vaguely thought it might come between Wednesday and Thursday. I had to learn that it changes in relation to them; but that change is not a movement;

if we say that it 'moves on', that is only a metaphor. No doubt our measurements of time are based on observations of the heavenly bodies; but the relation is not a simple one; thus we use an artificial 'clock time', which differs perceptibly from 'sun time' as measured from noon to noon each day. Again, it may be that we could have no consciousness of time without being aware of change; but this need not be movement; we could use clocks which told the time without moving hands or shifting patterns of figures; for instance, by lights that changed colour. The present, then, need not be regarded as an instant; and it may well be misleading to say that it moves.

Secondly, Augustine's problems derive in part from his assumptions about the verb 'to be'. He suggests that if we say 'X is Y', we imply that 'X is'; and this entails that 'X is real' and that 'X is permanent'. Hence the present is disqualified, because it has no permanence in relation to the scale of dates; it is always with us, but it is not always Tuesday. And the past and the future are disqualified, apparently, by the mere fact that they are not present. When Augustine says, 'The past and future are not there, so how can they be measured?' (16.21), he is raising a philosopher's difficulty, not a practical one. In ordinary life we find no special difficulty in answering such questions as 'How long were you waiting for your friend?' or 'How long will this bad weather continue?'; or again, 'If this journey begins (or began) on Tuesday and ends the next Friday, how long does it last?' Augustine seems to concede the latter point (21.27); but he does not seem to have observed that phrases like 'measuring time' are ambiguous. It is one thing to measure, or to estimate, time as it elapses; it is a different process if we try to remember or predict a lapse of time, or to calculate from already established measures like the days of the week.

Augustine goes on to propound a theory of time which seems an extraordinary mixture of acuteness and naivety. He begins by observing that it is common knowledge that there are three times, past, present and future (17.23). But if these times 'are', or exist, where are they? Wherever they are, they must be there now; if they merely will be there, or were there, they are not there now, and so are not anywhere, and so do not exist (18.23).

This leads to the conclusion that what really exists now (and so, is all that really exists) is my memory of the past and my conjectures about the future. He sums up this view in the lapidary phrases: 'It is not correct to say, there are three times, past, present and future; but it might be correct to say, there are three times, a present concerned with the past, a present concerned with the present, and a present concerned with the future'; these he identifies as 'memory, observation and expectation' (20.26).

I will briefly state the objections to this theory, so far as I understand them.

(1) Augustine is mistaken in suggesting that things can only exist if they 'are somewhere'. Much depends on the sense of 'being' or 'existing'. There are just five regular solids; but saying this does not imply any location. In a somewhat different sense, Augustine certainly holds that God exists; but there is no ordinary way in which he is located.

(2) The notion that the future must be somewhere *now* is difficult to pin down, since it seems difficult to see what it denies. Augustine contrasts it with the notion that the future *will be* somewhere (18.23 *ad init.*); but we cannot make predictions about the future taken as a whole. We might indeed say loosely, 'the future will be past'; but this comment applies, not to the future as such, but to any future event that we care to define. We are not suggesting that at some moment there will be no more future events.

(3) The notion that time can be understood purely in terms of our consciousness is arresting, and largely original, but has obvious drawbacks. In explaining it, Augustine seems to be thinking largely in terms of his own consciousness; but even if we correct this limitation, and consider the whole human race, it seems obvious that events have occurred which nobody remembers, and that events will occur which nobody expects. Augustine is clear enough about the distinction between memories or expectations and present realities; but he does not seem to consider that a task which I mean to undertake may not simply pass from the future to the present; it could very well turn out quite different from what I expected.

(4) Augustine's psychological treatment of time may serve his purpose of suggesting the relative unreality of time as contrasted with eternity (29.30); but in other ways it frustrates his real objective, since he set out with the intention of understanding God's act of creation. But he clearly wishes to present this as a real event in the past, even though no human being remembers it. It may be that he is influenced here by assumptions about the sufficiency of Scripture, which could suggest that the biblical record of the creation narrates the events, and all the events, exactly as they occurred. But this defence will not stand. The Bible often sets down very general descriptions, like 'He made the stars' (Gen. 1:16). It also says that God made a definite number of them (Ps.147:4); but we do not know their number, and the Bible does not tell us. Indeed it says that God's acts in creation far surpass our understanding. It is impossible, then, to argue that such acts in the past are in some sense real because they exist in our memory.

If this treatment of Augustine's theory seems too confident or too dismissive, I must remind the reader of the limitations of this book, which sets out to provide an elementary and comprehensible introduction to difficult problems. The last thing I intend to do is to close the door on further discussion.

After setting out his own conception, Augustine turns to consider the accepted Platonic view, which defines time in terms of the movements of the heavenly bodies (23.29 ff.). He points out that these luminaries might cease to move; but we could still count the rotations of a potter's wheel, or distinguish between long and short syllables in our own speech. Again, we can distinguish between the rotation of the sun, and the time it takes, for it is conceivable that the sun should go faster or slower. He finds a biblical basis for this suggestion; Joshua made the sun and moon stand still (Josh. 10:12 ff.), but this did not bring time to a stand, for the battle continued. Augustine's criticism seems both valid and original.

In his later writings Augustine seems to abandon the distinctive theory of time which we have just considered. He can still identify time with motion (e.g. *Gen. ad Litt.* 5.5.12) besides saying, more cautiously, that it depends on motion (*Civ. Dei*

11.6). Moreover he insists that time began with creation (*ibid.*); and although he explains the 'days of creation' in non-temporal terms (*Gen. ad Litt.* 5.5.12, cf. *Civ. Dei* 11.7), he also explains that the first man was created *in* time after the primary creative action (*Gen. ad Litt.* 6.5.7, 6.6.11, *Civ. Dei* 12.15–16). It should follow that time is not a product of the human consciousness. But Augustine himself does not note this change of view. He turns away from the theory set out in the *Confessions*; he does not formally withdraw it.

Augustine's treatment of time has led us to consider the connections between being and permanence, and between being and location. The keystone of his philosophy, however, is the union of being and value. We may approach this obliquely by considering its opposite, already mentioned on p. 223, the theory of evil as negation. Augustine argues that 'any nature, so far as it is, is good'; evil therefore is a defect, a simple absence of goodness (*On Free Will* 3.36; cf. *Conf.* 7.12.18 etc.). This view has an obvious attraction for him, in view of his concern to maintain the essential goodness of all God's creation, in opposition to Manichaeism. But it is not his own invention; it is found in Origen and Athanasius, who themselves are partly indebted to pre-Christian Stoicism. Its undoubted appeal to the mind rests upon its coherence with Platonic ontology, that magnificent construction of thought which holds that all values arise as things realize their true being and approximate in their measure to that supreme reality which is also supreme goodness.

Despite its august connections, I believe the negative theory of evil is inadmissible. Three objections can be stated.

First, even if otherwise successful, the negative theory could apply only to 'natures', i.e. to things themselves and their necessary properties. ('By a "nature" I mean that which is usually called a substance', *On Free Will* 3.13.36). But much of the evil we observe in the world is not inherent in things taken singly, or considered as species; it results from what A. N. Whitehead has called 'the mutual obstructiveness of things'. The prophet who foretells that 'the leopard shall lie down with the kid', Isaiah 11.6, implicitly condemns the present age in which leopards live by preying upon gentle and graceful creatures which we should like to see preserved. And it seems unrealistic to argue that there is nothing wrong with leopards as such, but only with their way of life, since the agility and the natural weapons which we admire in the leopard are precisely related to their predatory habits and would be pointless if the creatures were tame. In any case the reluctant admiration which the leopard excites in us cannot be extended to wolves or hyenas. Realists who wish to pursue these arguments can find far more horrific examples in Sir Charles Sherrington, *Man on his Nature*.

Secondly, the theory in fact breaks down in quite obvious cases. Malice is not describable as a mere absence of good will; this would result in indifference; whereas malice is a positive motivation, destructive in tendency. We should observe that, whatever the difficulties of combining various good qualities (see pp. 126–7), it seems far more obvious that vices conflict with one another; the ruthless tyrant has to be energetic if he is to do harm; add indolence to cruelty, and you deprive him of his power. Such arguments, which could be developed, suggest that evil is parasitic on goodness; a really evil power results, not from combining every possible form of evil, which is no doubt impossible, but from perverting potentially good qualities and enlisting them in designs which are destructive of goodness. There is no comfort to be found in Augustine's view that evil is a negation and must therefore extinguish itself (*Conf.* 7.12.18). Evil is more like a fire; there is no limit to its destructive potential so long as there is any good remaining for it to devour.

Thirdly, as we have observed, this treatment of evil is only the negative side of the theory which identifies goodness with being (see pp. 123–6), and rests upon assumptions about the force of the word 'being' which modern logicians have rightly rejected. The basic argument can be represented as a kind of equation: 'X is' = 'X is itself' = 'X is its true self' = 'X is what it ought to be' = 'X is good'. Therefore being implies goodness; conversely, badness must be simply an absence of being. Supporters of the theory of course do not see it in this light; they operate with a series of conventions which lay emphasis on the noble and attractive theme of a cosmic scale of values, and distract attention from the awkward questions of logical propriety which threaten to undermine the whole scheme. To explain these objections one would have to describe the developments in logic pioneered by Frege; one easily intelligible point, however, is that the verb 'to be' has several different functions which are logically distinct. (I have given a brief summary in my *Divine Substance*, pp. 7–19.) 'X is' may mean simply 'X exists'. If one names it as 'X', it must be a distinguishable phenomenon; if one classes it as 'an X', one assumes that it has some claim to be so regarded. But what is assumed here is that it *qualifies* to be regarded as an 'X', it has the standard characteristics which we associate with the term. And a thing can *qualify* to be regarded as a disease or a poison; the fact that it exactly fits that description gives it no claim to be regarded as good.

Modern logical analysis, therefore, has helped us to criticize a form of argument which I think must now retire from serious discussion. It is less easy to see what further help such logic can provide. We have already noted (pp. 124–5) that 'existence' is a term which can be applied very variously to different kinds of subjects; it raises problems which are not solved by mere attention to the existential quantifier. And certainly it need not be assumed that there are no logical links between existence and value; as a simple example, we have argued that all-inclusive badness is inconceivable, and cannot exist. Nevertheless the criticisms just expressed may perhaps excite dismay. Over the centuries the Platonic ontology has proved a valuable support for Christian philosophers, and Christians have come to rely on it and take it for granted. Yet it is worth remembering that it formed no part of the original message of Christ or his Apostles; it was a godsend to the Church, whether by fortunate chance or literally by a divine dispensation; something that could be adopted and used and ultimately worked into the whole fabric of Christian orthodoxy. In much the same way, the settled fabric of the Roman Empire came to be regarded as a divinely ordained institution within which the distinctively spiritual work of the Church could proceed. Augustine lived to see this order threatened with collapse; and his response was not to labour over shoring up the old fabric, but to venture boldly on a new construction, the City of God, which gave a charter to the next twelve centuries of Christianity. We shall do well if we try to imitate his wisdom and imagination. Many lovers of Augustine cannot conceive of a Christian philosophy divorced from Platonism. But we have had to consider this prospect, and set out, like Abraham, not knowing what country we are to inherit. It is only our faith that assures us of a city 'whose builder and maker is God'.

Bibliography

Asterisks denote introductory works

GENERAL HISTORIES OF ANCIENT GREEK PHILOSOPHY

*Armstrong, A. H. *An Introduction to Ancient Philosophy*, London 1947, 4th edn 1965

Guthrie, W. K. C. *A History of Greek Philosophy* I–VI, Cambridge 1962–81

Röd W. (ed.) *Geschichte der Philosophie* I–III, Munich 1976–85

Totok, W. *Handbuch der Geschichte der Philosophie*, Frankfurt am Main I 1964, II 1975 (bibliographical survey)

Vogel, C. J. de *Greek Philosophy: a Collection of Texts, with some Notes and Explanations*, Leiden I 4th edn 1969, II 3rd edn 1967, III 3rd edn 1973

*Zeller, E. *Outlines of the History of Greek Philosophy*, rev. W. Nestle, Eng. trans. L. R. Palmer, 14th edn London 1971

I

FROM THE BEGINNINGS TO SOCRATES

Barnes, J. *The Presocratic Philosophers* I–II, London 1979, 2nd edn 1982

Diehls, H. *Die Fragmente der Vorsokratiker* I–III, 10th edn by W. Kranz, Berlin 1961

Freeman, K. *The Presocratic Philosophers*, Oxford 1946

*— *Ancilla to the Presocratic Philosophers*, Oxford 1948

Grant, R. M. 'Early Christianity and pre-Socratic philosophy', *Harry Austryn Wolfson Jubilee Volume*, Jerusalem 1965, I pp. 357–84

Hussey, E. *The Presocratics*, London 1972

Kirk, G. S., Raven, J. E. and Schofield, M. *The Presocratic Philosophers*, 2nd edn Cambridge 1983 (revision by Schofield of 1st edn by Kirk and Raven, Cambridge 1957)

Lloyd, G. E. R. *Magic, Reason and Experience*, Cambridge 1979
Röd, W. *Geschichte der Philosophie I: Die Philosophie der Antike 1: von Thales bis Demokrit*, Munich 1976

2

SOCRATES AND THE PLATONIC FORMS

The Sophists

Classen, H. J. (ed.) *Sophistik*, Wege der Forschung 187, Darmstadt 1976
Graeser, A. *Sophistik–Aristoteles* (= W. Röd (ed.) *Geschichte der Philosophie* II), Munich 1983
Kerferd, G. B. *The Sophistic Movement*, Cambridge 1981

Socrates

Beckman, J. *The Religious Dimension of Socrates' Thought*, Waterloo, Ont., 1979
Guthrie, W. K. C. *Socrates*, Cambridge 1971, 2nd edn 1979
Vlastos G. (ed.) *The Philosophy of Socrates*, New York 1971

Plato, introductory literature

*Crombie, I. M. *Plato, the Midwife's Apprentice*, London 1964
Grube, G. M. A. *Plato's Thought*, London 1935, 2nd edn 1980
Hare, R. M. *Plato*, Oxford 1982
Raven, J. E. *Plato's Thought in the Making*, Cambridge 1965
For a full bibliography, together with recent specialist articles, see Richard Kraut, *The Cambridge Companion to Plato*, Cambridge 1992.

3

THE PHILOSOPHY OF PLATO'S MATURITY

Allen, R. E. *Studies in Plato's Metaphysics*, London 1965
Annas, J. *An Introduction to Plato's Republic*, Oxford 1981
Crombie, I. M. *An Examination of Plato's Doctrines*, 3rd edn London I 1969, II 1971
Cross, R. C. and Woozley, A. D. *Plato's Republic: a Philosophical Commentary*, London 1964
Friedländer, P. *Platon* I–III, Berlin 1928–30 (3rd edn of I–II 1964, III 1975)

Irwin, T. *Plato's Moral Theory: the Early and Middle Dialogues*, Oxford 1977, 2nd edn 1979
Robinson, R. *Plato's Earlier Dialectic*, 2nd edn Oxford 1953
Ross, W. D. *Plato's Theory of Ideas*, Oxford 1951, repr. 1963
Solmsen, F. *Plato's Theology*, New York 1942
Vlastos, G. (ed.) *Plato I: Metaphysics and Epistemology*, New York 1971
Wippern, J. *Das Problem der ungeschriebenen Lehre Platons*, Wege der Forschung 186, Darmstadt 1972

Platonism

See Bibliography 6; also, for the Christian era:
Armstrong, A. H. (ed.) *The Cambridge History of Later Greek and Early Medieval Philosophy* (= *LGP*), Cambridge 1967
Cassirer, E. *The Platonic Renaissance in England*, Eng. trans. J. P. Pettegrove, Edinburgh 1953
Feibleman, J. K. *Religious Platonism*, London 1959
Ivanka, E. von *Plato Christianus*, Einsiedeln 1964

4

ARISTOTLE

*Allan, D. J. *The Philosophy of Aristotle*, London 1952, 2nd edn 1970
*Barnes, J. *Aristotle*, Oxford 1982
Düring, I. *Aristoteles: Darstellung und Interpretation seines Denkens*, Heidelberg 1966
Gill, M. L. *Aristotle on Substance*, Princeton 1989
Jaeger, W. *Aristotle, Fundamentals of the History of his Development*, Oxford 1934, 2nd edn 1948
*Lloyd, G. E. R. *Aristotle, the Growth and Structure of his Thought*, Cambridge 1968
Owens, J. *The Doctrine of Being in the Aristotelian Metaphysics*, Toronto 1951, 3rd edn 1978
Ross, W. D. *Aristotle*, London 1923, repr. 1977
Waterlow, S. *Nature, Change and Agency in Aristotle's Physics*, Oxford 1982

Aristotelianism

Lynch, J. P. *Aristotle's School*, Berkeley, Los Angeles and London, 1972
Moraux, P. *Der Aristotelismus bei den Griechen*, Berlin I 1973, II 1984
Sorabji, R. (ed.) *Aristotle Transformed: the Ancient Commentators and their Influence*, London 1990

Wehrli, F. *Die Schule des Aristoteles, Texte und Komm,* 10 vols., Basel 1954–9, 2nd edn 1967–9

5

EPICURUS AND THE STOICS

Long, A. A. *Hellenistic Philosophy: Stoics, Epicureans, Sceptics,* London 1974
Long, A. A. and Sedley, D. N. *The Hellenistic Philosophers.* i: *Translation and Commentary;* ii: *Greek and Latin Texts with Notes and Bibliography,* Cambridge 1987
A Cambridge History of Hellenistic Philosophy is being prepared by Jonathan Barnes, Jaap Mansfeld and Malcolm Schofield

Epicurus

Arrighetti, G. (ed.) *Opere,* Turin 1960, 2nd edn 1973
Bailey, C. *Epicurus: the Extant Remains,* Oxford 1926, repr. Hildesheim 1975
— *The Greek Atomists and Epicurus,* Oxford 1928
Festugière, A. J. *Epicurus and his Gods,* Oxford 1955
— *Epicure et ses dieux,* 2nd edn Paris 1968
*Rist, J. M. *Epicurus, an Introduction,* Cambridge 1972

Stoicism

Arnim, H. von *Stoicorum Veterum Fragmenta* i–iv (=*SVF*), Stuttgart 1903–24, repr. Stuttgart 1968
Bevan, E. *Stoics and Sceptics,* Oxford 1913
Pohlenz, M. *Die Stoa. Geschichte einer geistigen Bewegung* i–ii, Göttingen 1948–9, 2nd edn 1978
Rist, J. M. *Stoic Philosophy,* Cambridge 1969
— (ed.) *The Stoics,* Berkeley, Los Angeles and London 1978
*Sandbach, F. H. *The Stoics,* London 1975

6

THE MIDDLE PLATONISTS AND PHILO OF ALEXANDRIA

Armstrong, A. H. (ed.) *The Cambridge History of Later Greek and Early Medieval Philosophy* (=*LGP*), Cambridge 1967
Dillon, J. *The Middle Platonists,* London 1977

Krämer, H. J. *Der Ursprung des Geistesmetaphysik*, Amsterdam 1964
Theiler, W. *Die Vorbereitung des Neuplatonismus*, Berlin and Zürich 1934, repr. 1964
Zintzen, C. *Der Mittelplatonismus*, Wege der Forschung 70, Darmstadt 1981

Philo

Bréhier, E. *Les idées philosophiques et religieuses de Philon d' Alexandrie*, Paris 1908, 3rd edn 1950
*Chadwick, H. 'Philo', in A. H. Armstrong, *LGP* pp. 135–57
Goodenough, E. R. *An Introduction to Philo Judaeus*, Cambridge, Mass., 1940, 2nd edn Oxford 1962
Runia, D. T. *Philo of Alexandria and the Timaeus of Plato* I–II, Leiden 1986 (contains survey of recent work on Philo, pp. 7–31)
*Sandmel, S. *Philo of Alexandria, an Introduction*, Oxford 1979 (N.B. for criticism of Goodenough)

7

THE PHILOSOPHY OF LATE ANTIQUITY

Scepticism

Annas, J. and Barnes, J. *The Modes of Scepticism*, Cambridge 1985
Bevan, E. *Stoics and Sceptics*, Oxford 1913
Brochard, V. *Les Sceptiques grecs*, Paris 1887, 2nd edn 1923
Stough, C. L. *Greek Scepticism*, Berkeley 1969

Gnosticism

Förster, W. *Gnosis, a Selection of Gnostic Texts*, Eng. trans. ed. R. McL. Wilson, 2 vols., Oxford, 1972, 1974
*Grant, R. M. *Gnosticism and Early Christianity*, New York 1959
Jonas, H. *Gnosis und spätantike Geist* I–II, Göttingen 1934, 3rd edn 1964
— *The Gnostic Religion*, Boston, Mass., 1958
Robinson, J. M. (ed.) *The Nag Hammadi Library*, San Francisco 1977, 3rd, revised edn 1988
Rudolph, K. *Die Gnosis. Wesen und Geschichte einer spätantiken Religion*, Göttingen 1977, 2nd edn 1980
— (ed.) *Gnosis und Gnostizismus*, Wege der Forschung 262, Darmstadt 1975
*Wilson, R. McL. *Gnosis and the New Testament*, Oxford 1968

Neoplatonism

Armstrong, A. H. *Plotinus*, in *LGP* (Bibliography 6) pp. 195–268
Dodds, E. R. *Proclus, the Elements of Theology*, Oxford 1933, 2nd edn 1963
Rist, J. M. *Plotinus, the Road to Reality*, Cambridge 1967
Wallis, R. T. *Neoplatonism*, London 1972
Zintzen, C. (ed.) *Die Philosophie des Neuplatonismus*, Wege der Forschung 436, Darmstadt 1977

8

THE DEBATE ABOUT CHRISTIAN PHILOSOPHY

Armstrong, A. H. (ed.) *LGP* (Bibliography 6) especially pp. 133–505
*— and Markus, R. A. *Christian Faith and Greek Philosophy*, London 1960
Chadwick, H. *Early Christian Thought and the Classical Tradition*, Oxford 1966
Forell, G. W. *History of Christian Ethics*, Minneapolis 1979
Gilson, E. *History of Christian Philosophy in the Middle Ages*, London 1955, new edn 1980
*Norris, R. A. *God and World in Early Christian Theology*, London 1966
Osborn, Eric *The Beginnings of Christian Philosophy*, Cambridge 1981
Stöckl, A. *Geschichte der christlichen Philosophie zur Zeit der Kirchenväter*, Mainz 1891, repr. 1968
Ueberweg, F. and Geyer, B. *Die patristische und scholastische Philosophie*, 11th edn Berlin 1928
Wolfson, H. A. *The Philosophy of the Church Fathers*, vol. 1 only published, Cambridge, Mass, 1956

9

GREEK AND HEBREW CONCEPTIONS OF GOD

The influence of Greek thought on early Christian theology

Chadwick H. in *LGP* pp. 158–92
Harnack, A. von *Lehrbuch der Dogmengeschichte*, 5th edn Tübingen 1931
— *History of Dogma* (Eng. trans. of the above, from the 3rd edn, by N. Buchanan), London 1894, repr. 1961
Hatch, E. *The Influence of Greek Ideas and Usages upon the Christian Church*, The Hibbert Lectures 1888, London 1891, repr. New York 1957

Hengel, M. *Judaism and Hellenism*, Eng. trans. J. S. Bowden, London 1974

Pannenberg, W. 'The appropriation of the philosophical concept of God as a dogmatic problem in early Christian theology' (Eng. trans. from *ZKG* 70 (1959) pp. 1–45) in Pannenberg, *Basic Questions in Theology*, vol. II pp. 119–83

Stead, G. C. 'Die Aufnahme des philosophischen Gottesbegriffes', *Theologische Rundschau* 51 (1986) pp. 349–71 (critique of Pannenberg's paper)

Representations of God

Daniélou, J. *Gospel Message and Hellenistic Culture*, ed. and trans. J. A. Baker, London 1973, especially pp. 303–43

Eichrodt, W. *Theology of the Old Testament* I, Eng. trans. J. A. Baker, London 1961

Festugière, A. J. *Le Dieu inconnu et la Gnose* (= *La Révélation d'Hermes Trismégiste*, vol. 4), Paris 1954

Grant, R. M. *The Early Christian Doctrine of God*, Charlottesville, Va., 1966

*Kaiser, C. B. *The Doctrine of God*, London 1982

Prestige, G. L. *God in Patristic Thought*, London 1936, 2nd edn 1952

Schmidt, W. H. *The Faith of the Old Testament*, Oxford 1983

10

PROOFS OF THE EXISTENCE OF GOD

Dalferth, I. U. *Existenz Gottes und christliche Glaube*, Munich 1984

Hick, J. *Arguments for the Existence of God*, London 1970

— *Faith and Knowledge*, Cornell 1957, 2nd edn London 1967

Lilla, S. R. C. *Clement of Alexandria*, Oxford 1971, especially pp. 118–226

Mackie, J. L. *The Miracle of Theism*, Oxford 1982

Pease, A. S. 'Coeli enarrant', *Harvard Theological Review* 34 (1941) pp. 163–200

Swinburne, R. *The Existence of God*, Oxford 1979

11

GOD AS SIMPLE UNCHANGING BEING

Creel, R. E. *Divine Impassibility*, Cambridge 1986

Farrer, A. M. *Finite and Infinite*, Westminster 1943

Gilson, E. *Being and Some Philosophers*, Toronto 1949, 2nd edn 1952
Hartshorne, C. *The Divine Relativity*, New Haven 1948, 2nd edn 1964
— *Man's Vision of God*, Chicago 1941, repr. Hamden, Conn., 1964
Kenny, A. *The God of the Philosophers*, Oxford 1979
Maas, W. *Unveränderlichkeit Gottes*, Munich 1974
Mozley, J. K. *The Impassibility of God*, Cambridge 1926
Owen, H. P. *Concepts of Deity*, New York 1971
Pike, N. *God and Timelessness*, London 1970

12

HOW GOD IS DESCRIBED

Bevan, E. *Symbolism and Belief*, London 1938
Geach, P. T. *Providence and Evil*, Cambridge 1977
Hick, J. *Evil and the God of Love*, London 1966
Lampe, G. H. W. *God as Spirit*, Oxford 1977, especially pp. 34–94
Stead, G. C. *Divine Substance*, Oxford 1977
— 'The concept of Mind and the concept of God', in *The Philosophical Frontiers of Christian Theology*, ed. B. Hebblethwaite and S. Sutherland, Cambridge 1982, repr. in Stead, *Substance and Illusion in the Christian Fathers* (London 1985), no. XIV

13

LOGOS AND SPIRIT

Chadwick, H. in *LGP* pp. 137–92
Dodds, E. R. 'The Parmenides of Plato and the origin of the Neoplatonic One', *Classical Quarterly* 22 (1928) pp. 129–42
Grant, R. M. *The Early Christian Doctrine of God*, Charlottesville, Va., 1966
Kelly, J. N. D. *Early Christian Doctrines*, London 1958, 5th edn 1977
Kretschmar, G. *Studien zur frühchristlichen Trinitätstheologie*, Tübingen 1956
Mackey, J. P. *The Christian Experience of God as Trinity*, London 1983
Stead, G. C. 'The origins of the doctrine of the Trinity', *Theology* 77 (1974) pp. 508–17 and 582–8 (= *Substance and Illusion* (see Bibliography 12) no. VI)
Wainwright, A. W. *The Trinity in the New Testament*, London 1962

14

UNITY OF SUBSTANCE

Dinsen, F. *Homoousios. Die Geschichte des Begriffs bis zum Konzil von Konstantinopel (381)*, Diss. Kiel, 1976; most valuable, though unfortunately difficult to obtain

Kelly, J. N. D. *Early Christian Creeds*, London 1950, 3rd edn 1981
— *Early Christian Doctrines*, London 1958, 5th edn 1977

Prestige, G. L. *God in Patristic Thought* (= *GPT*), London 1936, 2nd edn 1952 (most informative, but fanciful as regards this subject; for criticism, see Stead, 'Significance', below)

Ricken, F. 'Nikaia als Krisis des altchristlichen Platonismus', *Theologie und Philosophie* 44 (1969) pp. 321–41

Stead, G. C. 'The significance of the Homoousios', *Studia Patristica* 3 (1961) pp. 397–412 (= Texte und Untersuchungen 78), reprinted as *Substance and Illusion* (see Bibliography 12) no. 1
— *Divine Substance*, Oxford 1977
— 'Homoousios', *Reallexikon für Antike und Christentum* (forthcoming)

15

SUBSTANCE AND PERSONS

Dinsen, F. *Homoousios*, see Bibliography 14

Dörrie, H. 'Hypostasis', *Nachr. Akad. Göttingen* 3 (1955) pp. 35–92, repr. in *Platonica Minora*, Munich 1976, pp. 12–69

Fedwick, P. J. (ed.) *Basil of Caesarea, Christian, Humanist, Ascetic*, Toronto *c.* 1981

Hammerstaedt, J. 'Hypostasis' in *RAC* (forthcoming)

Holl, K. *Amphilochius von Ikonium in seinem Verhältniss zu den großen Kappadoziern*, Tübingen 1904

Köster, H. 'Hypostasis', in G. Kittel and G. Friedrich, *Theological Dictionary of the New Testament*, vol. 8, Grand Rapids, Mich., 1972, pp. 572–89

Otis, B. *Cappadocian Thought as a Coherent System*, Dumbarton Oaks Papers 12 (1958) pp. 95–124

Ritter, A. M. *Das Konzil von Konstantinopel und sein Symbol*, Göttingen 1965

Stead, G. C. 'Why Not Three Gods?', in *Studien zu Gregor von Nyssa*, ed. H. R. Drobner and C. Klock, Leiden 1990, pp. 149–63

Witt, R. E. 'Hypostasis', in *Amicitiae Corolla, Essays Presented to J. Rendel Harris*, ed. H. G. Wood, London 1933, pp. 319–43
The last is not easy to obtain, but remains the best full survey for those unable to read German.

16

CHRIST AS GOD AND MAN

Grillmeier, A. *Christ in Christian Tradition*, 1st edn London 1965, 2nd edn 1975
— and H. Bacht. *Das Konzil von Chalkedon* I, Würzburg 1951, 5th edn 1979
Hengel, M. *The Son of God*, London 1976
Kelly, J. N. D. *Early Christian Doctrines*, London 1958, 5th edn 1977
Liebaert, J. *L'Incarnation I, Des origines au Concile de Chalcédoine*, Paris 1966 (or the German original, entitled 'Christologie', Freiburg 1965)
Young, F. M. *From Nicaea to Chalcedon*, London 1983

Prosōpon and persona

Andresen, C. 'Zur Entstehung und Geschichte des trinitarischen Personbegriffs', *Zeitschr. für die neutestl. Wissensch* 52. (1961) pp. 1–39
Nédoncelle, M. 'Prosopon et persona dans l'antiquité classique', *Revue des sciences religieuses* 22 (1948) pp. 277–99.

Phusis

Köster, H. 'Φύσις', in G. Kittel and G. Friedrich, *Theological Dictionary of the New Testament*, vol. 9, Grand Rapids, Mich. 1974, pp. 251–77
Thimme, O. Φύσις, τρόπος, ἦθος . . . *Wesen und Charakter in der altgriechischen Literatur*, Quackenbruck 1935

17

TWO NATURES UNITED

See Bibliography 16 adding:
Fortin, E. L. 'The Definitio Fidei of Chalcedon and its philosophical sources' *Studia Patristica* 5 (1962) (= Texte und Untersuchungen 80), pp. 489–98

Otto, S. *Person und Subsistenz*, Munich 1968
Prestige, G. L. *GPT*, especially pp. 265–301
Relton, H. M. *A Study in Christology*, London 1917

18

PHILOSOPHY, FAITH AND KNOWLEDGE

General

Andresen, C. *Bibliographia Augustiniana*, 2nd edn Darmstadt 1973
Brown, P. R. L. *Augustine of Hippo*, London 1967
*Chadwick H. *Augustine*, Oxford 1986
Flasch, K. *Augustin: Einführung in sein Denken*, Stuttgart 1980
Gilson, E. *Introduction à l'étude de S. Augustin*, 4th edn Paris 1969
— *The Christian Philosophy of St. Augustine* (trans. from 2nd edn of the
    above), London 1961
Kirwan, C. *Augustine*, London 1989
Markus, R. A. *Marius Victorinus and Augustine*, in A. H. Armstrong, *LGP*
    pp. 329–419
O'Meara, J. J. *The Young Augustine*, London 1954
Portalié, E. *A Guide to the Thought of St. Augustine*, London 1960

Philosophy, faith and knowledge

König, E. *Augustinus Philosophus. Christlicher Glaube und philosophisches
    Denken in den frühschriften Augustins*, Munich 1970
Madec, G. '"Verus philosophus est amator Dei", S. Ambroise, S.
    Augustine et la philosophie', *Rev. sc. phil. et theol.* 61 (1977) pp.
    549–66
Nash, R. H. *The Light of the Mind: Augustine's Theory of Knowledge*,
    Lexington, Ky 1969

19

FREEDOM AND GOODNESS

Pelagianism: grace and free will

Evans, R. F. *Pelagius: Inquiries and Reappraisals*, London 1963
Ferguson, J. *Pelagius*, Cambridge 1956
Plinval, G. de *Pélage, ses écrits, sa vie et sa réforme*, Lausanne 1943

Freedom and goodness

Burnaby, J. *Amor Dei*, London 1938
Evans, G. R. *Augustine on Evil*, Cambridge 1982
Holte, R. *Béatitude et sagesse*, Paris 1962
Sorabji, R. *Time, Creation and the Continuum*, London 1983

20

OTHER WORKS MENTIONED IN TEXT OR NOTES

Andresen, C. 'Zur Entstehung und Geschichte des trinitarischen Personbegriffes', *Zeitschrift für die neutestamentliche Wissenschaft* 52 (1961) pp. 1–39

Barnes, T. D. *Athanasius and Constantine: Theology and Politics in the Constantinian Empire*, Cambridge, Mass., and London 1993

Baynes, N. H. *Constantine the Great and the Christian Church*, London 1931, repr. with new preface 1972

Bienert, W. A. *ZKG* 90 (1979) pp. 151–75

Camplani, A. *Le Lettere Festali di Atanasio di Alessandria*, Rome 1989

Davies, W. D. *Paul and Rabbinic Judaeism*, London 1955

Dennis, T. J. 'Gregory on the resurrection of the body', in *The Easter Sermons of Gregory of Nyssa*, ed. A. Spira and C. Klock, Patristic Monographs Series 9, Philadelphia 1981, pp. 55–74

Dörrie, H. 'Der Platoniker Eudoros von Alexandreia', *Hermes* 79 (1944) pp. 25–39 (= *Platonica Minora*, Munich 1976, pp. 297–309)
— 'Ὑπόστασις, Wort- und Bedeutungsgeschichte', *Nachr. Akad. Göttingen* 3 (1955) pp. 35–92 (= *Platonica Minora* pp. 12–69)
— 'Was ist spätantike Platonismus?', *Theologische Rundschau* 16 (1971) pp. 285–302 (= *Platonica Minora* pp. 508–23)
— 'Physis' in *Der Kleine Pauly*, vol. IV, Munich 1972

Edwards, P. *Encyclopedia of Philosophy*, New York 1967

Eichrodt, W. *Theology of the Old Testament*, London 1961

Festugière, A. J. *La Révélation d'Hermès Trismégiste* 3, Paris 1953

Frege, G. *Die Grundlagen der Arithmetik*, Eng. trans. as *The Foundations of Arithmetic*, Oxford 1950, 2nd edn 1953

Geach, P. *God and the Soul*, London 1969

Gottschalk, N. 'The earliest Aristotelian commentators', in *Aristotle Transformed: the Ancient Commentators and their Influence*, ed. R. Sorabji, London 1990

Kenny, A. *The Aristotelian Ethics*, Oxford 1978

Kirk, K. E. *The Vision of God: The Christian Doctrine of the* Summum Bonum, London 1931

Lebreton, J. *Histoire du dogme de la trinité*, Paris 1910, 8th edn 1927, 1928. Eng. trans. of vol. 1, *History of the Dogma of the Trinity . . . to Nicaea*, London 1939

Loofs, F. *Nestorius and his Place in the History of Christian Doctrine*, Cambridge 1914

Osborn, E. *Ethical Patterns in Early Christian Thought*, Cambridge 1976

Rad, G. von *Das erste Buch Mose, Genesis*, Göttingen 1956. Eng. trans. *Genesis, a Commentary*, London 1961

Richard M. 'L'introduction du mot "hypostase" dans la théologie de l'incarnation', *MSR* 2 (1945) pp. 5–32, 243–70

Ritter, J. *Historisches Wörterbuch der Philosophie*, Darmstadt 1971–

Schwartz, E. *Kaiser Constantin und die christliche Kirche*, Leipzig and Berlin, 1913

Sherrington, Sir Charles *Man on his Nature*, Cambridge 1940, 2nd edn 1951

Silva-Tarouca S. I., C. *S. Leonis Magni Tomus ad Flavianum Episcopum Constantinopolitanum*, Rome 1932, 5th edn 1959

Simonetti, M. 'All'origine della formula teologica una essenza / tre ipostasi', *Augustinianum* 14 (1974) pp. 173–5

Stead, G. C. 'Ontology and terminology in Gregory of Nyssa', in *Gregor von Nyssa und die Philosophie*, ed. H. Dörrie, M. Altenburger and U. Schramm, Leiden 1976, pp. 107–27 (= *Substance and Illusion* (see Bibliography 12) no. IX)

—— 'Individual personality in Origen and the Cappadocian Fathers', in *Arché e Telos. L'antropologia di Origine e di Gregorio di Nissa*, Studia Patristica Mediolanensia 12, Milan 1981, pp. 170–91 (= *Substance and Illusion* no. XIII)

—— 'The freedom of the will and the Arian controversy', in *Platonismus und Christentum, Festschrift für Heinrich Dörrie*, ed. H.-D. Blume and F. Mann, Münster, Westfalen 1983, pp. 245–57 (= *Substance and Illusion* no. XVI)

—— 'Why Not Three Gods?', in *Studien zu Gregor von Nyssa* (Festschrift for A. Spira), ed. H. R. Drobner and C. Klock, Leiden 1990, pp. 149–63

Studer, B. *Gott und unsere Erlösung im Glauben der alten Kirche*, Düsseldorf 1985

Tillich, P. *The Courage to BE*, London 1952

Troeltsch, E. *Die Soziallehren der christlichen Kirchen und Gruppen*, Tübingen 1912. Eng. trans. *The Social Teaching of the Christian Churches*, London 1931

Index of names

Adam, 72, 88, 190, 231–2
Aenesidemus, 64
Albinus, 66, 83, 115, 177
Alexander of Alexandria, 170–1, 177, 200
Alexander of Aphrodisias, 63, 82, 89, 108, 209
Alexander the Great, 31, 43
Ambrose, 12, 42, 135, 169, 220
Anaxagoras, 11, 12, 114
Anaximander, 4–6
Anaximenes, 5
Andresen, C., 196
Andronicus of Rhodes, 54
Anselm, 82
Antiochus of Ascalon, 54, 65
Apollinaris, 190–5, 200, 205–7, 211–12
Apollodorus, 237
Apuleius, 66
Arcesilaus, 40, 44, 63
Aristippus, 43
Aristophanes, 15
Aristotle, 4, 12–17, 24–7, 31–40, 45, 48–9, 52, 55, 63–7, 81–3, 86–9, 99, 104–7, 111–14, 123, 130–3, 136–7, 146, 159, 165, 179–84, 199, 209, 212, 236
Ps.-Aristotle, 58, 108
Arius, 90, 143, 166–70, 191, 206
Arius Didymus, 176, 209, 237
Arnim, H. von, 85
Arnobius, 112
Arrian, 45
Artemon, 157, 189
Aspasius, 63
Athanasius, ix, 68, 83, 112, 117, 132, 135–8, 141–3, 155–9, 166–72, 178, 189–95, 203–7, 241
Athenagoras, 117

Atticus, 64–7
Augustine, ix–xi, 64–5, 74, 81–6, 89, 91, 109, 112, 116–19, 131, 147, 155, 219–44

Barth, K., x
Basil the Great, 12, 65, 83–6, 91, 94, 117–18, 130, 159, 172, 182, [185]
Basilides, 68, 107, 189
Baynes, N. H., 169
Bienert, W. A., 166
Boethius, 32, 64, 83
Boyle, R., 12, 13

Calvin, x, 234
Cappadocian Fathers, 155, 159, 162, 173, 177–86, 195
Carneades, 44, 51, 63, 88–9
Celestine, 192
Celsus, 144, 178
Chadwick, H., 80, 93, 153
Chrysippus, 44, 83, 147, 175, 178, 237
Cicero, 44, 63, 67–8, 112, 115, 219, 235
Cleanthes, 44, 50
Clement of Alexandria, 8, 14, 66, 83–6, 92, 112–13, 116–17, 132–7, 142, 147, 167, 178, 189, 199
Constantine, 65, 90, 166, 169, 182
Cornutus, 63
Crates, 44
Cratylus, 8
Cyril of Alexandria, 83, 191–5, 198, 204–5, 210–15
Cyril of Jerusalem, 112, 178–9

Davies, W. D., 150
Democritus, 11–13, 41, 63
Dennis, T. J., 91

258

Index of subjects

allegory, 57–8, 67, 86, 91–2, 99–100, 144
anthropomorphism, 7, 12, 42, 100–2,
    120, 188; denied, 58, 103, 133, 188
atomism, 11–13, 41–2, 46–8, 209

being, 9, 11, 25–6, 34, 37, 58, 108, 113,
    121–8, 223, 238, 241–4

Craftsman, 26–7, 55–6, 68, 104–5, 146;
    cf. Demiurge
Creation, 12, 14, 59, 61, 66–9, 86–9,
    105–7, 114, 116, 146, 154, 235–6,
    241

Demiurge (Gnostic), 70, 72, 107
determinism and free will, 50–1, 71, 80,
    84–5, 88–9, 128, 221, 231–5

evil, 20, 27, 74, 90, 147, 178, 230–1,
    241–3

faith, 89–90, 109–13, 223–4

Gnostics, Gnosticism, 69–72, 144, 147–9,
    158, 167–8, 189–90

hypostasis, 156, 159, 162–3, 173–82,
    192–8, 210–14, 223

knowledge, 16, 18, 23–6, 41, 72, 111,
    224–5

Logos, 8, 46–8, 58–60, 75, 106–7, 132,
    139, 150–8, 188, 190–215

mind (*nous*), 12, 21–2, 27, 55–6, 72–3,
    136–8, 145, 225–7
mixture, 48, 143, 208
Monad, 6, 56–8, 60, 153–4, 209

one, senses of, 19, 27, 56, 105, 127, 153

providence, 8, 11, 14, 27, 45–7, 50, 58,
    60, 97–9, 146; denied, 35, 42, 51,
    104

revelation, 90, 220, 224

sceptics, scepticism, 40, 44, 54, 63–4, 83,
    112–14, 147, 224, 236
sensation, sense perception, 11, 41, 141,
    225–7
spirit (*pneuma*), 47, 98, 138–9; Holy
    Spirit, 152–72
survival of death, 5, 8, 11, 14, 17, 29, 45,
    87, 92; denied, 42; as reincarnation
    5, 23, 30, 65, 88, 92

time, 10, 66–7, 235–41
triadic theology, Trinity, 75, 93, 120–1,
    151–9, 167–72, 221–3

261

1985